A Funny Life

Also by Michael McIntyre

Life & Laughing

Michael McIntyre

A Funny Life

MACMILLAN

First published 2021 by Macmillan
an imprint of Pan Macmillan
The Smithson, 6 Briset Street, London EC1M 5NR
EU representative: Macmillan Publishers Ireland Ltd, 1st Floor,
The Liffey Trust Centre, 117–126 Sheriff Street Upper,
Dublin 1, D01 YC43
Associated companies throughout the world
www.panmacmillan.com

ISBN 978-1-5290-6365-3 HB
ISBN 978-1-5290-6366-0 TPB

1 3 5 7 9 8 6 4 2

A CIP catalogue record for this book is available from the British Library.

Typeset in Baskerville by Jouve (UK), Milton Keynes
Printed and bound by CPI Group (UK) Ltd, Croydon, CR0 4YY

Visit **www.panmacmillan.com** to read more about all our books
and to buy them. You will also find features, author interviews and
news of any author events, and you can sign up for e-newsletters
so that you're always first to hear about our new releases.

For The Captain

A Funny Life

Prologue

Hello! Welcome to the Prologue. Which might actually be the Preface, as I'm really struggling to understand the difference. If you're reading this Prologue and start to think, 'Hang on a minute, this is a Preface', please accept my apologies.

Apparently this section is called the front matter of the book. Personally, I normally skip this bit and just crack on with the book from Chapter One. The reason I do this is that the front matter normally has Roman numerals instead of page numbers. I don't read very often so I'm always quite proud of what page I've reached, like a child. I can't be wasting my time reading pages of a book before page 1. I'm also an embarrassingly slow reader; I could be reading for half an hour and my wife asks, 'What page are you on, darling?' And I'd have to answer, 'VII', like we were living in ancient Rome. There's a certain amount of pride too in how many pages I can write in my own book and these ones don't count towards the total. When people ask me how long my book is I'll have to say, 'It's 344 pages but then there's another 8 pages in Roman numerals.' It's like when someone asks how long my wife and I have been married I always have to add on the time we were together before the wedding: 'We've been married sixteen years, but we've been together for twenty.' In future I think couples who got together before the pandemic will have to mention that their relationship survived that too: 'We've been married four years, we've been together six years, and shared three lockdowns.' So you'll notice at the bottom, the number 2. No Roman numerals here. This book has started. Soon you'll be on page 3. You're really motoring.

I felt the need to write this Prologue (or Preface, or is it a Foreword?) as it is my second book so I wanted to remind you of what happened in the first one and set you up for this one. Like when you watch a new episode of a TV series and an American with a deep voice says, 'Previously on . . .' This can actually be quite annoying as most of us binge watch and have just seen the previous episode. I doubt very much any of you are binge reading my two books, so I think this is necessary.

My first book was entitled *Life & Laughing*. I thought of calling this one *More Life & More Laughing*, the next one *Still Alive & Still Laughing*, before the final, and most likely incomplete, instalment, *Barely Alive & Dribbling*. But the thinking was that you, the reader (or prospective reader if you're standing in a bookshop perusing the first couple of pages. Go on, buy it! It's good. I've read it, for the audiobook, which is also available), shouldn't feel like you can't read this one, without having read the first.

Michael McIntyre

I loved working on my first autobiography and felt honoured and surprised to be asked to write it in the first place. My agent, the infamous cigar-chomping comedy management juggernaut Addison Cresswell, called me up in early 2009.

'Michael! Addison!' he barked, his accent heavily influenced by East End gangsters.

His voice was uniquely gruff like he was coughing up words. He started every phone conversation by introducing himself, even though I had Caller ID. He knew about Caller ID because when I rang him, he would always pick up and say,

'Michael.'

But then strangely introduce himself again,

'Addison.'

Even though I'd phoned him on his personal mobile phone and he literally had one of the most distinctive voices on earth. I think he just liked to give himself a big introduction, and frankly he deserved it, as speaking with him was always full of exciting showbiz plans and gossip. He truly was a whirlwind of a man.

'I'm going to get you a book deal,' he announced.

My first thought was that he was telling me about the 3 for 2 offer at Waterstones. Writing a book had literally never crossed my mind. I had been working hard at stand-up comedy for years, but I had only just started to find real success.

'I've set up meetings with all the major publishers for you to write your autobiography,' he continued.

I found the prospect incredibly daunting but I knew not to question him. The best thing to do with Addison is just strap in and enjoy the ride. Trust him. He was the most feared and respected player in the comedy industry. He represented or had represented a who's who of British comedy: Jonathan Ross, Lee Evans, Peter Kay, Jack Dee, Alan Carr . . . Who was I to argue?

'Right, this is what's going to happen. We're meeting all the big publishers at 1 p.m. at the office next Tuesday.'

'We're meeting them all together?' I asked, confused.

'No, I just want them all to arrive at the same time and have to sit waiting with each other in reception. I'm just being honest with ya. Only one publisher, Penguin, is interested in you. The others took a bit of convincing to come. I'm just being honest with ya. I want Penguin to think you're the hottest comedian in town, generate a bit of heat around you. Get the price up. Nobody wants to miss out on The Beatles.'

'Am I The Beatles? All of them?' I asked, hoping he thought that much of me.

'No, yes, I don't know. Are ya? That's not the point.' Addison ploughed on. 'The point is you might be The Beatles and they don't want to miss out. We got to make 'em think that. I know what I'm doing.'

'Won't they talk to each other in reception?' I worried.

'No chance. They're rivals. They'll just be eyeballing each uva. We'll meet with them one by one and then get Penguin in last. By that time they'll be shittin' themselves that they ain't gonna get ya. Just let me do my job. I know what I'm doing.'

These are phrases Addison used all the time, 'Just let me do my job' and 'I know what I'm doing', but the main one was 'I'm just being honest with ya', and when he said it you really had to brace yourself as he never held back. Once when I was in the midst of having a suit fitted at a tailor's in Soho, he approached the delicate subject of my weight gain in the following way:

'Michael, are you planning on gaining more weight or losing weight? Because I suggest losing weight. You're getting fat. I'm just being honest with ya.'

The tailor, mumbling through a safety pin in his mouth, a tape measure draped over his shoulders suggested, 'I could open the side panels in the shirt if you want, to give you more room.'

'Open the panels?' Addison said, half hugging and half head-locking me. 'It's not about opening the panels, it's about closing his fucking mouth when there's cake around. I'm just being honest with ya. You're fat, sort it out.'

I was usually quite confident at meetings, especially when it was just Addison and me. Addison was a performer who knew his act inside out. He would launch into show business anecdotes which I and, more often than not, the people we were meeting with, had heard him tell before. But we never laughed any less. Not because they were hilarious – a story told over and over will inevitably get diminishing returns. If Addison didn't get the response he felt a story deserved he would immediately launch into another one (that we'd also heard before) to try to top it. To underline how much Addison was a performer in his own right, he would always have one final story that concluded every meeting and every phone call: 'I'll end on this,' he'd say before launching into his closing tale.

A Funny Life

Addison held court in every room. I was supposed to be a hotshot new comedian but I could barely get a word in, not that I cared. This was Addison's world, wheeling and dealing. He was the star of this show, not me. Many times we left meetings together and he would whisper to me, 'You were great', and I had barely said a word. Maybe on reflection he was just talking to himself.

The prospect of a string of meetings with publishers made me nervous. I felt out of my depth. I'm not much of a reader. Reading is a hobby. There are lots of hobbies I don't do. People don't judge me for not stamp collecting, trainspotting, baking or knitting. There's just something about reading that makes people who read a lot snobby towards people who don't. When I tell people I don't read very often, they give me a certain look as if they're re-evaluating the esteem they previously held me in. I'm worried that's what you're thinking now, as you obviously are a reader. Often people don't believe me.

'You don't read? Don't be silly, of course you do,' they'll say, looking over the top of their reading glasses, even if they're not wearing reading glasses.

They wouldn't have said, 'You don't fish, don't be silly,' or 'You don't hula hoop? Are you being serious?'

'My wife reads non-stop, at least a book every week!' I always tell people straight after the revelation of my non-reading, as if her excessive reading makes up for my shortfall and reading statistics are best averaged out between couples.

My problem with reading is that I read very slowly and my

mind wanders. So I have to re-read what I have already read very slowly again, only for my mind to wander again. This cycle continues until I literally fall asleep no matter what time of day it is. The process of reading has a strangely hypnotic effect on me. This is why when I do read I'm so proud of what page number I'm on. A few years ago I went away to an Austrian weight-loss clinic for a week and returned a stone lighter and decided the new improved me should try reading again. The sight of me in bed with a book and not watching TV made my seven-year-old son Ossie deeply distressed, as he genuinely thought I was an imposter posing as his father. Who was this slim reading man lying on Daddy's side of the bed? It looked so alien to him. Was it an alien? So he burst into tears and then literally slapped me open-handed across the face. 'Stop reading! Stop it! You don't read, Mummy reads, you look weird, I want Daddy back, get Daddy back from Austria, I don't want you,' he screamed, before striking me again.

So as I sat in the boardroom of Addison's TV production company, Open Mike, in the heart of London's Soho, waiting to meet a string of publishers, I felt apprehensive, nervous and out of my depth. Surely these learned literary lovers would judge me more than anyone. How can I write a book if I hardly read them? And they're bound to ask me about whether I had read certain books. All I could do was pray those books were made into movies I had seen. To be honest, the only books I can remember finishing are *The Secret History* by Donna Tartt, *The Catcher in the Rye*, Neil Simon and Jackie Mason's autobiographies, and *Gazza*, which was an unauthorized biography of the footballer Paul Gascoigne I read when I was a kid. The rest of them made me either fall asleep or get violently attacked by my children.

'Right, let's get the first one in here,' Addison barked into the phone from the boardroom like Lord Sugar on *The Apprentice*.

Reception was full of representatives from all the major publishing houses, among them James Brown from Penguin who was the only person who actually wanted to meet me and potentially sign me up. The rest were all gathered as part of Addison's elaborate mind-game production. In walked a cardiganed lady sporting what is now described as a lockdown haircut but was then ahead of its time. She actually had a book sticking out of the pocket of her knitwear. I harboured a faint hope that it was *Gazza* so we could have a mini book club session. 'A wonderful read,' I would have enthused. 'The passage about Vinny Jones grabbing his testicles was exceptional. I still pick that book up occasionally. A timeless classic.'

Addison bounded to his feet like the bell had just gone off at the beginning of a WWE wrestling match and thrust out his hand.

'Penelope, Addison Cresswell.'

'Hello,' she meekly replied before turning to me saying, 'And you are?'

She didn't even know who I was.

Addison quickly butted in. 'That's Michael, now let's get down to business. I've spoken to Jonathan and he might be up for it if the deal's right.'

Jonathan? What's going on?

It turned out she was there for a meeting with Addison about Jonathan Ross. Addison just wanted James Brown from Penguin to think she was there to see me. So for twenty minutes or so I played the part of Addison's mute colleague. Maybe she thought I was his personal assistant or on work experience. The rest of the meetings followed a similar pattern as it transpired that all the other publishers were there to have meetings regarding other comedians Addison represented. A few of the publishers recognized me and said hello before discussing possible books by Jack Dee or Alan Carr. While I was feeling like the least popular comedian in the country, James Brown from Penguin was sitting in reception believing the opposite. He had waited while all his main publishing rivals were being ushered in one by one to vie for my coveted signature behind the closed door of the boardroom.

'Just Penguin left?' Addison uttered into the phone to the receptionist. 'Great, send him in.'

At long last my would-be publisher James Brown entered the boardroom for a meeting that was actually about me. His friendly face was smiling from ear to ear and I immediately felt relaxed with him. Strangely, he was carrying a brand-new boxed 32-inch television.

'Michael, so good to finally meet you,' he said as he shook my hand with both of his, laughing wildly before I'd even opened my mouth. 'You're so funny!'

'I've got a present for you from everyone at Penguin,' he

continued as he plonked the TV down on the table. 'It's HD-ready! Hahahahahaha!' he laughed.

'What's going on?' Addison interjected. 'We gonna watch TV together? I thought we were doing a book deal?'

'It's from your joke,' beamed James, 'about HD-ready TVs. I love that one.'

There was a strange time before HD TV, you might remember, when you would buy new TVs that said 'HD-Ready' in the top right-hand corner. I had made jokes about them on *Live at the Apollo*, personifying TVs who were HD-ready: 'I'm ready, whenever you want to get HD, I want you to know that I'm ready', and worried TVs who didn't have the HD-ready sign: 'I don't want you to get HD, please don't get HD, I'm just not ready.'

I couldn't believe it. Penguin thought I was so hilarious they were buying me presents about my jokes. If only I had also made jokes about Ferraris, luxury holidays and gold bullion. Nothing relaxes me more than when I know someone finds me funny, and James was clearly my biggest fan. He went on to recount most of the jokes I'd ever told and then laughed wildly at them. I was having the best gig of my life and I hadn't had to tell a single joke myself.

'We're hugely keen to work with you, Michael,' he said, wiping away tears from his performance of all my material. 'Celebrity autobiographies have been doing really well for us, especially by comedians. We think yours will be a huge success. Have you read many autobiographies?'

'Errr . . .' I hesitated, 'I read *Gazza*.'

James cracked up laughing again, assuming I was joking.

'To be honest I don't really read,' I continued. 'Reading sends me to sleep.'

James started guffawing. I loved this guy. I wanted him cloned to fill the front row of all of my gigs.

'A good book,' I continued, launching into some of my actual stand-up material, 'is called a page turner. Surely that's the minimum expected of a book, that the pages turn. Do people ever say, "I wouldn't recommend this book, the pages don't turn, it's more of a block than a book."'

With every laugh from James, Addison was adding money to the deal. He had teed him up perfectly and would soon go in for the kill.

'As you can see, James, there's a lot of excitement about Michael. We've had all the major publishers here and we've got several offers on the table. So if you're serious about this it's going to take a pretty substantial offer as it looks like there's a bidding war developing. I'm just being honest with ya.'

What transpired over the coming days was indeed a bidding war between Penguin, and themselves. I kept saying to Addison, 'Just take the money.' 'I know what I'm doing,' was his inevitable response. When the deal was finally struck I subsequently learnt that Penguin were elated to have 'won' the race for my signature and went out for celebratory drinks.

Although it was never my plan to write a book and still isn't my plan to read one, I found the six months I spent writing my first book the most enjoyable time of my career. Having a chance

to reflect on my life and be at home with my family and not touring and performing was much needed respite. *Life & Laughing*
ended with what I perceive to be my big break at the televised
Royal Variety Performance in 2006. I was thirty years old and
after being a uniquely tremendous loser in love I had met and
married Kitty, the love of my life and mother of our then newborn son Lucas. Kitty was, and remains, out of my league. I
don't know who determines the leagues. I'm sure with gruelling
exercise and Hollywood plastic surgeons there can be occasional
promotions and relegations, but Kitty is far too many divisions
above me for me to ever catch up. Go on, flick to the picture
section. I'll wait . . . See what I mean. Without her I would be
a shadow of the man I am. Over the years I have pointed to
unshaven, dirty, badly dressed men in the street who have obviously fallen on hard times. 'You see that man over there, darling,
the one with the two Lidl bags,' I would say as we stopped at
traffic lights. 'That's me, if I'd never met you', and she would just
nod in agreement. She knows and understands me better than I
know myself. Every morning when I wake up dazed, confused
and foggy brained – Who am I? Where am I? What year is it? – I
see her sleeping next to me and it all comes flooding back and I
feel an overwhelming sense of joy that she's my wife.

After years of debt and lack of success on the comedy circuit,
Life & Laughing culminated in a moment of real triumph. I
remember striding off that stage at the London Coliseum, the
applause of the bejewelled and bow-tied Royal Variety audience
ringing in my ears. I glanced at Prince Charles looking down on

me from the Royal Box, his face grinning and wobbling. 'He's an incredibly funny chap,' I imagined him muttering to Camilla, 'I'm sure the public will take to him, like they did to Diana. No offence darling.' It was a momentous night and a huge relief that I had delivered when it mattered most. I phoned Kitty from a payphone after the show – I have no idea why I used a payphone when I must have had a mobile phone in 2006 and been surrounded by people with mobile phones who could surely lend me theirs. Maybe I did use my mobile phone and my memory has just romanticized the moment, like I was in an old black and white movie. But I clearly recall being in a phone box outside the theatre in Covent Garden, rather unromantically surrounded by sexually graphic business cards of local prostitutes and the smell of urine. Kitty was at home sleeplessly waiting for news. I told her that I couldn't have done any better, that all the struggling and striving had been worth it. My performance was calm and confident. I knew what I was doing on that big stage. I was ready. Everything that had gone before was just learning and preparation and now, the real stuff, the exciting stuff, was about to start.

It was the beginning . . .

1

My mother would use the expression 'I slept like a baby' when I was growing up and I was sure she was referring to a good night's sleep. So when I had a baby of my own I was expecting to marvel at their ability to sleep soundly. It turns out that either this expression is misleading, or my poor mother used to spend her nights screaming and shitting the bed. Having a baby is the most momentous and magical thing that ever happened to me. But as soon as you've performed the miracle of creation, your main focus becomes getting the baby to sleep, for as long as possible. A sleeping baby is the Holy Grail of parenting. The whisper of my wife's voice telling me that, 'He's asleep' was definitely the highlight of my early years of fatherhood. For when your baby is sleeping, the worrying for their well-being is paused and you, like them, can relax. Many times, Lucas would cry for hours, his distress distressing Kitty and me tenfold: 'What's wrong with him?' 'He's really not OK.' 'Is it wind? It seems worse than wind.' 'He's turning blue.' 'Should we call the doctor?' Then as if by magic he would exhaust himself to sleep, rendering Kitty and me paralysed, not wanting to make a sound in case he woke up again. Relying on lip reading to communicate with each other. Slowly, and with more care than any bomb disposal expert has ever taken, we would place him in his Moses basket. It was only then we could enjoy a fleeting moment of peace, momentarily free from parental high anxiety. Gazing lovingly at him, his soft breath making his tiny tummy rise and fall in his cosy Babygro. This would last about forty seconds before the panic set in again: 'Is he breathing?' 'He's breathing funny.' 'Something's wrong.' 'He's turning yellow.' 'I don't know if he is breathing properly.' Then we would poke him, wake him, he would restart screaming and we would spend another three hours trying to get him back to sleep, before poking him awake again.

Nothing prepares you for fatherhood. Initially a father's role isn't remotely as intense as a mother's. Kitty was in labour for thirty-six hours with Lucas, although she adds an hour every time she tells the story of his birth. I think the last time she told the story it was sixty-three hours. Hold on, I'll ask her now . . .

. . . I stand corrected. She was actually in labour for sixty-four hours.

My only two duties on day one of Lucas's life were to cut the umbilical cord and put him in his car seat for his maiden voyage home. Thankfully I did these in the correct order, avoiding a frightful sight in the back seat of our Volkswagen Polo and an unnecessarily uncomfortable journey for my wife. The cord cutting was as easy as it sounds. I was handed the scissors by the midwife, which avoided me having to find them, which is a life-long struggle: 'Where's the scissors? Have you seen the scissors? I just put them down, they've disappeared?' I've long been convinced that when you're not looking scissors come to life and shuffle off on their two pointy legs and hide from you for their own entertainment. But no such problems in University College Hospital on 29 June 2005, as I slotted my thumb and forefinger into the fit-for-purpose mini-scissors and liberated my son from his mother, giving him his first taste of independence. The car seat however was the single most difficult undertaking of my life to date. Why I thought I didn't need to read the instructions and practise before the birth, I will never know.

'Is the car seat ready, Dad?' said the midwife in her thick Irish accent as we descended in the hospital lift with Lucas swaddled tightly in Kitty's arms, his jet-black hair already slightly more on-trend than mine. I had never been called 'Dad' before so wondered how the Chinese gentleman in a wheelchair who was sharing our lift could possibly be her father. But it was me she was talking to. How surreal. Even after nine months to get used to the idea, it still hadn't registered.

'Yes, yes. The car seat's in the car,' I reassured her. Not realizing I may need another nine months to work out how to fit it.

We walked super slowly down Gower Street in Central London in what felt like a new world, both to Lucas and to us. Everything suddenly seemed so loud and threatening. Cars screeching and hooting. Cyclists whizzing by. Workmen shouting.

It was terrifying. Even though the car was less than fifty metres away it felt like a marathon. Lucas looked so vulnerable. Finally we made it to the car and I opened the back door.

'What the fuck?' said Kitty when she saw the car seat still in its box on the back seat. 'I've been in labour for forty-one hours' (she had told the story five times at that point) 'and you haven't sorted out the car seat? You only had one thing to do, Michael. One!'

'I also had to cut the umbilical cord, darling. I had two things . . .' I started saying in my defence before I too was cut off.

'Just sort it out now,' she shouted as she sat in the back seat squashed up against the large unopened Maxi-Cosi car seat box. I caught Lucas's tiny eye as Kitty scooched over. He seemed to look at me and then back to his mother as if to say, 'This guy? You married this guy?'

I immediately started to panic, furiously ripping at the box that didn't seem to grant me any obvious point of entry. It was Sellotaped along the edges. I pulled at the corners with all my strength but the tape just stretched further and further, determined not to let me in. I started to hack at the box with my car key, puncturing little holes that mimicked the ignition of the Volkswagen Polo but in no way helped open the box. Then a eureka moment, as I realized I had pocketed the umbilical cord scissors. A few snaps of the stretched Sellotape later and I finally got the box open. Lucas watching on surely concluded that his dad has one skill and one skill only, to cut things with tiny scissors.

I'm sorry to report that getting into the box was the easy part.

What followed was excruciatingly challenging. First the seat had to be strapped into the car using the seat belt. Then I was confronted with six metal clasps that all had to fit together like a *Crystal Maze* puzzle in order to buckle the baby in. There seemed to be an infinite number of combinations these clasps could potentially fit. Every time I assembled them all together, I tried to push them into the buckle but they would not click in. Why wouldn't they click in? Just click the fuck in! I remember Lucas crying, Kitty mumbling, 'I can't believe this is happening' and my futile attempts failing over and over again. I was sweating, cursing, wailing. At one point I asked for an epidural. The relief when the clasps finally clicked into the buckle is indescribable. I genuinely thought it would never happen, or take so long that Lucas would have grown out of the baby seat or be old enough to drive us all home.

I was assigned further fatherly duties over the early years of Lucas's life, but one thing Kitty and I always shared was the 'early shift'. This is when one of us would get up early with the baby to allow the other much needed sleep. We alternated daily without fail, this normally being indicated with one of us responding to Lucas's 5 a.m. wake-up with a satisfied mumble of 'It's your turn' from the cocooned comfort of the duvet. And it was these words I heard the morning after my triumphant Royal Variety Performance. 'But, darling, I was home very late and had a few drinks after the show . . .'

'It's your turn,' she firmly sleep talked back to me, turning away to find additional comfort for her lie-in.

A Funny Life

Lucas was eighteen months old now. A toddler. He was as uneasy on his feet as I had been the night before, staggering home after several celebratory glasses of cheap red wine. The evidence of my late-night raid of the fridge greeted me a few hours later as I tried to locate a jar of baby food to warm up for Lucas, hoping I hadn't drunkenly eaten them all myself as a kebab substitute. I popped Lucas on the floor to play with his box of toy cars while I boiled the kettle, the now familiar whiff of a full nappy regularly drifting my way as I prioritized my coffee over him sitting in his own shit.

The three of us, Kitty, Lucas and I, were renting what the chain-smoking estate agent had described as a 'one and a half bedroom, half bathroom' flat in Alma Road with its identical Victorian terraced houses on the outskirts of Muswell Hill in North London. We had moved there from our 'one bedroom, one shower room' rented flat just up the road. Simple maths will tell you that we had gained half a bedroom and half a bathroom by relocating. Kitty especially was desperate for a relaxing bath, having only been able to shower for two years and bath Lucas in a blow-up baby bath in the living room. She was also eager for Lucas to have his own room. So we were seduced by the flat in Alma Road with its tiny box room for Lucas and half bathroom, which was like a normal bathroom but with half a bath, a shortened bath that you could only sit in bolt upright.

'You can lie down with your feet dangling outside the bath and resting on the toilet seat,' the estate agent helpfully suggested.

'It also takes half as long to run as a normal bath,' he added, doing his best to sell the property.

We had two boxes to tick and the flat on Alma Road half ticked both of them, so was technically an upgrade. We were so blinded by the half bedroom and half bathroom we completely overlooked how awful the rest of the flat was, in particular the 'galley' kitchen, as the estate agent had optimistically described it. It was no bigger than an average coat cupboard and painted in a colour that seemed inspired by the contents of Lucas's nappy. When we viewed the property the estate agent, whose teeth seemed more yellow every time he opened his mouth, was so expecting us to hate it that he actually blurted out, 'Really?' when Kitty proclaimed she loved the flat, would like us to move in immediately and started running herself a bath.

Alma Road was the latest in a series of rented flats in North London that always cost us £200 per week. Kitty and I had moved to Crouch End a few years previously as £200 went a lot further there than in Hampstead and Belsize Park, where we had grown up. We were very happy in our ground-floor flat in Crouch End: it had an abundance of badly assembled Ikea furniture, a drawer full of Allen keys, a quaint little terrace and, although we didn't realize it was a luxury at the time, a whole bath. We were happy there until I had an argument with the busybody old lady Pamela, who lived directly above us. Pamela was in her seventies and short, maybe 5 foot on tiptoes. Her grey hair was brutally cut, more than likely by herself. An angry woman whose face wrinkles had not been forged from smiling, she was constantly knocking on my door with utterly unreasonable complaints. Whenever I could just see a wisp of grey hair through the peephole, I knew I was in trouble.

'Must your wife blow-dry her hair? It's very noisy. I don't have a hairdryer. I just brush it,' she would spit, and then scuttle off without waiting for a response.

But nothing wound up Pamela more than leaves. Autumn was living hell for her. She was always banging on our door and ordering me to sweep up the leaves that had fallen overnight.

'It's disgusting,' she would snap as if it was dog poo everywhere and not a few discarded yellow and orange London plane tree leaves.

I normally appeased her as it didn't seem worth falling out with someone living above us who was obviously not altogether sane. But things came to a head one morning when she knocked furiously on our door. I opened it to find her even more incensed than usual, which was elevated by the fact that Kitty was blow-drying her hair at that very moment.

'LEAVES!' she shouted, pointing at the ground around her. 'WHY? WHY HAVEN'T YOU SWEPT THEM?'

'Pamela, it's my porch, I'll sweep them when I want, or not sweep them at all,' I said, for the first time showing some resistance.

What happened next is barely believable. She scrunched up her little wrinkled face, clenched her little wrinkled fist and punched me square in the jaw, an uppercut that had a surprising amount of power behind it. She then cocked her hand and said, 'Do you want some more?'

I was in shock. It really hurt. What was I supposed to do? I couldn't retaliate. There are rules in life and I'm pretty sure that 'Don't hit old ladies' is one of them. So, I'm humiliated to admit, I slammed the door and then called the police. Within the hour there was another heavy knock on the door. I looked through the peephole, worried I'd see Pamela's wisp of grey hair again or several wisps from a posse she had gathered at the bingo to finish me off. Instead, I saw two of the burliest police officers I'd ever seen. They must have each been about 6½ foot tall. I immediately regretted my knee-jerk decision to involve the law. I gave them a full account of the incident that they read back to me whilst trying not to laugh.

'So, Mr McIntyre, at approximately 10.30 a.m. you were assaulted by your neighbour Pamela because you failed to sweep the leaves from your porch. She is described as being in her mid to late seventies, grey hair, glasses, hearing aid in the right ear, a slight hunch and approximately 5 foot tall.'

'Yes,' I reluctantly said, flushed red with embarrassment, masking the hint of redness from Pamela's blow.

They paid Pamela a visit and warned her about her future conduct and made her agree to write me a letter of apology. A few days later I received her letter. The first four pages were an essay about why I should sweep up the leaves, then a page on how pointless hairdryers are, and the final line read, 'I'm sorry I beat you up.'

We then moved to central Muswell Hill into the aforementioned characterful flat with no bath. The flat was on the top floor, making it impossible for any psychopathic pensioners to live above us. The estate agent proudly announced it had a large 'unofficial' roof terrace, which was actually just a roof. Every building ever built has an 'unofficial' roof terrace. Though it did have a lovely rustic charm, beautiful oak floors and was tastefully furnished by the landlord in what was described as shabby chic. Kitty and I had only ever experienced shabby, so the addition of chic was extremely enticing. However, we realized on moving in that the pros of living just off the High Street were actually outweighed by the cons. For one thing the beautiful church directly opposite the flat wasn't a church anymore, it had been converted into an O'Neill's, an enormous Irish pub. Our bedroom window overlooked the pub and night after night drunk men would urinate against the wall opposite us. After the initial upset this caused Kitty and me, we turned it into a game. Every time a man exited the pub we would guess if he was a 'pisser' or not. By the time Lucas was born, Kitty was winning, having correctly identified well over a hundred 'pissers'. It turned out she had a remarkable talent for guessing when men needed a pee, a skill she honed nightly. 'Second door on the left,' she would impressively say to our houseguests before they had a chance to ask where the loo was.

The final straw was when one man was so intoxicated he

decided not to piss against the wall but to lean his back against it and piss out, away from the wall towards Kitty and me watching at the window, with his apparatus on display. It was horrifying, we both felt so dirty. It was one of the rare occasions we preferred a shower to a bath, to help wash away the memory.

'Are you hungry?' I asked Lucas as he played on the exposed floorboards of the small dining area outside our 'galley' kitchen in Alma Road.

I wasn't expecting a response as at that stage his entire vocabulary consisted of two words, 'car' and 'map'. I would joke onstage that he might be trying to escape. If his next words were 'passport' and 'credit card' I would know for sure.

'Car,' he replied, which I took as a yes as I hoicked him into his highchair.

I had heated up some kind of fruit compote that he was reluctant to open his mouth for. I had to be silly and pull funny faces until his mouth fell open and I would shove as much of it in as possible which he would half eat and half spit out, the food often landing in the gaps between the floorboards.

'Daddy had a good show last night,' I said.

'Car,' he said, but he seemed interested.

'It's going to be on TV next week,' I continued.

'Car,' he replied. Although this might actually have been what he meant as the film *Cars* was his absolute favourite, he watched it every day of his life.

'We can watch *Cars* afterwards,' I promised.

'Map,' he said, as more fruit compote spilled from his mouth.

It was good father–son time, a man to man. I was proud of myself. There's something about being a comedian as a profession that is weird. It is, by its nature, not very serious. It can't be. But it's as serious as any job that is done primarily to put food on the table, even if most of it falls on the floor. I had responsibilities; another nappy whiff reminded me of my most immediate one, but beyond that I had to build a life for my family. It was a bizarre feeling having performed for 2,000 people the night before, knowing that in a week millions would see that performance on TV. It was a limbo laced with panic that there had been something wrong with the cameras or sound, it wasn't recorded, would not be broadcast, wasn't as good as I thought, or wasn't any good at all. But it was exciting, really exciting. For the first time, I saw a future where I lived somewhere with a bath that my whole body could fit in, where the coat cupboard was for coats and not the kitchen, where my wife could blow-dry her hair without fear of her husband being sucker punched by a septuagenarian, and I could look out of my bedroom window to see a view that didn't contain drunks pissing.

'Now, is it time to get that nappy changed?' I asked Lucas, his face, Babygro and the floor covered in fruit compote.

'Car,' agreed Lucas.

2

Weeks had passed since my Royal Variety Performance was broadcast and after the initial flurry of praise and congratulations from friends and family, it was starting to feel like it never happened. I was recognized in public only once by a woman eating alone in Zen, a Chinese restaurant in Hampstead. I was elated when she said I was the best new comedian she'd ever seen and would be following my career closely. Although this high was soon cancelled out by another diner who mistook me for a waiter and asked for some more soy sauce, after Kitty had sent me to the loo saying I needed a pee. So I was waiting for my phone to ring and constantly checking it. I was impatient for things to take off. My diary still contained the same old depressing club gigs. Nothing had changed.

Addison was, of course, the key to everything. My relationship with him was embryonic. He was my manager but he was busy managing the careers of comedy superstars. I had to compete for his time and attention. Whenever I saw his name pop up on my phone it was thrilling. He had seen me perform for the first time less than six months earlier, and since then I had entered into his whirlwind of star making. Before that, comedy seemed like a miserable business as I spent my twenties gigging around the country in small comedy clubs with older and often bitter comics. I had forgotten that glamour and glory was actually possible in this business. Addison had injected that into my life, I'd had a taste and was craving more. But he made me nervous. He had an aura and bluster all of his own, but that's not just what made me nervous. He wielded so much power and influence and I didn't want to blow my opportunity for him to wield it for me. I was on the bottom rung of an industry that Addison not only knew inside out but very much helped to create. He was a true impresario with an eye for talent. As a student at Brighton Polytechnic in the late seventies, he promoted music events and booked up-and-coming bands like U2 and Madness. Alternative comedy and cabaret was burgeoning and in 1981 Addison set up Off The Kerb from a tiny office in Peckham, South-East London, to promote shows in clubs and universities featuring the likes of Phill Jupitus, Julian Clary and John Hegley. Soon he was representing future household names Jack Dee and Lee Evans and began building an industry he went on to dominate.

It was Danny Julian, who had worked for Addison since he was a teenager, who began managing me at Off The Kerb without Addison having seen me perform. I've never known anybody who can equal Danny's energy, enthusiasm and above all positivity. Whenever I mention Danny in this book, it's important that you imagine him in his natural habitat: sitting at his cluttered desk with a telephone headset strapped on whilst swivelling on his swivel chair and constantly nattering on the phone with at least four calls waiting. When I first joined Off The Kerb in 2005, Danny instantly revolutionized my life as a jobbing comedian. I was not only gigging regularly and making a steady income, but doing my preferred gigs with friendly comedy-loving crowds instead of unfriendly alcohol-loving ones. But in my first year at the agency I had only spoken to Addison once on the phone and never met him personally. This only added to his mystique. I owed my former agent money, money I didn't have. I had received a legal demand for an amount far beyond what I thought I owed and it terrified me. I asked Danny for advice and he said, 'Let me ask Addison, he'll know what to do.' My heart immediately pounded. I didn't want to trouble the almighty Addison with my lowly problems. The line went dead as I was put on hold. Moments later Danny was back: 'Ad wants a word.'

'With me?' I said, my voice breaking like a teenager.

'Deep breath, mate,' Danny said, understanding fully how I felt, before the line went dead again. Oh fuck, I'm about to speak to Addison Cresswell. For those of you who have seen *The Godfather* (I'm assuming all of you), I suddenly understood exactly how the hitman Luca Brasi felt when he met Don Corleone for the first time, sweat pouring from his brow as he nervously recited what he would say to him: 'I am honoured and grateful that you have invited me to your home . . .'

'Michael. Addison.' It was the first time I had heard his voice. Up to this point in my life, my ears were unaware that an octave so low existed on the vocal register. I could feel my brain expanding to cope.

'I am honoured and grateful . . .' I began, but Addison talked over me. No pleasantry, no introduction, just business.

'I understand you owe money to your old agent. Just pay him off, in full. Whatever he wants, it's just not worth it. Clean break.'

And with that he was gone and the comfort of Danny's voice restored, along with my heart rate. Addison's interlude in my phone call with Danny was akin to when you're on a train and then suddenly another train unexpectedly hurtles past in the opposite direction for a few shocking seconds. I was of course in no position to pay back my former agent in full and couldn't heed his advice. Instead I ended up writing a letter begging him to accept what I could afford, which he thankfully did.

The first time I met Addison in person was over six months later at the Edinburgh Festival in 2006, a few days before he first saw me perform and a few months before he would get me on the Royal Variety, but then I was nothing to him. I was in the Pleasance Courtyard, which will forever be the place to be at the festival. A large courtyard that served as a hub for several venues all around it. There was a huge multicoloured blackboard displaying the names of all the shows appearing at the Pleasance and what time they began, some with the much craved for 'Sold Out' sign alongside. The courtyard was always full of hustle and bustle, people drinking beer and wine from plastic cups and queuing for shows. Pleasance staff in matching yellow polo shirts crying out among the chattering and laughing assembled comedy fans, 'The house is now open for Al Murray!' or 'Queue on the left please for Frank Skinner!' I loved walking through the Pleasance Courtyard as a comedian performing at the festival. It was my first little taste of celebrity, as occasionally a punter would approach me and tell me they enjoyed my show or recognize me from my posters pasted all over town wherever space could be found among the thousands of competing shows. I remember Jimmy Carr, who was already a TV star then, walking though the courtyard in a white suit literally like a god, turning heads and igniting excited conversation.

One August night after I had just come offstage, I was loitering in the courtyard scanning for a friendly face when I noticed a gaggle of comedians surrounding an unseen figure who was very much holding court. There he was. It was Addison. He was not a small man, but seemed smaller than I was expecting. His infamous reputation had made him grow so much in my mind I was expecting him to resemble a *Tyrannosaurus rex* – he had certainly sounded like one on the phone. He was wearing what I soon came to realize was his uniform, a shiny dark blue suit and crisp white shirt. He was in constant motion and extremely animated, bobbing and weaving like a middle-weight boxer. I knew this moment was inevitable and was thrilled that it had come after I had just performed a decent show. I had that post-show inner glow of confidence after a good gig, when I felt at my most relaxed and sharpest. If I was Popeye, I would have just gulped my spinach. I sidled over and joined the audience of comedians surrounding Addison, including Shappi Khorsandi. He was mocking her and others, but everyone was laughing, including Shappi. Suddenly, mid-story, I caught his eye.

'Who the fuck are you then?' he said, like I had just broken into his home in the dead of night.

'Michael McIntyre,' I meekly replied.

'This is Michael, you know Michael? Isn't he with Off The Kerb? He's brilliant,' Shappi kindly said, as she introduced Addison to a comedian his own agency had represented for over a year. Addison then moved alarmingly close to my face.

'Ahhhhh, you. Yeah. Apparently you're like Jack Dee on acid. That's what they tell me. You don't look funny. You look like a schoolboy.'

I was speechless. I seemed to have lost all that post-gig confidence. Like Popeye checking the Best Before date on the can of spinach after his muscles failed to bulge. Addison just ignored me and launched into another boisterous story from his wild days at the Edinburgh Festival, as if he'd forgotten about me already. But he hadn't forgotten about me, he was showing off for me. When he reached the punchline, cueing raucous laughter from his disciples, he returned to the uncomfortable distance just in front of my nose and goaded, 'Follow that then if you're so funny. You ain't got nothing. Follow that.' He also sprinkled a few 'C' words in to enhance his point. It was the most extraordinary encounter. I didn't know if he was challenging me or just a totally unpleasant lunatic. I told Danny about this unfortunate meeting and was met with advice that I would subsequently be given by everyone who knew Addison.

'That's Ad, mate. You best stay away from him when he's had a drink,' followed by a reassuring, 'You'll love him, trust me. And he's gonna love you too, as long as you keep doing what you do best, making people laugh.'

Well, I did what I do best when Addsion saw me perform for the first time a few days after that awkward first meeting, and Addision did love me. So much so that he convinced the BBC to squeeze me onto the bill at the Royal Variety. But now he had disappeared. Why wasn't he calling? What's the plan now? Let's go. I kept suggesting to Kitty that I call him, but she kept correctly insisting I be patient and play it cool, something I typically failed to do when I did phone him, by accident.

I was at London Zoo with Kitty and Lucas. Lucas loved the zoo. We had an annual pass and, boy, were we going to make the most of it, going every Wednesday without fail. Lucas's jaw never failed to drop when he saw the animals. 'Look, Lucas, it's a big grizzly bear,' I would enthuse while Lucas pointed and giggled. 'Ohh look, Lucas, it's a slithering snake!' And all three of us would impersonate the snake to its face, 'Sssssssssssss.'

We went to the zoo so many times that the animals started to recognize us. The tigers would give us a familiar nod as we walked past, 'All right, mate.' I remember a camel rolling her eyes when she saw us approach for the millionth time, 'Them again.' An orang-utan once handed me a copy of the *Time Out Guide to London*, 'Surely there are other things to do in this city.'

Kitty and I were busy impersonating sheep in the farm section of the zoo when I checked my mobile phone for the hundredth time since we arrived and was confused to see Addison's name lit up on the screen. Was he calling? But it's not ringing. It didn't ring. What's happened? Under his name was a timer counting upwards 9.45, 9.46, 9.47.

'Oh fuck!' I'd pocket dialled Addison.

'Addison?' I said into the phone, but there was no answer. It had gone to his voicemail. I quickly cancelled the call. Length of call 10.03. A cold sweat enveloped my whole body as I tried to recall what may have been recorded in the last ten minutes. Looking back at the enclosures we had passed at the zoo, it became apparent Addison's answerphone was mainly filled with monkey noises, 'Uh-Oh, Uh-Oh, Uh-Oh, Uh-Oh, Uh-Oh', culminating in me saying, 'Oh fuck, Addison.'

'I phoned Addison!' I squealed, prompting a muddy pig to stop scoffing from a trough and stare at me. Kitty and Lucas, who were deep in conversation with a sheep, ignored me. 'Baaaa, Baaaaa, Baaaaa.'

'I phoned Addison!' I repeated with more urgency.

'What did he say, darling?' Kitty finally asked. 'I thought we agreed you were going to play it cool and not call him.'

'I phoned him by accident. I bum dialled him just now, I don't know how it happened, I left a ten-minute message on his phone of us making monkey noises and now he's going to think I'm an idiot or that I'm taking the piss out of him. I ended the call by saying "Oh fuck, Addison" because I noticed what I'd done. That's offensive. He might think I'm saying that to him. Or that I'm calling him a monkey or something . . .'

'Calm down, darling,' Kitty interrupted. 'This can be sorted out. Stop rabbiting on.' At which point two large white rabbits stopped carrot chomping and glared as if to say, 'Leave us out of this.'

'Just send him a text and explain. He'll find it funny. Stop panicking,' Kitty tried to reassure me.

'I'm going to call him. It's better,' I decided, as the sheep wandered off, annoyed at the lack of attention.

'You do what you want, but I think you should just text him,' Kitty shrugged.

I dialled his number, it started ringing on the other end but he didn't pick up. I hung up.

'It's the machine,' I said.

'Why didn't you leave him a message?' Kitty responded.

'No,' I said, 'it's better to talk . . .' As I was speaking the phone started to ring. ADDISON read the caller ID display. 'It's him!'

I picked it up.

'Michael. Addison,' came his usual guttural greeting.

'Addisooon! Hiya!' I replied overfamiliarly and launched straight into my explanation: 'I'm at the zoo and must have bum dialled you by accident and think I may have left a message on your phone making monkey noises.'

'I can't really hear you, Michael. It's a bad signal. I'm on a train. You've had an accident? Something about a bum and a monkey. You've had an accident with a monkey's bum? What are you on about? I'll call you in an hour when I'm off the train.' And he hung up.

'Well, what did he say?' Kitty impatiently asked.

'I think I made it worse,' I said, defeated. 'There was a bad signal and he only heard the words accident, monkey and bum.'

Addison didn't call back in an hour, or that night. I was beside myself with panic that my pocket dial had been misconstrued as cheeky or offensive. It was several worrisome days later when he finally phoned while I was in the bath at Alma Road with my feet dangling over the end, resting on the toilet seat.

'Michael. Addison. I haven't been calling cos I've been busy setting things up. There's a lot of excitement about you. You are what we call "hot", my friend. You free for lunch at the Ivy next Wednesday with the Head of Entertainment at the BBC?'

'Yes,' I said immediately.

'Great. 1 p.m. I'll get Danny to put it in your diary,' and he hung up.

'Darling!' I shouted from the bath, stomping on the toilet seat with excitement.

'What is it?' Kitty replied as she poked her head around the door.

'That was Addison! We're having lunch with the Head of Entertainment at the BBC, at the Ivy restaurant at one o'clock! Danny's putting it in the diary!'

'See, I told you to be patient,' she said. 'That's brilliant news, darling. When?'

'Next Wednesday.'

Lucas then bounded in, his frowning forehead hooding his eyes.

'No! Zoo!' he said, instantly doubling his vocabulary with his disgust at my having to change our plans.

3

Younger readers of this book won't remember a time before mobile phones, when telecommunications were restricted solely to the landline. Nowadays landlines are used mainly as substitutes when mobile phone signal is poor: 'I'll call you back from the landline'. The consequence of this is that most landline calls now start with the statement, 'Ahh, that's better.' A landline might suffer from the obvious roaming limitations, but it had some surprising perks that have now been lost. Undoubtedly the most fun thing in the golden age of landlines was the crossed line. Every so often, like a lottery, your phone line would accidentally cross another and you were suddenly all party to each other's conversations. If you kept quiet, they wouldn't know you were listening. It was exhilarating to eavesdrop on even the most mundane conversations of strangers.

I don't know if Kitty and I were missing the mischief we enjoyed in the eighties of overhearing people's conversations on a crossed line, but when a day or so after moving into Alma Road we clearly heard the neighbours having an argument, we both leapt from the sofa to squash our ears against the wall. The walls were so thin I think if I'd tripped I would have crashed through in what would have been a very awkward introduction. Flats in London are full of people having to overhear each other's lives. The sound of my wife's blow-drying may have tipped our previous neighbour Pamela into madness. A friend told me recently that his walls are so flimsy that his Alexa often responds to the instructions of the Death Rock-loving teenager who lives next door. Whereas most people complain about the sound of loud music, when it comes to the sound of people arguing, Kitty and I found ourselves fetching glasses from the 'galley' kitchen to wedge against our ears to enhance the experience.

'It's disgusting. Is that what you want? Am I not enough for you?' a female voice screamed.

'Just calm down, you're massively overreacting,' said a defensive male voice.

Kitty and I were enthralled, our ears glued to our glasses.

'Just fuck off!' the female voice screamed.

Then we both flinched in unison at the slamming of a door, before it went quiet. We never found out what the row was about, but we did learn they had made up by that Friday night, at 11.20 p.m. to be precise. Kitty and I had never missed an episode of *Friday Night with Jonathan Ross*. The show had become even more must-see now that Jonathan and I shared an agent, Addison, who was also the show's executive producer. Jonathan was undoubtedly Addison's golden boy. The previous year, in 2006, Addison had infamously secured Jonathan an £18m deal with the BBC. EIGHTEEN MILLION POUNDS!! Jonathan was the best in the business, but so was Addison. That deal alone was proof that with Addison as my agent the sky was the limit.

The conclusion of Jonathan Ross on a Friday night always signalled time for sleep. The off switch on the remote control hit just after the final credit of 'Executive Producer Addison Cresswell' had appeared. But on this Friday night after the TV went off, we heard a few more bars of the theme tune from the neighbours.

'They're watching Jonathan Ross too,' I said.

'What? Sleepy time now,' replied Kitty, not listening.

Then the neighbours, too, switched off their TV. Bedtime for all. Or maybe not. I was just falling asleep when I heard soft moaning coming from beyond the wall. I listened for a minute or so to make sure my ears weren't deceiving me.

'I think they're having sex,' I whispered to Kitty.

'No!' Kitty said with her eyes closed. 'No sex. Sleep time.'

'No, the neighbours. I think the neighbours are having sex,' I said.

'Really, I can't hear anything,' Kitty said as she sat up and then strangely turned her bedside light on. We both stared at the wall in front of us, which now had two head-height circular glass stains already visible from our new-found eavesdropping hobby.

'I think you're hearing things, darling,' Kitty said. 'I can't hear anything.'

'There! Listen . . .' I insisted.

'I can't hear anything,' she too insisted.

Then any doubt was instantly removed as we heard the woman next door yelp a very loud and sordid sexual instruction. Moments later we heard the unmistakable banging of the headboard against our shared wall which I was immediately worried would give way. What followed was well over an hour of escalating passion that put me to shame, not helped by Kitty at one point muttering, 'Wow, he's still going!'

It transpired over the forthcoming weeks that this occurred every Friday night, without fail. At no other time in the week did we hear anything erotic through the wall. If a couple are to remove spontaneity from their sex lives and schedule a weekly encounter, Friday night seems like a good time. It's the end of the working week, the weekend beckons, lie-in incoming. It makes sense. Then, unexpectedly, one Friday night we heard nothing. They weren't out. We heard them have dinner earlier. Their car was still there.

'They're not doing it. It is Friday night, isn't it?' I asked an equally confused Kitty.

'Maybe they had another argument or something. Not in the mood. Not tonight, Josephine,' Kitty speculated.

'Hang on a minute . . .' I said.

'Jonathan Ross!' Kitty said, finishing my sentence for me. 'The series ended last week.'

'You don't think Jonathan Ross plays a part in their arousal? His interviewing technique acting as some kind of foreplay?

They're not in the mood unless they've heard the comedic songs of Four Poofs and a Piano? Was it Addison's name, as the final credit on the show, that got them going?'

For weeks they refrained from any sexual activity on a Friday or on any night as Kitty and I waited for the new series of Jonathan Ross to test our theory. When the trails for the new series started a few months later we were more excited than anyone, for the strangest of reasons.

The big night arrived. Kitty and I watched the show, unable to enjoy it as we were only waiting for it to end. We knew the neighbours were in and watching it too as I kept muting our TV to hear theirs next door. Finally the show reached its conclusion. 'That's it fwar tonight, ladies and gentlemen, join me next week when my guests will be Tewwy Wogan, Julianne Moore, Will Fewwel and the Scissor Sisters,' Jonathan said as I turned the TV off in anticipation. After months of abstinence were the neighbours to return to their old sex schedule in line with the BBC's scheduling of their flagship chat show?

Disappointment. We heard them switch their TV off, and then nothing. Silence. It was over. The passion in their relationship must have just waned like with so many couples. It sounds creepy to say we were disappointed. We're not perverts. But we were disappointed. We wanted our theory to be proved correct. Just as we were losing hope we heard the lady next door break her own record for the loudest scream.

'Give it to me!'

Followed by the sound of the headboard banging against our wall, not heard since Jonathan had finished interviewing Jarvis Cocker in the spring.

Kitty and I were elated that our theory had been proved correct. Our neighbours could only have sex after *Friday Night with Jonathan Ross* had been broadcast. We both spontaneously applauded, whooping and cheering the coital cacophony coming from next door.

Then suddenly, mid-moaning, they fell silent.

'Why have they stopped?' Kitty whispered.

'Oh shit,' I whispered back. 'They heard us. Of course they did, the wall is so thin.'

Kitty and I were paralysed lying next to each other on one side of the wall, our neighbours too were paralysed in what I imagine was a less comfortable position on the other side. All four of us afraid to make a sound. But then, after a few very tense minutes, they started up again, so erotically charged by Jonathan's lisp or whatever it was, they had to keep going.

Kitty and I became more and more desperate to move out with every passing Friday night, and added 'detached' to our lengthening list of boxes to tick if we were ever in a position to spend more than £200 a week on rent. Looking back, we are grateful that Sky Plus hadn't been invented then, otherwise they might have been at it 24/7.

*

The day of my meeting with Addison and the Head of Entertainment at the BBC was a big day, underlined by the fact that Kitty let me off the 'early shift' with Lucas.

'Morning, darling,' said Kitty as she carried a tray into the bedroom. 'I brought you breakfast in bed.'

Breakfast in bed is a very kind and loving gesture that is always appreciated by one's partner despite the net result being crumbs that cling to the bedding for eternity. I found one just the other day that I believe was of the vintage, Valentine's Day 2002.

'Thank you, darling,' I said as she placed a tray on my lap whilst I was sitting up, wedging pillows behind me, salivating at a perfectly poached egg on toast to ready me for my big meeting.

'Are you going to wear that awful suit?' Kitty asked as Lucas toddled in, banging the walls with a wooden toy hammer, giving the neighbours a small taste of their own medicine.

'I only have one suit, darling, so I'll have to wear it,' I replied.

'Why don't you just wear those nice Marks and Spencer trousers and a shirt instead?' she suggested.

'I have to wear the suit, it's the smartest thing I own. Addison always wears a suit. All his acts wear suits,' I insisted.

The one and only suit I had was made by a Chinese gentleman called Rocky in Singapore. There are various gigs abroad that circuit comics play to expat communities. Suddenly, instead of driving for hours to gig in a UK city or town for a £200 pay cheque, you were in Tokyo or Dubai or Hong Kong. It was all expenses paid, including flying in the very exciting Premium Economy class, which was better than Economy but not as good as Business. I think the fork and spoon were metal, but the knife still plastic. There was also a label on the headrest that said 'Premium', so I could lean forward when passengers from Economy were walking past on their way to the loo to show my superiority, and point at it with my metal fork, ensuring they noticed. The hotels were 5-star luxury and all paid for, as was all the food at the hotel which was often wonderful all-you-can-eat buffets. The only thing that wasn't paid for was us, the comedians. I would earn less than a normal weekend gigging in Nottingham or Birmingham. I'd come home with about £300 and several pounds to lose from my waistline, now filled with free croissants, sushi, meze and mini-lemon tarts (often all on the same plate) from the buffet.

On my first trip to Singapore, some of the other comics I went with had all done the gigs before so were full of advice about where to eat and visit. Without wanting to be crude, the main tourist advice they gave for a day trip was to go to the shopping mall they had renamed 'Four Floors of Whores', which they frequented multiple times in what I assumed was a quest to contract a variety of sexual diseases. Although my focus was very much on the free buffet, my interest was piqued when the other comics said they were all off to visit Rocky, who I initially assumed was a local pimp. But no, Rocky was a tailor and apparently for £100 he would create a Savile Row quality bespoke suit for a price to be found nowhere else on earth. I discussed the expenditure with Kitty on a phone call that probably cost half as much as Rocky's fees, and the decision was made to purchase my first tailored suit.

Myself and my fellow comedians, probably best not to name them but safe to assume they all were middle-aged men in less than happy marriages, burst through the door of Rocky's little shop, jangling a bell on entry. Rocky embraced them all like old friends, probably in a similar way the whores did in the mall. And like the whores in the mall, and to my alarm, Rocky was soon on his knees face to face with my belt buckle. Although, thankfully, the similarities ended there as he proceeded to measure my inside leg.

Armed with my measurements and my selection of a safe dark blue fabric, Rocky presented me with my first ever suit on the morning of my Premium Economy flight home. In return he received approximately £100 and my email address. To this day I receive a monthly email from him asking if I want another suit. I haven't replied to a single one of his emails mainly owing to one fatal flaw in his tailoring, the zip. The zip would pull up beautifully, the clasps were sewn perfectly. The problem lay in the imperceptibly slow unzipping that would occur after about an hour of wear. I tried to remedy this with a safety pin but found the proximity of something so sharp to something so important way too stressful. So instead, I just had to keep remembering to pull it back up at regular intervals.

'If you're going to wear that suit, you must remember to keep checking your flies are up, Michael,' Kitty reminded as I mopped up the yolk of my egg on the morning of my big meeting, crumbs falling onto the bed sheets to remain for forever.

'Do you want me to text you?' she asked.

'To remind me to do my flies up?' I replied.

'Yes, you really don't want your flies undone. You're trying to make a good impression. It doesn't matter how charming and funny you are at lunch, if you stand up with your flies open it's kind of over.'

'You're right, that's why I'll remember,' I reassured her.

I was meeting Elaine Bedell. She was the Head of Entertainment at the BBC. I don't think I need to explain how important and powerful she was, it's all there in her job title. I was all too aware of this as I stood clutching my travel card on the Northern Line tube to Leicester Square in my bespoke Singapore suit, fiddling so much with my zipper that people were edging away from me. I arrived early but hung around nearby until 1 p.m. The original and infamous Ivy restaurant is located on West Street between Leicester Square and Covent Garden; London's longest-running theatre production, *The Mousetrap* at the St Martin's Theatre, is a few doors along. Over the years, when passing, I had attempted the impossible task of peering through the stained-glass windows on the Ivy's facade, wondering which celebs were dining within. Now I stood outside the door, checked my fly for the hundredth time since leaving home, and headed in.

The maître d' greeted me warmly. I felt like Roger Moore or Michael Caine, as I gave him the name of the reservation. He replied with the words nobody wants to hear and the coolest people have never heard, 'You're the first to arrive.' I really didn't want to be sitting on my own, needily waiting. I panicked. 'I'll come back,' I said and walked straight out at the very moment Addison and Elaine were arriving together.

'You leaving, Michael?' Addison asked, bemused.

'No, no, I just . . . lost my bearings. Hi, Elaine,' I said, deflecting the awkwardness.

'Hi, Michael, nice to see you,' she said.

We kissed each other hello on both cheeks without a hitch, and were led to our table as I scanned the dining room for celebrities, and saw only Christopher Biggins. Having recently seen Noel Gallagher in Take One, my local Chinese takeaway, I was starting to wonder what all the fuss was about. Addison seemed a bit more smartly dressed than usual and he was behaving slightly differently, more courteous, less bluster. Elaine was important, this was important. It was easier for me to shine with the more serious and diluted version of Addison. Elaine was very charming and friendly and obviously liked me. I dropped a few of my regular 'fancy restaurant' jokes. Jokes about how you pay all this money at the best restaurants and the first thing they give you is bread and water: 'Some bread for the table? Water for the table? It's a Michelin star restaurant and so far it's no better than an orphanage.'

'Michael's fantastic. Since his performance at the Royal Variety my phone hasn't stopped ringing. ITV are very excited about him, but you know how much I love the BBC. I feel it's his natural home.'

This was the first time I'd heard Addison say ITV in a meeting with the BBC, and it would certainly not be the last. Similar to the book deal he would secure me in the future, Addison's tactics were often based around the threat of taking his talent to someone's biggest rivals.

'We would love Michael on the BBC. We just have to find the right thing for him, the best thing, and not rush it,' Elaine gushed.

I was loving every minute of this, sipping my sparkling water between compliments. When the waiter came over to take our order I assumed Addison or Elaine would ask for more time as none of us had glanced at the menu, but they knew exactly what they wanted having eaten there countless times before and expertly reeled off their orders, along with a few personal preferences.

'And you, sir?' asked the waiter, turning to me. Not wanting to waste time I ordered the first thing I saw on the menu.

'I think I'll just have . . . the langoustine.'

I had never ordered langoustine before, nor eaten it. I had never even said it out loud and made as big a mess of the pronunciation as I was about to make eating it. I wasn't trying to be sophisticated or anything, I was just enjoying the meeting so much I wanted to get back to it. When the langoustines arrived I immediately regretted my decision as they lay on the plate staring at me with their eyes, their actual eyes. The waiter placed a finger bowl next to me. What have I got myself into? 'This soup's tasteless,' I said pointing at the finger bowl, starting to overdo my fancy restaurant jokes. The conversation continued to flow between the three of us as I tried to peel my first langoustine which, although dead, managed to roll its eyes at me. I saw a flicker of confusion in Elaine's eye as she noticed me struggling.

I wanted to salvage the situation and saw the lemon wedge as the perfect opportunity. My plan was to squeeze lemon all over my langoustines, chef-like, expertly. This was a mistake. Many of you would have squeezed lemons on food and 99 per cent of the time the juice shoots directly onto the food. Unfortunately, 1 per cent of the time it shoots off at an oblique angle, and this was one such occasion. I squirted the lemon juice past the eye of the langoustine and directly into the eye of the Head of Entertainment at the BBC. Naturally she screeched with surprise and it must have stung too.

'I'm so sorry!' I said as I passed her all the napkins on the table. Addison was rendered speechless as Elaine repeatedly batted her eyelid over her violated citrussy eyeball.

'It's fine, it's fine,' Elaine said, as her eye started to swell.

The rest of the lunch passed without incident. It was very much my nature to fixate and worry about the acidic attack, but Elaine was so kind and had a great sense of humour about it. I knew really it was just a good anecdote and hadn't affected how she saw me. Well, it had affected how she saw me, but you know what I mean. The lunch concluded with an exciting plan. Long term, Elaine felt I could be a future star on the BBC, and on Saturday nights in particular. But for now she was going to help me get my face on the box. She mentioned the long-running jewel in their crown *Have I Got News for You*. It was all rather dizzying. I kissed Elaine goodbye as expertly as before and she jumped in a taxi. As I was embracing Addison farewell, he seemed pleased with how it went.

'Good lunch, Michael, very positive. She likes you a lot, which is good news.'

'Thanks, Addison, it's really exciting,' I replied as he too jumped into the next taxi on the rank, before rolling the window down and pointing to my waistline.

'Oh . . . and your flies are undone.'

4

'Great news!' Danny announced into his phone headset in his customary upbeat tone.

'What is it?' I replied whilst watching Lucas playing with a limbless Spiderman at our local playgroup. Once a week Kitty or I would take Lucas to the local church hall, where he and other toddlers fought over buckets full of ancient and broken toys. Getting his hands on the Spiderman with no hands or legs was actually a pretty decent result; one week he played with a broken battery casing for two hours.

'I've got you on *8 Out of 10 Cats* next week,' announced Danny proudly.

'That's great,' I said, feigning excitement, my heart beating hard with instantaneous nerves.

8 Out of 10 Cats was a successful panel show hosted by Jimmy Carr, the darling of Channel 4. Jimmy and I had started on the bottom rung of the comedy circuit at around the same time. I had gigged with Jimmy at several 'open mic' comedy nights, where unpaid wannabe stand-ups who think they're funny each have five minutes onstage to find out if the audience agrees. Most give up and go back to the day job and a few, like myself, keep toiling. But Jimmy just sailed through and his career went stratospheric very quickly. I was going to explain the format of *8 Out of 10 Cats* to you but just had to google it myself. Basically, the format isn't relevant on most panel shows – every round of every panel show is a springboard for you and the other guests to be as funny and silly as possible. I've been funny and silly my whole life, so I thought panel shows would be a walk in the park.

Most panel shows tend to have two teams made up of a team captain and their guests. The team captains on my debut were regulars Sean Lock and Dave Spikey. The other guests were Swedish weather girl Ulrika Jonsson, the Channel 4 newsreader Krishnan Guru-Murthy and Johnny Vegas. I had never met any of them before. Ulrika seemed nice when she was doing the weather, Krishnan Guru-Murthy was always charming in his flamboyant ties when he read the news. A newsreader and a weather girl on a comedy panel show. If I was there to read the travel news I might have felt out of my depth, but comedy was my thing. I was going to be fine, surely.

Shortly before the show recorded, I was taken to make-up. I loved the idea of make-up, especially a bit of bronzer. A few brushes and you've got a healthy tan.

'Make me look like I've just come back from two weeks in Florida,' I asked the make-up artist.

'You'd like some bronzer?' she asked.

'No, it's hurricane season, I want to look windswept,' I joked, and she laughed.

This is great, I thought. I'm relaxed and being funny, I just need to carry on when the cameras are rolling. I looked at myself in the mirror as the make-up was applied to my face. I was looking better with every passing second, more like a TV star. My Singapore suit was looking as sharp as the safety pin holding up the zip and the shocking-pink shirt I wore was suitably attention seeking.

The sound man clipped a microphone on my pink lapel and hooked the battery pack on my belt in an always awkward procedure dominated by apologies. The wire is intrusively fed up the inside of your shirt, and you both long for it to pop out of the top while you find out whether the sound man has brushed his teeth recently.

I now looked and sounded the part and was led to a door with a neon 'Studio 1' sign above it. Everyone else appearing on the show was loitering, covered in their own less bronze make-up, chatting breezily and laughing. I introduced myself as confidently as I could and tried not to be perturbed by a wardrobe lady who was rolling a sticky de-fluffing device over my £100 Singapore suit before moving on to Jimmy's significantly more expensive one and to Sean Lock's and Johnny Vegas's shirts. With our fluff all intermingled on the de-fluffer, it was time for us to mingle for real. We stepped just inside the door of the studio; I could hear the floor manager addressing the audience but still saw nothing of the set. I was surrounded by wires and busy crew members. Jimmy and all the stars of the show were bathed in darkness waiting to be called into the limelight. One by one we were introduced to the audience. I stood there as the other guests disappeared out of sight onto the set being cheered to the rafters. The largest cheers reserved for the other comedians.

'Please welcome Michael McIntyre,' announced the studio floor manager.

Even I nearly said, 'Who?' A ripple of polite applause greeted me as I walked onto the set. It was surreal and disorientating. Having seen a programme on television and then being on the set is a weird experience, like you've jumped into the telly. The set looked vast, the distance between the guests so much bigger than I was expecting. Jimmy was quipping away with the audience to roars of laughter and the show hadn't even started yet. Every time Jimmy, Sean or Johnny uttered a word the audience erupted. For the first fifteen minutes I was in essence an audience member, laughing with everyone else. But in truth I was in shock and awe at how quick witted the other comics were. They had jokes prepared and were riffing and bantering hilariously. Sean and Johnny embarking on off-the-cuff comedic flights of fancy that made me want to retire. When Ulrika got a big laugh and then Krishnan Guru-Murthy an even bigger one, I realized I was being humiliated. Just when I thought things couldn't get any worse, Johnny Vegas turned his attention to me. When I say 'attention' I mean his comedy brain. Comedians will scan everyone and everything to be potentially mined for laughs and Johnny

Vegas, despite his haphazard persona, has a razor-sharp and brilliant comedy mind as I unfortunately discovered when I found myself and, in particular, my pink shirt, in his cross hairs. My pink shirt to Johnny Vegas was like a red rag to a bull.

'Who are you?' he literally said to me. 'What are you?'

I don't recall what I said back but the sound of my posh, camp voice sent him into a frenzy of ridicule, like I was in the front row of one of his gigs rather than an equal on a comedy panel show.

I just sat there with an inane grin and took it. I felt like some kind of a freak. I hated every second. Everyone was charming before and after the show, but when the cameras rolled it was dog eat dog, which was maybe a more apt name than *8 Out of 10 Cats*. Jimmy very kindly telephoned me late that night to see if I was OK and assured me that the show would look good.

'You'll be amazed at what they can do in the edit,' Jimmy said.

'Can they edit me out entirely?' I wanted to say, but didn't.

Jimmy was right. The show looked fine when it went out on the TV. I was quiet but had a few lines that were bolstered by added laughs in the edit. Laughs borrowed from somebody else who was actually funny. Our three hours of filming was condensed to a half-hour show that really zipped along. All of Johnny Vegas's cutting remarks were on the cutting room floor as if they never happened. But they did happen, and I was shaken by the experience.

Despite my horrifying debut the producers were pleased. They told me that chipping in occasionally is all they need.

'Three laughs in a half-hour show is great. We like that you didn't interrupt, especially when Sean really got going,' the producers said.

Rather than being penalized for having nothing funny to say, I was being complimented for not interrupting when funnier people had funny things to say. I assumed this was just lip service, but the producers were true to their word as they booked me soon after to appear on a one-off panel show celebrating the tenth anniversary of Channel 5, entitled *I Blame the Spice Girls*, in reference to the girl band launching the channel. They sent me an enormous pack of subjects that would be in the show and I took the decision not to read them. I thought I didn't need to prepare. Johnny Vegas gave me a baptism of fire but was very funny. He was riffing and improvising with such confidence, I thought that's what I should do.

Just before the filming I spoke to Danny on the phone from my dressing room.

'Are you prepared, mate?' Danny asked, on his hands-free as he cycled home, texts pinging throughout our conversation.

'No, I haven't written anything. That's not really my style. I'm just going to relax and be myself,' I replied.

'Are you sure that's wise, mate?' Danny said doubtfully.

'Definitely,' I said, 'I've thought about it a lot, this is the best way for me to play it.'

The show was hosted by Liza Tarbuck and featured two teams. I was with Frankie Boyle and Ben Miller and the other team consisted of fellow newbie at that time Jason Manford, Trisha Goddard and (oh fuck!) Johnny Vegas. While waiting in the wings, I felt more confident. I had some experience. A bad experience, but experience nevertheless. I knew what to expect; I was determined. My shocking-pink shirt was replaced by a less eye-catching blue and I felt ready for whatever Johnny Vegas would throw at me. Just before we were introduced onto the set, my confidence took another boost when Johnny Vegas came over and apologized for being a bit full-on with me before. He was gracious and genuine. If I wasn't to be the target of his comedy, I had a much better chance of shining myself.

Buoyed by my new relationship with Johnny, we all took our seats and the show began with me feeling positive. That didn't last long. My first clue that I may have made a mistake with my lack of preparation was when I saw that Frankie Boyle and Jason Manford had pages and pages of A4 sheets of jokes piled up on their desks as I sat in front of a now empty glass of water. My first contribution to the show was a hopeless impression of Nelson Mandela. I had never impersonated Nelson Mandela before. I don't know why I did it. It was so bad and not funny that nobody understood quite what was going on. I remember Johnny Vegas gazing at me, regretting his decision to give me an easy ride. My next attempt at humour was an 'off the cuff' joke greeted by total silence and also confusion: as my Mandela impression had been so weird most of the audience, who didn't know me, assumed that was my actual voice. I had totally lost the audience. Jason and Frankie took over and were amazingly funny as, of course, was Johnny. The recording lasted about four hours and I literally sat there in silence while the show went on around me. If I thought my *8 Out of 10 Cats* appearance was bad, this was infinitely worse. It is no exaggeration to say I became totally mute. Following another avalanche of hilarity from the other comics, the host Liza Tarbuck turned to me. Obviously the producers had asked in her earpiece to try to bring me into the show.

'What about you, Michael? Do you have anything to say on this?' she said to me, the mute Mandela.

I felt so exposed. So humiliated. Like a schoolboy who hadn't done his homework, which in a way I was.

'No,' was all I could muster in reply. Despondent, resigned, already thinking about other careers I could pursue.

'No?' questioned Liza.

It was as if time stood still. The loudly laughing studio audience fell silent. It was excruciating. You could have heard a pin drop – and if I had done I would have picked it up and stabbed myself with it.

'No,' I repeated.

When you do pre-recorded shows, everybody speaks for hours and you never know what will make the final edit. I was pretty confident that this particular exchange between Liza and myself would not make it onto the broadcast show. I was being paid to be funny and my only contribution to the last hour of the recording was the word 'no'. If the producers had booked my two-year-old son Lucas at least he would have added, 'car', 'map' and 'zoo'.

People make mistakes at work. My work was now on television, so my mistakes were public and witnessed by millions. The stakes are very high. If you mess it up, you won't be invited back; your reputation can crumble in an instant. My ego was shattered. The only thing that saved me after this horror story was that it was on Channel 5, not very public or witnessed by millions, in fact hardly anyone watched. Personally, the button marked '5' on my remote control at home had never been touched. Not once had Kitty or I pressed it. Even when Lucas played with the controls he stuck to 1 to 4. When the show was televised I actually forgot that it was on as Kitty and I were watching a DVD.

'You finish it if you're enjoying it. I just can't stay awake, darling,' she said with her eyes closed, often her last words of the day.

'It's OK, darling. I'll turn it off. We'll finish it tomorrow night,' I said, hitting the red button and plunging the bedroom into darkness.

'Oh shit!' I blurted, hijacking Kitty's drift to slumber.

'What is it?' she said in the darkness.

'The neighbours are watching the Channel 5 show that I was shit on!'

She listened closely and heard voices and laughter coming from the TV next door, Manford, Boyle, Vegas, Tarbuck.

'I can't hear your voice,' she said.

'You won't,' I admitted with regret.

Apart from the neighbours, I know of nobody who saw that show. Thankfully Addison wasn't there to witness it or *8 Out of*

10 Cats before it. He had missed both catastrophes and can't have watched them on TV as he made no reference to either when he called the following week.

'Michael. Addison. All good for *Have I Got News for You.* Danny's got the date in the diary. I'm coming down to this one so I'll see you there.'

I felt like throwing up. I had concluded that I simply couldn't do panel shows. I wasn't suited to them and although there were no serious repercussions from my Channel 5 disaster, another one and my career would be over before it had begun. It had only been a few months since the glory of the Royal Variety Performance and already I was in the last chance saloon. I was in no position to turn down such an opportunity, but I was finding out that opportunities for success are also opportunities for highly visible failure. I genuinely didn't know if I was cut out to succeed in a panel show environment. I struggled being surrounded by competing comedians. It was unsettling, not what I was used to onstage when it's just me dictating and expanding on my own thoughts without them being interrupted or spun in another direction.

I made the decision to prepare as thoroughly as I could for *Have I Got News for You.* For *8 Out of 10 Cats* and *I Blame the Spice Girls* I had been sent huge swathes of information about what questions would be on the show. I ignored all of them thinking it best to be natural and spontaneous. Well, that didn't work. Determined not to make the same mistake again, I was going to swot up. Unfortunately, the nature of *Have I Got News for You* is that you can't prepare. It's about the news, which can break at any time. 'Watch the news, buy the papers,' was the only response Danny got when we tried to get some information from the producers.

This was the big one for me. Addison would be there, Elaine Bedell would be there, the *Have I Got News for You* ratings are huge with up to 5 million viewers. This wasn't Channel 4 or Channel 5, this was BBC1. I spent the week watching every news broadcast and reading every newspaper. There was one major story that week about some British sailors who were taken hostage by the Iranians. Is that funny? How is that funny? In my favour was the smaller number of guests. There's a guest host, team captains Paul Merton and Ian Hislop who each have just one guest, one of whom was me. The other guest was Krishnan Guru-Murthy, the Channel 4 newsreader who I had been watching all week and had witnessed my humiliation at the hands of Johnny Vegas on *8 Out of 10 Cats*. How weird that he should be on another show with me. My immediate thought was that if I had another panel show shocker he might turn my continued failings into a news item.

'Don't tell me Johnny Vegas is hosting,' I asked Danny.

'No, it's Jeremy Clarkson,' Danny revealed.

Having not met Jeremy, I gulped. His persona was even more intimidating than Johnny Vegas. But then I smelt an opportunity. The main thing I had learnt from my brutal panel show experiences is that everything and everyone is fair game for a laugh, and boy did I need laughs. I had a few weak jokes prepared about Sea Lords from the Iranian hostage story and little else, so maybe I should go for Clarkson like Johnny Vegas went for me. I googled Jeremy Clarkson and found out that he had just come back from Barbados, where he had apparently played tennis with Prince Harry. So I concocted a whole little routine about it, impersonating Clarkson arranging his matches with the Prince in his trademark way, describing his shot-making like he describes cars, and an impersonation of the Queen reacting to the news that her grandson was playing tennis with Clarkson, 'What, that bloody chauffeur?' This is all I had, along with my off-the-cuff wit that had yet to make an appearance outside of one make-up room.

'I don't want to teach you how to suck eggs, just be yourself and do what you do,' was Addison's pep talk when he popped into my dressing room.

I've never really understood the 'sucking eggs' expression. The egg reference only served to make me feel more nauseous. And as for 'do what you do', well, I tended to die on my arse on these shows. With that he was gone, to hobnob with other powerful men in suits who he had invariably 'known for twenty years'.

Then came another knock on my door. It was my team captain, Ian Hislop. Ian always seemed frightening to me. As editor of *Private Eye* and regular on *Have I Got News for You* he had a razor-sharp wit. As someone who had only just started paying attention to the news that past week, I was intimidated. He couldn't have been kinder and more charming. He told me he had seen me on the *Charlotte Church Show* which was my very first appearance on TV and that he had told the producers to look out for me. I couldn't believe that Ian Hislop thought I was funny, nor could I believe he watched the *Charlotte Church Show*. He was a true gentleman, supportive, full of advice and wishing me well. I was on Ian's team, just the two of us. The show was so much more intimate than my previous two panel show horror stories. All the guests were huddled around; it felt like a dinner party with great guests and no dinner.

Prior to the cameras rolling each person has to say something to make sure their mic levels are correct. Everyone had a funny remark and I, true to form, just rambled a whole load of nonsense. Ian scribbled on his pad and placed a note in front of me – 'Relax', it read. *8 Out of 10 Cats* and *I Blame the Spice Girls* had been so competitive, I felt so alone, so isolated and above all, not very funny. But now I had Ian Hislop on my side, my saviour, who thinks I'm funny and not a weird posh camp unknown. I'll always be grateful to him for that. Kindness did exist in this new ruthless world I found myself in. Although it wasn't an example I was set to follow as my only hopes of survival on this show lay with my potential Clarkson takedown.

The first subject that arose was thankfully about the Iranian hostages. Because there were fewer participants, and because Ian and Paul had nothing to prove, the atmosphere felt inclusive. I delivered my pre-planned jokes and got some average laughs. 'Well done,' Ian whispered. Every time I said anything amusing, Ian would congratulate and encourage me. Paul Merton was quieter than I had expected, but would burst into life in his own magnificent, surreal and hilarious way. For the first time on a panel show, I was beginning to enjoy myself.

When Clarkson asked Paul Merton's team a question totally unrelated to himself, 'What other event overshadowed the pedalo accident?' I seized the moment and interrupted even though the question wasn't even directed to my team.

'Was it a tennis match involving you and royalty?' I interjected.

'Stick to the subject,' Clarkson uncomfortably replied.

But there was no chance of that as I launched into my seemingly spontaneous jokes about Clarkson on his holiday. The audience lapped it up. Jeremy laughed along and my new best friend Ian loved it, congratulating me afterwards saying it was in the spirit of the show to have a go at the host.

I had appeared on three panel shows and finally done OK. Thankfully, I did well on the one that mattered most. At last, I had appeared on a show I could tell my friends and family to watch and not pray they missed. I wanted to tell the neighbours to watch it but, having not met them personally, it would have been an odd exchange.

As I headed to the car that would whisk me home after the recording, Addison gave me a hug goodbye and whispered in my ear.

'Did well tonight. I thought you might have been fucked after that Channel 5 car crash.'

He *had* seen it. I was teetering on the edge, but had pulled it round. If Jeremy Clarkson hadn't played tennis with Prince

Harry maybe I would have dropped back onto the comedy circuit, back driving around the country in my fluff-covered suit, the days of wardrobe ladies rolling sticky de-fluffers over me never to return again.

But I was still in the game.

Just.

5

I struggle to call people by their actual birth names, I very quickly rename them. I don't know why I do this. I renamed Addison 'The Captain', Danny 'DC', an abbreviation of Danny Cool. I have literally never called my wife Kitty. It's strange writing 'Kitty' over and over again in this book as that isn't actually someone I know. I have so many names for her: 'Padder', on account of her constantly and busily padding around perfecting our home, 'Humsy', short for 'Best Human in the World', 'Shweeeeetieeee', which I shout in a sustained high-pitched voice, 'Maggie', I don't even remember why. The list goes on. But for all my nicknaming, one stands out as totally befitting. In the midst of my appearing more and more on TV I got a call from Fay Clayton, who was promptly renamed 'Big Fee Fay'. It was a call I will never forget.

At their worst, my debts amounted to over £30,000. I had become very familiar with seeing a minus sign before the total when I pressed 'account balance' at the ATM. A homeless person sitting beside a cash machine once told me he had no money.

'No money?' I said. 'I remember when I had no money. The good old days. Now I have minus money.'

Naturally I immediately realized the inappropriate nature of my joke and gave him a fiver, plunging myself into further debt.

As many readers will unfortunately know, debt is a terrible downward spiral that grows exponentially due to additional fines and charges imposed by banks and debt collectors. I remember Lloyds Bank charging me £30 a day if I slipped into an unauthorized overdraft. This was normally due to direct debits automatically leaving my account to pay bills. The very nature of having less than no money is that you obviously have no money. So why charge me £30 a day? How am I going to pay that? The same would happen with debt collectors. In extreme circumstances, if you can't pay a bill it gets passed to a debt collecting agency who write to you (always in angry capitalized red ink) demanding all the money you owe in full, plus charges of their own. Again, I have no money to pay the first bill, how can I pay that bill and your bill?

I blame nobody but myself for getting into debt in the first place. I was very naive when it came to interest rates, naive to the point of not understanding the actual concept. Growing up, my experience of borrowing money had been from my wealthy grandmother, who never asked for it back let alone charged interest. Blinded by the offers of money in big print from loans and credit cards, I never read the small print. If the font sizes were reversed, I might have avoided such a financial mess. I'm not blaming the font size. Actually, I am blaming the font size. If I ever went into politics, a ban on small print would definitely be part of my manifesto (I always thought that word sounded like a gay nightclub). How deceitful to hide key information in smaller, hard to read text. I once mooted to Shweeeeetieeee (actually, I'll stick with Kitty) that I should get laser eye surgery, having worn glasses most of my life.

'You have to be careful, Michael,' she warned, 'I've heard it can be dangerous, make sure you read the small print.'

I replied with a joke I'm pleased to squeeze into this book. 'I can't read the small print, that's why I want the surgery.'

So, through a combination of naivety and poor eyesight, Kitty and I had endured many sleepless nights burdened by our money worries. I was gigging regularly around the country and with my new-found television exposure the future was looking brighter, but I still had substantial debts and interest to pay. The day Big Fee Fay first called me, Kitty and I owned next to nothing. The flat was rented, our car leased, she was reading a book from the library and I was watching a rented DVD on the television I got from Curry's on a 'Buy Now, Pay Later' deal.

'Hi, is that Michael?' Fay asked when I picked up the phone, pausing the DVD.

'Speaking,' I replied. I always say 'Speaking' when someone asks if it's me on the phone. It's so annoying. I wish I didn't. It just pops out of my mouth automatically. Identifying yourself by describing what you're doing at that particular moment is weird. I may as well have said, 'Sitting' or 'Scratching'.

'My name's Fay Clayton, we haven't met. I work for Off The Kerb and book the corporate events. I've had an offer I wanted to run by you.'

'Hi Fay,' I said, using her birth name for the first and last time.

'It's for an event in Portugal for Sony, they'll fly you out the day before, then you perform the next day and fly back the morning after. They've offered five thousand pounds.'

'Offered? Me?' I asked, stunned. In truth I nearly fainted. I had never done a gig for five thousand pence, let alone five thousand pounds.

'Yes,' Fay confirmed.

'That's amazing. Really? Are you sure?' I asked, disbelieving.

'It's an annual event Sony do. Dara Ó'Briain did it last year and said it was fine, good audience. Danny's freed up your diary so if you're up for it I'll confirm with them.'

As she was speaking, I was staring at the Sony logo on my television. I'm finally going to buy this Sony TV outright, with their own money, I thought to myself.

'Yes, yes, yes. Are you kidding? Of course I want to do it! I've never earned anything like that before. I would do it for less!' I admitted. The truth being I would have done it for a suit with a working zip.

'That's not the attitude, Michael, we're trying to make you money,' Fay laughed.

'Thank you, thank you, thank you. This is amazing,' I

gushed. 'I love Sony. Sony are my saviour. Sanyo, Panasonic, Hitachi, Blaupunkt are dead to me! I'm Sony forever!'

'You should probably open the gig with that,' Fay suggested.

'I'm sorry to ask, but how long does it take them to pay?' I said, glancing at the pile of unopened letters, the ones with the windows on the front I assumed were bills.

'They pay upfront, you'll get the money as soon as you've done the gig,' Fay said.

'Holy shit! This is the best phone call I've ever received,' I yelped. 'From this day forth you shall be known as . . . Big Fee Fay.'

There are few things more exciting than being armed with good news to tell a loved one. This news is often delivered in a quiz format where the person receiving the news is asked to guess what it is – although this mini-quiz show is often ruined by them making a guess that is better than the reality. But thankfully not on this occasion.

'Darling,' I said, running into the 'galley' kitchen before retreating out again realizing we couldn't both fit in there.

'That was Fay from the office on the phone. I've just been offered a gig in Portugal for Sony. Guess what they're giving me?'

'I don't know,' Kitty said.

'Guess,' I insisted.

'A camcorder?'

'No, money. Guess what they're paying me?'

'£500?' she said, thankfully not ruining the surprise.

'It does begin with a five,' I said.

Her face fell. 'Fifty pounds? But they pay for travel and accommodation, don't they?' she asked, falling into my trap.

'FIVE THOUSAND POUNDS!' I screamed as we jumped around on the decaying wooden floorboards, prompting a bang on the wall from the neighbours. Bloody cheek. It was genuinely overwhelming. Like a lottery win. How was it possible to pay so much money for me to perform the same twenty-minute set I would be doing that night in Chiswick for £150.

I flew to Lisbon a few weeks later and strangely remember checking into the hotel more clearly than the gig itself. An olive-skinned, dangerously attractive and flirtatious receptionist batted her eyelids and then enquired about how many keys I wanted to my room, asking in her Portuguese accent, 'Do you want one key?'

What I heard was, 'Do you want wankey?'

'Do I want wankey?' I asked, flustered to say the least.

'I can give you wankey if you want. Or I can give you more?' she replied.

I recounted this exchange to the attendees of the Sony event the following night and the international male-dominated audience loved it. A Japanese man, perhaps not understanding it was a joke, actually approached me after the show and asked what hotel I was staying at.

Receiving the cheque from Off The Kerb in the post was joyous. Spotting the handwritten windowless envelope in the pile of the threatening envelopes I was accustomed to was exhilarating. Just two pieces of paper were inside, a compliments slip signed by the Off The Kerb accountant Ann, soon renamed 'Money Ann', and a cheque signed by Addison for a whopping amount. The total contained all the gigs I had done, plus the panel shows and the Sony corporate money. I stared at it in disbelief. I laughed at how it still said 'Only' after the written amount. 'Only?' I told a few jokes and a silly story about a hotel receptionist giving me a wank and now I have all this money. The full extent of my ambition as a comedian was to make people laugh and have financial security, not have to worry about money. It never crossed my mind I could have more than that. The thin walls of our flat may have belonged to someone else, but I still felt proud to be renting them, to be putting food on the table and fighting to just about earn a living. But this felt different. It felt a bit absurd. When it had always seemed so hard to earn money and stay afloat, is there really a world where it can be this easy?

Kitty and I went together to deposit the cheque at the Muswell Hill branch of Lloyds Bank, like we were taking our child to their first day of school. The cheque was in my wallet in my inside pocket which I had my hand upon the whole time. Anyone monitoring the CCTV might have thought I had a gun. I filled out the deposit slip with a biro chained to the desk, about to trust people with all my money who didn't trust me with their pen. I handed the cheque to a smiley bank teller whose face dropped with concern as soon as she read it.

'Please excuse me,' she said, standing up from her desk and whipping her blind down in front of her with more haste than if I was a peeping Tom at her bedroom window.

'What's going on?' Kitty asked me.

'How do I know?' I said.

Moments later a heavy door to the side opened. A door I hadn't noticed before. An enormous, in all senses, Eastern European security guard emerged with a suited man who I deduced was the bank manager, thanks to the word 'Manager' on his name badge.

'Mr and Mrs McIntyre?' he said.

'Yes,' we replied in unison, the ever-growing queue behind us staring in morbid fascination at the unfolding events.

'Please will you come with us?' he asked in a deathly serious tone.

What was going on? Did they think I had a gun? Did they think I was robbing the bank? Who robs a bank by depositing money first? If anyone's robbing anyone it's the £30 a day they charge me for going a pound overdrawn.

Kitty and I were taken into a small room, I'm not going to say cell, but that's how it felt. The bank manager sat opposite us and the burly security guard stood by the door. The manager fixed me in the eye and said calmly, 'Mr McIntyre. Where did you get this money?'

I couldn't believe it. I was being accused of gaining this money by some sort of nefarious means, having never deposited a cheque for anything like that amount before. Do banks not believe comedians can make this much money? Did Lee Evans have to launder his income? Did the bank manager see me on *I Blame the Spice Girls* and assume my career was over and that I must have turned to a life of crime? The whole thing made me flustered and panicked; thankfully Kitty stepped in.

'My husband earned that money. It's a bit embarrassing you hauling us in here when all we're doing is giving you our money. Hard-earned money.'

'May I ask what you do?' the bank manager said.

'I'm a comedian,' I replied.

The bank manager then uttered the single most annoying question I ever get asked after revealing my profession.

'Would I have heard of you?'

What I should have said was, 'Obviously not! If you had heard of me, you and your heavy over there wouldn't have performed this little FBI-style arrest, making us feel like Bonnie and Clyde.'

What I actually pathetically said was, 'I recently appeared on *Have I Got News for You.*'

This seemed to excite him. A quick google confirmed I had indeed been on TV. We were released, he took our money and I learnt a new phrase: 'BACS Transfer'.

I then went on a glorious run of performing at corporate events for what Noel Edmonds on *Deal or No Deal* would describe as 'life-changing money'. If this was a film (you never know) there would now be a montage of Big Fee Fay phoning me over and over intercut with me performing in front of men in suits for more and more money. In fact, while writing this I've thought of a montage in the film *Scarface* which is the kind of thing I want you to envisage. It's when Al Pacino keeps harvesting cocaine between shaking a crooked bank manager's hand as he deposits holdalls full of cash. It was like that, but with jokes instead of cocaine.

Many of these corporates took place at the Grosvenor House Hotel in a huge former ice rink that was now called The Great Room, which seated over a thousand people. Just about every night of the year there is an event being held there. Drive down Park Lane in the evening and you will invariably see gentlemen in bow ties loitering outside, sneaking in cigarettes between dinner courses. Inside, some huge industry bash will be in progress and chances are a comedian will either be hosting or performing. Corporate entertainment is the lucrative little secret of comedians and television personalities. Most of these events are annual and book a new comedian each year. 'Last year we had Alan Carr', 'Jack Dee was brilliant. Or was it Rob Brydon?' were words I was often met with when I arrived.

There are hundreds of events every year, and if you get a good reputation you can take your seat on the gravy train and you're laughing, even if the audience aren't. Because corporates are notoriously tough. You get paid ten times more for ten times less of a response. The ice may have disappeared from The Great Room at the Grosvenor House Hotel but the frosty atmosphere remains for comedians. The reason corporate events are tough is simple. The audience is often dominated by men who aren't there for comedy. They are there to network, to feast and drink excessively, all at the expense of their employer. The audience in a comedy club have paid to laugh, they've literally bought into the idea of comedy. They sit in rows, facing the stage, looking for the funny in every word that comes out of the comedian's mouth. At a corporate event they sit at huge round tables with only half the table facing the stage – and their view is often blocked by massive centrepieces. The comedy tends to be after dinner but the room is so vast there are still plates being cleared, coffee being served, wine being poured, people going to or returning from the loo. To top it off, nearly everyone is in conversation with each other, as if nothing at all is going on onstage. They're chatting, flirting, relaxed, having a good time, guffawing at their own jokes. Often there's an auction too with money being raised for a good cause. A Comic Relief style incredibly sad film is played on massive screens enticing the now tearful audience to bid to help stop children dying. A minute later I'm onstage telling a joke about a Portuguese hotel receptionist offering to wank me off, to total silence and disapproving groans. The whole thing is a nightmare.

I tried to adapt my act to respective events, with varying results. My first awards hosting was the Kitchen and Bathroom Awards (who knew there was such a thing). It went OK despite this relatively weak opening:

'Last year I hosted the Attic and Downstairs Loo Awards, so for me this is a big step up, a dream come true.'

Other openings I was more proud of, but got less of a response. At the Customer Service Awards I walked on the stage and said in a monotone voice, 'The hosting of this award ceremony is important to me. Please wait and I will be hosting as soon as possible . . . The hosting of this award ceremony is important to me. Please wait and I will be hosting as soon as possible . . . The hosting of this event may be recorded for training purposes.'

Nothing. No laughs. Over a thousand people who worked in Customer Service didn't get that joke and just waited patiently for me to start.

It sounds like I'm making these up but I'm not. At the Health and Safety Awards, I was introduced, ran onto the stage, tripped (on purpose) and fell over screaming, 'My leg! My leg!'

Again, nobody got the joke or even rushed to my aid. I dusted myself off and began the ceremony.

Probably my worst experience, and I can't remember what the event was as I have obviously wiped it from my mind, was when I was struggling away onstage getting the occasional titter and someone from the audience threw a lump of sugar at me from the sugar bowl on their table. It was white sugar, naturally, a brown sugar user would never behave in such a manner. It hit me square on the forehead. This got an uproarious laugh from the audience, something which none of my jokes had thus far been able to trigger. Before I had a chance to think of a witty response another sugar lump was thrown, this time whizzing past my head. Cue more laughter from the audience. Anyone listening to a recording of this gig would think that I'd turned the audience as they were now in hysterics. Soon the whole room were throwing sugar lumps at me until I walked offstage, having endured both the unkindest and sweetest experience of my life. Following this event, Big Fee Fay inserted a clause in all of my corporate contracts entitled 'You Throw I Go', which permits me to immediately leave and still get paid if anything is thrown at me. It's not a clause that hugely endorses my ability as a stand-up comic, but it had unfortunately been proved to be necessary.

Not all corporates were this bad. I am pleased to say that the 'You Throw I Go' clause has not been activated since. Mainly, I just about survived by developing a corporate-specific set of jokes. These were jokes never too far away from a punchline – the patience for a longer story or routine simply wasn't there. Once the audience were lost there was no regaining their focus unless something was hurled at me.

There's no denying many of these highly paid occasions were soul destroying and damaging to my confidence. When I was on the comedy circuit I was unknown and broke, but I was confident in my ability. Panel shows and corporates were knocking my confidence. I needed to return to the purity of stand-up, to showcase what I had been honing and perfecting for years. The best place to do that has always been the Edinburgh Festival. Off The Kerb booked me into the 150-seat Pleasance Above every night for the month of August at the 2007 festival. Just me performing for an hour to whoever had paid to see me. The venue was one of the theatre spaces at the Pleasance Courtyard, the same place I had first met Addison the year before. Giant strides had been made in the last year. My Edinburgh poster was now adorned with 'As seen on *The Royal Variety Performance, Have I Got News for You* and *8 Out of 10 Cats*'. I chose not to add, 'And hopefully not seen on *I Blame the Spice Girls*'.

But I didn't become a comedian to pop up on panel shows and be average or to dodge sugar cubes while trying to entertain men in suits who cared more about the hospitality than me. I became a comedian because at its best, stand-up comedy is magical. In a room filled with people, one person is facing everyone else and rendering them helpless with face-hurting laughter.

I wanted that one person to be me.

It was time to get back on track.

6

There is a small storage room on the top floor of the Edinburgh University Students Association under the eaves of the roof. Go there now and this quiet, dust-gathering space will most likely be filled with unwanted furniture, filing cabinets of old exam papers or boxes of stationery resting against the cracking walls. Unless it is August. In August this storeroom is emptied, its walls covered with black drapes, a lighting rig and sound system installed, and fifty fold-up plastic chairs are placed two rows deep, transforming it into the Pleasance Attic, the venue at the Edinburgh Festival where I performed my first show in 2003. Near silence fills that room for eleven months of the year, and for the many nights I played there struggling to find my voice, the near silence remained. But for one magical night, I made people laugh more than I ever had before. Everything clicked into place and I became the version of myself that made me want to become a comedian in the first place. Kitty was on the train from London to see me and I was to meet her straight after the show at Waverley Station. I was excited and distracted by her arrival and tired from the relentlessness of performing a show every night. I normally sipped water before and during the show but on this night I ordered a Jack Daniel's from the bar at the Pleasance Courtyard and walked onstage drinking it. I was done caring. I abandoned my average jokes and improvised the whole hour to raucous laughter. For one night only, an island in a sea of mediocrity, I could make anything funny.

The Perrier Award, a silver trophy in the shape of a bottle of Perrier, is given to what is adjudged to be the best comedy show at the festival. I'll never understand the association between sparkling water and comedy and why Perrier decided to sponsor this award. But no British comedian can look at a bottle of Perrier without being immediately transported back to the intensity and anxiety of comedy's most important competition. Judges are dispatched to every one of the hundreds of shows in the hope of unearthing the next big thing and giving them a boost on their way to stardom. Five comedians are nominated, and on the final Saturday in August the winner is announced. The five chosen ones leave Edinburgh on the road to success, their faces splashed all over the newspapers, their name buzzing around broadcasters. Whereas everyone else leaves on the same path to obscurity they came on, back to the comedy clubs to dust themselves off and try again the following year. Frank Skinner, Lee Evans, Eddie Izzard, Jack Dee, Peter Kay and Graham Norton are just some of the names who had either won or been nominated in the years leading up to my debut in 2003. I struggled to sell tickets in my fifty-seat attic venue. When you are totally unknown your show's success depends upon enticing journalists in to review it. A favourable review can be photocopied and glued to the front of your posters all around Edinburgh. During the festival every inch of wall space in the city has a comedian's poster promoting their show pasted on it. Any comedian seen in WHSmith buying Pritt Stick has probably received a good review and is off to glue it all over town. As the days of the festival tick on posters begin to be adorned with 4- or 5-star reviews. Often just a strip of paper that reads: THE METRO**** or THE TIMES****. Darlings of Edinburgh that year like Adam Hills and Reginald D. Hunter would soon be barely visible under the galaxy of stars stuck on their posters. The combination of positive reviews and word of mouth will start to shift tickets until that magical SOLD OUT sign is whacked over your name for all to see in the Pleasance Courtyard. There is a clear trajectory in Edinburgh that can lead to fame.

At my debut festival in 2003 I decided I didn't want to know if there was a journalist at my show to review me. I thought it would add to my nerves and affect my performance, but not knowing may have been worse as I began to suspect every audience member of being a critic, especially the ones who weren't laughing. This was my first experience of critics. On the one hand I desperately needed them, but on the other their presence or suspected presence compounded my anxiety, the paranoia clipping my wings. Every day I would buy the papers early from the newsagent and scan websites to see if my show was among those being reviewed, and every day it wasn't. For over half of the festival my posters didn't have a single review glued on them.

I even made a joke about it to my sparse audience: 'It seems like every comedian here has at least one 4-star review for their show and I haven't even had a review. Everywhere I look I see four stars. I walked past a petrol station and even the unleaded is having a better festival than I am.'

My posters looked conspicuously bare, my hopeful face smiling as potential punters passed by, on their way to see the hot shows of the festival. A few members of my audience even told me they were only there as their first choice show had sold out. Heading into the last week of the festival I went to bed after another poorly attended show in front of around twenty people and logged on to the Chortle website. Chortle is by far the most successful and popular website specializing in UK comedy. I don't know how many people viewed it, but I knew for certain that every comedian read it, every single day. Still my name did not appear in the reviews section. In the morning when I opened my laptop the same Chortle page remained on the screen from the night before. I refreshed it and my name appeared. Having searched for my name so many times it felt surreal to finally see it. My heart raced. I breathlessly scanned the words, trying to read them all at once. But the key to the review wasn't the content, it was the golden stars below my name. Two of them. Two stars. That's what I had been waiting for. I felt sick and embarrassed. Getting a bad review is far worse than getting no review at all. I wanted to un-refresh the screen, to return it to how it was the night before. I had longed for my name to pop up on the homepage; now I longed for it to be erased. A 4- or 5-star review and I'd be off to buy Pritt Stick. A 3-star review would have been meaningless but not harmful. But two stars heralds me as one of the worst shows at the festival. My already avoided show was one to avoid. I had sold about thirteen tickets for that night's show. Would people return them?

This was my first experience of having to deal with a bad review. Although they become easier to shake off, it's never pleasant. Years later I received another 2-star review, this time in the *Guardian*, which I discovered whilst flicking through a free copy at Heathrow airport in transit to Scotland for the next leg of my tour. I genuinely wasn't overly bothered by the review. It was written by a man who simply doesn't find me funny. He had slated every single one of my shows. He's not a fan; why he keeps coming to see me, I'll never know. Also, I comforted myself with the fact that *The Times* and the *Telegraph* had reviewed the very same show and given me a far more favourable four stars. I was taking it in my stride as I strode down the tunnel to the aircraft. That was until I realized every passenger walking onto the plane was also being handed a free copy of the *Guardian* newspaper. I sat up tall in my seat to see nearly the whole plane slowly making their way to page 38 where my big smiling face was joined by a vitriolic assassination of my ability in my chosen profession. A woman sitting across the aisle was reading the paper from cover to cover and seemed to be discussing many of the articles with her husband. I cowered in my window seat hoping she hadn't seen me just two seats along. She turned the page onto my review and grinned the whole way though reading it. She finished reading, turned to her husband, held up the page for him to view and said, 'Ouch.' To which her husband replied, 'Oh yes, he's terrible.' Up to then I'd made it a point to avoid that big red emergency lever on the door, but pulling it suddenly seemed quite an attractive idea. 'Two-star comedian throws himself out of plane over the Highlands of Scotland' would have been the headline in the following day's *Guardian*, probably still around page 38.

More recently I performed in Oslo, Norway. I had a hugely enjoyable and successful show with the audience giving me a standing ovation at the end. The next morning, again at the airport, I saw a review in the local paper written in Norwegian. There was no star rating visible so I had no idea if it was positive or negative.

'This is great,' I said to my tour manager. 'I know in my heart that last night's gig went well. I always know myself how well a show has gone. I don't need validation or criticism from a reviewer. I don't understand a word of what this review says and I don't care to. This is how I should treat all reviews in future, as if they are written in a foreign language.'

It felt like an epiphany. If words can wound, don't read them. The review should be excellent. I got a standing ovation. If it was a bad review then who cares? The audience loved the show, who cared if a spiteful critic in their midst didn't. The Norwegian

My darling wife Kitty and I: so inseparable we decided
to glue our heads together.

Laughing at everybody else's jokes on *8 Out of 10 Cats* while failing to make any of my own.

A corporate event where I'm getting as much attention as the patio heaters, and probably as many laughs.

Finally getting laughs on TV with the very supportive Ian Hislop.

Addison (*left*) and Danny in the early days at Off The Kerb. Addison looks very young, and Danny seems to be an actual child.

Kitty and Lucas at Alma Road. A good example of how a baby dominates your life.

'Michael. Addison.'

My 2007 Edinburgh Festival poster.

A very nervous night for me. Not sure if I'm posing or needing a hug.

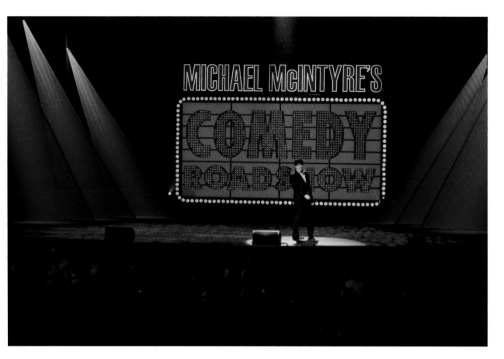

Not sure where this was, but it was definitely my favourite city of them all.

My pre-show ritual of questioning whether anything I have to say is funny.

Just before the BAFTAs. So, this is why I needed a pee! You know the rest.

At the Hammersmith Apollo in 2008, recording my first DVD *Live & Laughing*.

The man who is always behind me. My wingman (and boatman in this photo) Paul Tonkinson.

Former heavyweight champion Scott Welch, and Addison trying his best to look like former heavyweight champion Scott Welch.

An amazing night in an arena although I assume, like the audience, you're watching the screen and didn't notice me standing there.

This photo sums up life on tour more than any other. Although Terry probably only took the picture to check if he needed petrol.

Ossie and I at our country house in Wiltshire holding a defensive position between horsefly attacks.

words in the paper looked like gibberish and that's exactly what they should be to me, and my self-esteem.

Unfortunately, my epiphany was interrupted by a Norwegian gentleman in a hi-vis waistcoat who must have worked at the airport. He approached me and said, 'Michael McIntyre, right? I wanted to come to your show but couldn't get tickets. Sorry about that review in the paper, man, that guy has no sense of humour.'

I was then compelled to google translate the whole review. The word 'overrated' came up a lot. This led again to me considering pulling the big red emergency lever on the door, this time on the Scandinavian Airline's plane.

'Overrated comedian throws himself out of plane over the fjords of Norway' my hi-vis friend would have been reading the next morning.

There's a joke I always make when checking into a hotel that seems appropriate to drop in here. Whenever the receptionist asks, 'Would you like a newspaper in the morning? They're complimentary.' I always answer, 'Not to me they're not!'

Another brutal 2-star review in *The List*, Edinburgh's equivalent of *Time Out*, meant that my entire 2003 Edinburgh Festival star tally came to four. I resisted the temptation to con people by strapping CHORTLE AND THE LIST**** on my posters. But then, out of the blue (or grey, as I was in Edinburgh), I got a huge stroke of luck. That one and only night when I was properly funny, a judge for the Perrier Award was in the audience and persuaded the other judges on the panel to nominate me for the Perrier Best Newcomer Award, which I was eligible for as it was my debut. It was a magnificent and unexpected surprise to receive the news in the final week of the festival. I glued PER-RIER BEST NEWCOMER NOMINEE across all my posters and sold out my last few remaining shows.

I didn't win. Not for a moment did I think I would. But the experience of going to the ceremony with the champions of the festival who were nominated for the main award, whose star-covered faces I had been walking past for a month, was inspiring. Next year. Next year, I kept saying to myself. Next year, I will be as good as that one night, every night. Nobody will stop me. Next year, I will be nominated for the main award. I will win. I have a year to prepare. I have glimpsed how good I can be and some-one else has too. This is real. I can do this. Next year.

Next year came, and the one after, and the one after that and each time I was overlooked for a nomination. I know I was close because the judges are given free tickets and I knew when they had been allocated, and they always watched my show several times up to and including the night before the announcement. I was always in the running. On the longlist. Close. But after the final discussions, never made the shortlist. My annual wait for the phone to ring on the day the nominations are announced was excruciating and had always been deeply disappointing.

2007 was my chance to finally get nominated for the Perrier Award. I had momentum after my breakthrough performance at the Royal Variety and a strong showing on *Have I Got News for You*, and I was battle-hardened by my experiences at corporate events. A Perrier Award win or nomination would not only cement me as the next big thing but give me the industry stamp of approval that I craved. I would feel like a proper comedian. Like I belonged with the best. I couldn't think of anybody successful in comedy who hadn't received a nod from the Perrier panel for the main award.

Kitty and I decided to take Lucas and spend the month in Edinburgh together as a family. I invested some of my corporate earnings in a second-hand Seat to get us there. For those of you unfamiliar with Seat, they're a Spanish car manufacturer pronounced 'see-at' not 'seat'. I didn't invest in a second-hand seat in the hope it would magically transport us to Scotland. I bought a gold Seat Altea 1.6 TDI outright for £6,995.

'We have some great finance deals at the moment, sir,' the Seat salesman said from the passenger seat as I sat in the driving seat of the Seat after a test drive.

'No thank you,' I proudly announced. 'I'll be paying in full.'

Finally I understood the concept of finance. The car cost £6,995 but over five years the same car would cost closer to £9K. I wanted my days of debt behind me. I was counting every penny earned and every penny spent. The irony of my used-car purchase was that I had just hosted the Used Car Awards in Birmingham the week before for a significant chunk of the cost of the car. The winner of Best Used Car of the Year, the BMW X5, was unfortunately still beyond my price range.

'Take a seat,' the Seat salesman invited as he motioned to a seat opposite his seat at the Seat sales desk. 'Are you sure I can't interest you in any of our finance deals?'

'Absolutely certain,' I insisted, as I paid the £6,995. Which was actually £6,994 as I found a pound coin under the front seat of the Seat.

Our gleaming new (used) golden car was packed full on the morning of our seven-hour, 400-mile drive from London to Edinburgh. Lucas was strapped tight in his car seat, a skill I had long since mastered. He was such a good passenger for nearly the entire journey, but for the last hour there were signs of his patience running out. Spitting out the biscuits we offered, throwing his bottle, refusing to clap his hands to 'If You're Happy and You Know It'. Kitty and I continued with our desperate attempts to keep him entertained. The tenth rendition of 'The Wheels on the Bus Go Round and Round' sent him over the edge. Lucas initiated full tantrum mode. High-pitched screaming drowned out our singing. He was rightly fed up. I angled my rear-view mirror to see tears streaming down his scrunched-up red face. Kitty and I both knew what had to happen. A daring move that surely all mothers of young children have performed in the car. A move I have witnessed many times over the years.

Kitty turned to me, barely audible over Lucas's wailing, and announced like an FBI agent, 'I'm going back.'

I nodded with full understanding, decelerating the car to 60 mph, placing both hands on the wheel, holding it steady in the slow lane.

She clicked open her seat belt and pirouetted 180 degrees in the passenger seat, cars whizzing all around us on the A1 Northbound. She then carefully and deliberately clambered between my seat and hers. Momentarily wedged as she gathered her bearings, her bottom filled my rear-view mirror. The final move of the front to back motorway mum transfer was a spinning flourish as she landed alongside an immediately pacified Lucas.

The words 'Mummy's here' signalled that the manoeuvre was complete. She clicked in her seat belt and I accelerated to over 70 mph whilst weaving back to the middle lane.

For the remainder of the journey Lucas teetered on the brink of tears and kept nodding when Kitty asked him if he felt sick. Drizzle in the air indicated we were close. The Seat's windscreen wipers kicking in for what would be a very busy month for them too. The TomTom satnav sucked onto the windscreen led the way to our rented flat down the cobbled roads of Edinburgh's New Town.

I had agreed to meet the local estate agent Jennifer outside the property. 'There she is!' I said, spotting a lady wearing a dark trouser suit and holding a clipboard.

'Hurry up. Hurry up,' Kitty said for the thousandth time, 'Let us out!'

I pulled up right next to Jennifer who pulled out her most welcoming smile.

'Hulloooo!' she beamed, speaking in a thick Scottish accent. 'Welcome to Edinburgh.'

I pretty much ignored her as I leapt out of the car to release Kitty and Lucas. But as soon as I did, the overeager Jennifer leaned into the car to greet Lucas.

'You must be wee baby Lucas then? Give us a smile?' she said.

A Funny Life

Lucas looked at Jennifer and rather than smiling, projectile vomited all over her. Her trouser suit and the unsigned contract for the flat were covered in sick. There was even a splash on her cheek. In shock, Jennifer abandoned all decorum.

'Fucking fuck fuck for fuck sake,' she screamed, surely breaking a record for the number of F-words in a sentence.

Adding additional F-words to sentences is a skill many Scots are born with, but Jennifer was in a league of her own. Her next sentence was even more impressive as she placed her next F-word within another word.

'Well, that's fan-fucking-tastic, isn't it?' she said, brushing sick off her suit with her hand.

Kitty and I were mortified and blamed ourselves for thinking Lucas could sit in a car for over seven hours. Even though the ride in the Seat was as smooth as the many reviews I read suggested, it was too much to ask of a two-year-old. Kitty and I profusely apologized and we all rushed up the three flights of stairs to the flat we had rented for a month but never been to before. Lucas was crying again as Jennifer's sick-covered hand tried to get the keys into the lock. The original plan, of course, was for Jennifer to show us around room by room like estate agents do. But instead she burst through the door, ran into the bathroom and slammed the door behind her.

A damp Jennifer emerged soon after and I signed the sick-stained contract whilst continuing my chorus of apologies. The flat was spacious with high ceilings, a feature so many Edinburgh flats benefit from, as do electricity companies with what must be astronomical heating bills. The furniture was lived-in but taste-ful. I asked Kitty if she liked the flat but it always takes her time to decide. 'Just wait, let me settle in, I'm not sure yet,' she always says when arriving at new accommodation. She needed to be happy; with me working every night she and Lucas would be alone a lot. Whilst waiting for Kitty's verdict my attention turned to the latest love of my life, my golden Seat Altea 1.6 TDI and the terrifying possibility it may have Lucas's vomit on the back seat.

'See if there's any stain remover in the kitchen,' Kitty sug-gested when I asked her for advice. 'If not, is there fizzy water? Check the fridge.'

I opened the fridge door, and there it was. A single, unopened bottle of Perrier. I removed it from the fridge and held it in my hands.

My festival had started with me getting my hands on a bottle of Perrier.

For it to end that way was the dream I was now ready to make a reality.

7

The Edinburgh Festival is relentless. Having a show every night demands a daily routine that hopefully results in being at my funniest between 8 p.m. and 9 p.m. That single hour was all that mattered. Peaking for those sixty minutes could change my life. Unfortunately my natural peak is first thing in the morning when I wake up. That's when I am by far at my sharpest and most switched on. I'm a morning guy. I wake up, make myself a coffee, sit at my desk and between sips am at my most creative. This lasts about three hours before I gradually decline until I am a shadow of my morning self by mid-afternoon. As I write this you will be pleased to learn that it is 8.08 a.m. There isn't a word in this book written after midday, and if there had been, it would certainly have been rewritten the following morning.

Unfortunately for me, comedy clubs tend to open after dark and not at first light. 'After dinner' speakers, for example, have infinitely more lucrative careers than 'After breakfast' ones. So my solution at the 2007 Edinburgh Festival was to treat every day as if it were two days. The morning was exclusively family time, like a family mini-break in Edinburgh. The three of us would head out on daily excursions on rotation for the whole month. Sometimes we just went for a simple walk around the Royal Botanic Garden or Princess Street Gardens beneath Edinburgh Castle. Whenever we felt brave enough we attempted to climb Arthur's Seat. For those of you unfamiliar with this Edinburgh landmark, this isn't the Spanish car of a man called Arthur that we clambered on top of; it's an extinct volcano that is now a mountainous hill with panoramic views of the city at its summit. Thankfully Edinburgh has a zoo where Kitty, Lucas and I could enjoy our favourite pastime of impersonating animals to their faces. I even employed a Scottish accent for my monkey grunts that didn't impress the Scottish monkeys who stared at me with dead eyes, a reaction I had become accustomed to from various corporate events I had recently endured. But Lucas loved it, giggling away before issuing his next destination directive, 'Penguins!' And off we trotted to annoy them too. Several times we drove our new Seat outside Edinburgh to Deep Sea World, an enormous aquarium filled with thousands of species of fish, all of whom Lucas disdainfully ignored because they hadn't been cast in the film *Finding Nemo*. Once we had located Nemo, and the slightly less popular Dory, Lucas would point and scream, 'Nemo! Nemo! Dory! Dory!' Then we would about turn, bypass all the other fish once more and head back to the city.

Lunch was grabbed at one of Edinburgh's many charming

child-friendly eateries where I would hoist Lucas into a highchair, a chair favoured by toddlers and tennis umpires. 'Juice,' a thirsty Lucas would demand, or maybe he was saying 'Deuce' and humorously making a similar comparison. Kitty or I shovelled baby food, heated in a bowl of boiling water, into Lucas's unco-operative mouth while recounting the highlights of the morning's entertainment through a series of unanswered questions: 'Did we see Nemo?' 'Did we get to the top of the mountain?' 'Did you say hello to the penguins?' All the while redirecting dribbling baby food back towards his mouth.

Having eaten it was back to our rented flat where the three flights of stairs finished us all off. Lucas always had an afternoon nap, and during that year's festival my routine followed a similar pattern, although I preferred to use the more grown-up phrase, 'siesta'. My new Spanish car seemed to be having an increasing influence over my life. Psychologically my siesta signalled the end of the day, the family part of the day. This was no power nap; it was a two- to three-hour deep sleep. When I awoke at about 6 p.m. I had artificially created another morning in the same day. 'Morning guy' was now 'Evening guy'. The countdown to show-time had begun. I was refreshed and focused.

Instead of the all-important coffee 'Morning guy' favoured, 'Evening guy' filled the fridge with cans of the highly caffeinated drink Red Bull. According to the advert, 'Red Bull gives you wings'. I had read it takes an hour for the ingredients of Red Bull to enter your bloodstream and for their full uplifting effects to take hold. I needed my wings to appear at 8 p.m. so I placed it in my bag alongside my show notes and scribbles for me to take my first sip at 7 p.m. on the dot.

'Say goodbye to Daddy,' Kitty would say to Lucas, snuggled on the sofa, engrossed in either his *Cars* or *Finding Nemo* DVD.

'Bye Daddy,' his new little voice would obey as I picked him up, only managing to kiss the back of his neck as his eyes remained fixed on the TV.

'Good luck, darling. Have a good show. You'll be brilliant. We're fine here. I love you,' Kitty encouraged every night as we kissed in the open doorway.

My walk through the city to my venue was ritualistic. I sipped my Red Bull as my mind spun with the key phrases of my jokes and the ideas behind them. It was never enough just to remember the words; if I was going to be at my best I had to remind myself why everything in my show was funny, which would inevitably make me laugh. What a sight I must have been, marching along as the Red Bull kicked in, mumbling and laughing to myself.

Five minutes before my show is due to start the audience, murmuring with anticipation, file into the Pleasance Above and take their places on the raked seating facing the empty stage and a makeshift curtain behind. On the other side of that curtain I stood, sharp and switched on from my slumber, caffeine coursing through my veins, my adrenaline levels rising as I listened to the Pleasance staff instructing the audience, 'Move all the way down the rows, please.'

The small auditorium is lit for the audience's arrival then

dimmed just before the show. This moment always gives me a clue as to what kind of audience they are. A good crowd will spontaneously 'Oooh', cheer and applaud when the lights go out; a tough crowd will just sit and wait in silence. At that year's festival the audience always whooped and cheered every night when the lights went down. They were as excited and up for it as I was. The atmosphere was electric.

After the house lights are extinguished, the stage lights are illuminated and music signals my arrival. Each Edinburgh Festival I had chosen a different track that would play as I walked onstage. This carefully chosen tune gets the audience and mostly myself in the mood. At the previous year's festival my walk-on music was 'Miss You' by The Rolling Stones. It's a song that made me feel much cooler than I actually am and gave me a bit of a Jagger swagger when I emerged from behind the curtain.

Have a listen to it now on your phone. Type it into Spotify or YouTube.

See what I mean? I challenge you not to feel like a cooler version of yourself right now.

I also loved the poignancy of the lyrics as I was at that festival alone without Kitty and Lucas and missed them terribly. The song energized and focused me just before the show to make the most of the sacrifice I was making being absent for a month. Making the most of the sacrifice of course meant being nominated for the elusive Perrier Award, which did not happen. I had missed out with 'Miss You'. What was to be the song that enabled me to take that final step and be the stand-out stand-up show at the festival? After much deliberation I selected 'Take Me Out' by Franz Ferdinand.

I'll wait if you want to have a listen . . .

The song has a tremendous opening that raised my already fast heart rate to dangerous levels. Still to this day, when I hear it I am transported back to 2007 and waiting behind the curtain at the Pleasance Above for the first minute of the song, my name being announced moments before the hook kicked in so that I would stride onto the stage as the music crescendoed. Whenever 'Take Me Out' is played on the radio all the adrenaline I experienced at 8 p.m. on those Edinburgh nights instantly pumps through my body, and at 1.04 mins into the song I find myself shouting, 'Good evening, ladies and gentlemen! Let's do this! It's showtime! Bravo!' Fine when I'm driving alone, but a bit weird when I'm in the back of a taxi, shopping or boarding an aeroplane.

The fact that Franz Ferdinand is a Scottish band was no coincidence. We were in Scotland, the audience was full of Scots. It's standard fare for comedians to start their performance with some 'local' material. Audiences love jokes personally tailored to them, their culture, accent, local news. It's an icebreaker before getting into prepared routines. At the Edinburgh Festival the trend was more and more for comedians to have a central theme running through their show, an insightful informative narrative with a sprinkling of jokes. The idea of having a theme confused me. I just wanted to make people laugh as hard as possible and for as long as possible. My theme was comedy itself. The comedians who inspired me like Billy Connolly, Richard Pryor, Eddie Murphy, Robin Williams, Jackie Mason, Eddie Izzard had no narrative arc to their shows. They just cracked me up. If people are laughing non-stop for an hour until their faces hurt, my job is done. That was my only goal.

I quickly realized that the 'local' jokes were working better than anything I had prepared. What started as chatty, throwaway lines were built night after night into my best routines. I had jokes about kilts, the new tram being built, Scottish money, the new Scottish parliament building, Scottish patriotism and, of course, Scottish weather. I explored and expanded these local jokes every night until they were getting bigger laughs than I'd ever had before. They set up the rest of the show with waves of laughter that I kept riding until the hour was up. I was determined to never let the audience stop laughing, hitting them with the next jokes before they had time to take their next breath.

In the first week of the festival, while mumbling and laughing to myself walking across North Bridge on the way to my show, I heard a voice call out to me.

'Michael McIntyre?' a fast-talking Scottish female voice cried as if my name was all one word.

I turned to see the infamous, and by far the most feared critic in Edinburgh, Kate Copstick, who wrote for the *Scotsman* newspaper. A slight woman with dark-rimmed glasses and a shock of frizzy black hair, her nickname, Caustic Copstick, was well earned, having slayed comedians' dreams for years. Other than her, there was a handful of top comedy critics in Edinburgh, the main ones being Dominic Maxwell from *The Times*, Dominic Cavendish from the *Telegraph*, Brian Logan from the *Guardian* and Bruce Dessau from the *Evening Standard*. Often they had a dual role and also sat on the judging panel for the Perrier Award. The power they wielded cannot be underestimated. Occasionally I would see them scuttling around town on the way to or from shows, or loitering in the Pleasance Courtyard. They kept a low profile, tended to be alone, often holding a copy of the publication they wrote for or a bottle of Perrier I assumed they got free. They seemed to exist mostly in the shadows, with comedians whispering out of earshot, 'You know who that is, don't you?' But not Kate Copstick. She swept through the streets of Edinburgh like the Wicked Witch of the West, green smoke billowing in her wake, cackling 'Ahahahahahaaa', as comedians cowered behind bins and fled for the hills fearing she would destroy them with a vicious 1-star review.

'Michael McIntyre?' she repeated even faster than the first time, as I stared at her in disbelief.

I had never spoken directly to a critic before. Many times I had rhetorically shouted, 'What the fuck do you know?' when reading their reviews alone at the kitchen table, but had never experienced any personal interaction. Kate Copstick hadn't reviewed any of my previous shows. I had no idea she even knew who I was. I had hoped she didn't.

'Do-you-always-talk-to-yourself?' she asked at breakneck speed.

'Sorry . . . I didn't realize . . . I was just . . .' I stuttered, worrying she had overhead the jokes I was rehearsing to myself and would give them a scathing review in the *Scotsman* or immediately, right to my face.

'I-came-to-your-show-last-night,' she announced, fully aware the power of that statement would rock me onto the back foot, if not over North Bridge itself, plunging me to my death on the railway tracks beneath.

'Oh . . .' was all I managed to reply as my nervous hand loosened its grip on my can, Red Bull dribbling onto the street.

And then she was gone, in a flash. When the green smoke cleared I was left dumbstruck in a puddle of energy drink. I called Kitty.

'Hi darling, everything OK?' she answered.

'I don't know. I just ran into Kate Copstick while I was walking to my show,' I revealed breathlessly.

'The critic? From the *Scotsman*? The one you read aloud at breakfast, laughing at her reviews of other comedians?'

'No! I never do that,' I denied. 'Not always. Anyway, she spoke to me.'

'Oh wow. What did she say?'

'She said she saw my show last night.'

'And?' Kitty asked, impatiently.

'And? Nothing. She said nothing. That's all she said and then walked off really fast, like an Olympic walker does. She gave no indication as to whether she did or didn't like the show,' I said, worried.

'Well we'll just have to wait until the review comes out,' said Kitty, typically rational.

'I'm going to throw up,' I replied, typically irrational. 'How am I supposed to do the show tonight? This has disrupted my daily routine. I've spilled all of my Red Bull. I'm late. I'm totally freaked out.'

'Calm down, Michael. Just forget about it now. There is nothing you can do about it. You have to focus on tonight. Every show is as important as each other. OK?'

Despite Kitty's advice my fragile mind crumbled into despair and distraction. I then had by far the worst show of my festival thus far and cursed myself for my brittle self-confidence the entire walk home. My fear about Kate Copstick's review in the *Scotsman* was now compounded by my fear that other critics or Perrier judges had witnessed the disappointing show I had just performed.

My mind raced as I quietly slid into bed alongside my sound asleep wife. I googled the *Scotsman* newspaper on my laptop to check the reviews by Kate Copstick, but couldn't see my name among the catalogued carnage of her criticism. A sleepless night followed, with frequent checks of the time until 6 a.m. when the newsagent's opposite opened.

'Twenty-eight Red Bulls?' the shopkeeper enquired when I entered setting off a jangling bell, as he referenced the only other time I had been in his shop.

'Just this, please,' I said, placing a crisp copy of the *Scotsman* broadsheet on the counter, not yet knowing my fate within it.

Outside the newsagent's I frantically searched the pages, standing next to a bin where I was certain the paper would soon be discarded in disgust. My heart raced as I reached the Edinburgh Festival pull-out section, and there it was, my big smiling face on the front page.

Michael McIntyre at The Pleasance Above by Kate Copstick. Five stars.

FIVE STARS!!! The newspaper's fate instantly switched from street bin to framer's. Never in my wildest dreams did I think a critic would give me five stars. Edinburgh critics traditionally laud shows with themes, praise and celebrate shows for originality not hilarity. What I do as a comedian was usually sniffed at by critics, but here was the supposed sniffiest of them all, and she loved me. The impact of Kate's endorsement (she's Kate now, because I love her too) was instant. That very day I sold all the remaining tickets for my entire Edinburgh run. My confidence was boosted to record highs. The audience now came expecting a 5-star show and I was ready and prepared to give them just that.

Leading up to the day the Perrier Award nominations were to be announced, my thoughts weren't on being nominated, they were on winning. Having performed three times before at the festival, I knew who was having a good Edinburgh, who there was a buzz around, who was the talk of the town. In 2007, I knew it was me. I realized that all the other years, as disappointing as they were, were just a build-up to now.

This was my year.

When the day itself came I was sick to my stomach with nerves.

'What shall we do this morning?' Kitty asked at breakfast. 'Deep Sea World? We haven't been to the zoo in three days?'

'I don't think I can do anything. I'm too nervous,' I said, staring at my porridge in a trance.

'It's out of your hands now. You've done everything you can. When is the announcement?' Kitty asked.

'I think midday or 1 p.m., around then. I don't know what I'll do if I'm not on the list again.'

'I know it's hard, Michael. But you'll be fine if you're not nominated again. There are so many routes to success. This isn't the only one. Nothing can change how well this festival has gone and how much people are loving your show.'

At that moment my phone rang. It was Addison. Did he know something? Did he have the inside track? My nerves deepened.

'Hello?' I answered.

'Michael. Addison,' came his familiar intro, before he set about contradicting everything Kitty had just said. 'Big day today. We need this nomination. Would be great for us. Everyone's in town, the BBC, ITV, Channel 4, everyone's talking about you. I know people close to the panel and let's just say it's looking very good. I think you'll get nominated and you've got a good chance of winning it on Saturday. I'll call you later when we know for sure.'

Everything hinged on this announcement.

I chose to wander around the streets of Edinburgh on my own as time slowly ticked towards midday, arriving back at the flat just before the announcement was due to find Lucas sitting on the sofa sipping an apple juice. I was so riddled with anxiety I just nodded to him like he was an acquaintance at a bar as I checked my watch for the thousandth time. I then noticed him spilling his juice all over himself as he was drinking from a glass and not his usual beaker.

'You're back. Any news?' Kitty asked with trepidation as she entered the living room.

'Darling. Why is Lucas drinking from a glass?' I asked.

'No!!' she screamed, rushing towards him and swiping the glass from his clutches. 'He didn't drink that, did he?' Kitty demanded, panicked.

'Yes, when he wasn't spilling it.'

Kitty put the glass down and started stripping off Lucas's wet clothes.

'What's wrong?' I asked.

'It's pee. It's my pee,' Kitty alarmingly revealed.

'What?' I asked, totally baffled.

At that very moment my phone rang. It had gone past midday, the results were out. It was Addison, but rather than his customary introduction he opened with,

'Fuck 'em.'

'What? What's happened?' I asked, my heart sinking.

'Brendon Burns, Andrew Lawrence, Andrew Maxwell, Tom Binns and something called Pappy's Fun Club, that's the list, you're not on it. I can't believe it, I thought you'd be there. I'm honestly shocked,' Addison sympathetically said.

I hung up the phone and just shook my head at Kitty. I had been overlooked again, for the third year in a row. I felt utterly crestfallen. Of course I knew that hundreds of comedians were gunning for the same thing. My disappointment stemmed from the fact that I knew I was close. Every year it had been confirmed that I was on the longlist, down to the last ten, but never down to the all-important last five. What was it about me that when it came to the final reckoning I wasn't chosen?

Kitty hugged me in silence. There was nothing to say. It felt like the whole month was again in vain.

'It's never good news,' I finally said, dejected.

'I have some good news,' Kitty said. 'I'm pregnant.'

8

A man's home is his castle. My castle was currently a one and a half bedroom, half bathroom rented flat on the outskirts of Muswell Hill. Ikea furniture dominated every room. The walls were bare other than one print of a Chagall painting called *The Lovers*, a romantic picture of a couple embracing on a bench under the moonlight as an angel flies across the night sky. Kitty and I fell in love with this poster and decided we should frame and hang it on the wall of our rented living room. The task of framing and hanging fell to me, the man of the house. As this was just after we'd moved in, I was yet to do any debt-busting corporate or TV work, so was still only purchasing the cheapest of everything; 'low to high' was my online search criteria. Browsing the Argos catalogue, the cheapest frame turned out to be a clip frame. In essence it is a frame, without a frame, just a piece of glass that clips in front of the picture. Having bought the frameless frame I was disappointed to discover that it also lacked glass and merely consisted of a floppy transparent Perspex sheet and a rectangular piece of MDF of the same size. Thankfully it was the perfect size for *The Lovers*, who I clipped in between, before holding it aloft for Kitty to view.

'It's blurry,' she remarked. 'Really blurry.'

'It is, isn't it?' I agreed. 'I thought it would be glass. I don't think I can take it back now that I've opened it.'

It was years later when we realized there was a protective plastic sheet covering the Perspex that we had failed to peel off. A frustrating discovery, but a wildly satisfying moment when finally unpeeled.

Hammering into my rented wall to hang the clip frame resulted in an enormous chunk of plaster breaking off and falling to the floor. I should have anticipated the wall's fragility, having complained daily about the noisy and perverted neighbours. Despite the mess I was making, my masonry nail failed to penetrate the wall enough to remain inserted. The role of the painting shifted from decoration to something to hide the damaged wall, like the Rita Hayworth poster Andy Dufresne used to conceal his escape tunnel in *The Shawshank Redemption*. Any hope of that disappeared when a final swing of my hammer created a crack that ran all the way up the wall. As I watched it travel I feared the whole row of Victorian terraced houses might tumble.

'We need to buy our own place,' I said to Kitty, sitting beneath the cracked wall, where the blurry *Lovers* now just about hung, on our return from Edinburgh.

The flat we rented in Edinburgh was twice the size of our

place in London, making our homecoming additionally depressing. Now, with a new baby coming to stay with us for the next eighteen years or so, upsizing was a priority.

'Everywhere is so expensive,' Kitty replied with the frustration shared by all renters.

'We have to get on the ladder before it's too late,' I said with all the urgency of a man swimming back to a boat having spotted a shark while in open water.

You may recall 2007 was the height of the housing market. In fact the housing market was so out of control that it led to a global financial crisis and house price crash the following year. Not that we knew that then. Nobody knew that then, apart from that one guy in the film *The Big Short*. The perception about house prices was that they would increase exponentially forever, and if you didn't get on the first rung of the ladder you would be left behind. People's houses were making more money than them. Older people who had bought in the sixties or seventies couldn't stop giggling: 'Hahahahaha! We bought the house for £3,000 in 1971 and now it's worth £2.6m!' 'At least £3m now, darling!' their spouse would correct. 'The one down the road, smaller than ours, just sold for £2.9m. We're thinking of adding a basement and a loft conversion, then it will be worth upwards of £4m! Hehehehehe!'

Kitty and I had a budget of around £300K having saved £30,000 to put down as a 10 per cent deposit. Having been £30,000 in debt less than two years before I was giddy with pride that I had turned our fortunes around. However, when mentioning the size of my deposit at the local estate agency, rather than a round of applause I was met with despondent groans. 'It's unlikely you'll find what you're looking for with that. Not around here.'

The lesson I learnt from the TV programme *Location, Location, Location*, without ever watching it, is that location is important. We wanted to live in either Crouch End or Muswell Hill, where we had been renting (or 'burning money' as I now called it) for several years. We soon found that the further away we went the further our money went. For the price of a small flat in Crouch End we could buy a whole house in the less fashionable Wood Green, only ten minutes' drive further north, and still have money left over for the additional locks and panic alarms needed to keep out the local gangs and crack addicts. More and more middle-class families were moving to areas that estate agents claimed to be 'up and coming' but really were as grim as ever. People were buying anything just to get on the ladder. It was frantic. I would phone estate agents having seen a promising dwelling online but always be met with the same responses: 'Too late. It's gone. Sold this morning.' 'Sold above the asking price the day it came to market.' 'That one is still available. Hold the line. Sorry, someone's just walked in and bought it for cash.'

One flat we saw online looked perfect for us. Just off Crouch End Broadway, it had three bedrooms, the excitement of 'outside space' and most importantly was under budget at £295,000. I phoned the estate agent in question immediately.

'Hi, I'm calling about the flat for sale on Nelson Road.'

'Do you wanna make an offa?' the exceptionally cocky estate agent asked.

'I haven't seen it yet. I've just seen a picture on the internet,' I said.

'There a biddin' war on that one. Beautiful place. Lots of interest. What's your offa?'

'I can't make a bid on a flat I've never seen in person. Can my wife and I see it today? We can go right now? We're in Muswell Hill, we can be there in five minutes.'

'No chance, mate. Gotta make a bid now. Trust me, you'll love it. What's your situation? What are you looking for?' the ever more annoying estate agent asked.

'We need three bedrooms, as we have a two-year-old and my wife is pregnant. We'd like to live in a conversion, nothing modern. A garden would be amazing . . .'

'Make an offa,' the estate agent interrupted, 'it's perfect for ya, you don't want to miss out.'

'I haven't seen it,' I repeated. 'This is by far the biggest purchase of our lives. There's no way I can make an offer when I've only seen three photos on the internet. That's totally absurd.'

Kitty, my beautiful aproned pregnant wife, was draining pasta in the 'galley' kitchen when I approached to update her on the phone call.

'So? Is that flat still available?' she asked as steam from the boiled water filled the tiny space.

'Yes,' I confirmed.

'Amazing. When can we go and see it?' she said.

'I made an offer,' I announced, bewildered at myself.

'You what?' Kitty said, totally confused.

'The estate agent was very persuasive. He said we'd lose it and that there was a bidding war and it was perfect for us. I had to buy it or we'd miss out.'

'What are you talking about? He doesn't know what's perfect for us. Have you gone mad? How much did you offer?'

'£380,000,' I revealed.

'What the fuck? We don't even have that.'

'I had to secure it. He gave me the number of a mortgage advisor who can get us the extra money at a really good rate,' I replied, having been truly hypnotized by the estate agent's sales techniques.

'Have you gone mad? Call back and withdraw the offer,' Kitty demanded.

'It's south facing. We're not losing the money, as property prices will continue to rise. It's an investment,' I continued, repeating verbatim the estate agent's spiel.

At that moment my mobile phone rang.

'Mr McIntyre. Jaimie Russell from Foxtons. The vendor has rejected your offer, let's go 390. You don't want to miss out. But I have to do it now. She's holding on the other line. Shall I do it? We have to go now, mate.'

My mind was in a spin. Jaimie Russell was one of the most convincing men I had ever spoken to.

'OK, 390,' I said, before Kitty grabbed the phone out of my hand and told Jaimie Russell from Foxtons in no uncertain terms that we couldn't afford the flat and the stress of the housing market had made her husband lose his mind.

Then she went quiet, listening for a few minutes as Jaimie spoke.

'Uh-huh . . . Yes . . . Of course . . . Totally . . . Mmm . . .' she said, before ending with, 'OK, 410.'

This time I snatched the phone from her and cancelled the call.

We looked at various properties within budget but they were unliveable. There was simply too much competition, too many people vying for a limited number of homes, clambering to get on or climb the ladder with all the credit banks were irresponsibly dishing out. One flat we saw claimed to have a 'shared garden', which turned out to be shared with four other flats and divided by actual lines, painted on the grass in what resembled lanes on a running track. Each flat owned a strip of grass, one person wide, where they could stand with their family and friends one behind the other, but if they wanted to stand next to each other they would be trespassing. On a sunny day there would be four barbecues at the end of four queues of people.

We thought we'd hit the jackpot when we saw an affordable three-bedroom flat advertised in upmarket Hampstead. We raced to view it and, although pokey, the dream location more than compensated. Knowing the levels of competition we faced, Kitty and I immediately started negotiating on the price within minutes.

'But you haven't seen the bathroom?' said the estate agent,

who had sold two other flats on his mobile phone while we were looking round.

'Of course,' Kitty and I replied in unison, thinking it was only a formality.

'It's a shared bathroom,' the estate agent revealed, 'which is reflected in the price.'

It transpired that the bathroom was down a flight of stairs and in the landlord's flat below.

'You'll have your own key,' the estate agent said as he unlocked the flat below and walked us down a messy corridor in somebody else's home, to another locked door.

'I'll be out in a minute,' came a male cry from within, following the estate agent's knock.

Not only was the bathroom in someone else's flat, it was occupied. Moments later, accompanied by the sound of a flushing loo and the scent of air freshener, a heavyset Middle Eastern gentleman opened the door. Before he had a chance to apologize, Kitty and I had bolted and were scampering down the stairs, cursing each other for believing we could afford to live in Hampstead.

Kitty and I soon concluded that we would continue to rent until house prices came down or our deposit went up. For our deposit to increase I needed my career not to falter after the disappointment of Edinburgh. Brendon Burns, a brash Australian comedian, had won the Perrier Award. Brendon was also represented by Off The Kerb, so naturally heat-seeking missile Addison swooped in to capitalize on his success. I liked Brendon and was happy for him but couldn't help feeling jealous and worried that Addison would lose faith in me. Apart from bringing comedians up through the ranks, he was managing all his big stars and increasingly focused on high-flying Alan Carr. A clue was that he often accidentally called me Alan on the phone. Kitty claimed that was a good sign as he saw me as the next big thing like Alan, whereas I just assumed his mind was elsewhere.

The truth was that Addison's faith in me was sky high. Having seen my Edinburgh show and the audience's response he was determined to get me on TV, showcasing what I was best at: stand-up comedy. The BBC flagship stand-up series *Jack Dee Live at the Apollo*, filmed at the Hammersmith Apollo, had run for two years. Prior to that there had been no successful purely stand-up TV shows. Most had attempted and failed to recreate the intimacy of a comedy club for television, but the key to the success of *Live at the Apollo* was its grand scale. *Live at the Apollo* supersized and glamorized stand-up, taking it from an underground club atmosphere to, with over 3,000 seats, London's biggest theatre. Smoke billowed as comedians emerged from the lifting neon *Live at the Apollo* sign, greeted by a ballyhoo of lights, thunderous music and applause. The set was beautifully lit, as were the audience, with celebrities filling the first few rows. Host Jack Dee introduced one guest comedian per show, who performed a substantial half-hour set. Big name turns like Joan Rivers, Jo Brand, Lee Mack, Julian Clary and Dara Ó'Briain had appeared thus far.

Live at the Apollo became an instant success as it had been created by someone who knew how to make stand-up comedy shine on TV. The show was the creation of a man with an instinct for what television audiences wanted more than live audiences, someone who understood the importance of production values and comics performing longer sets so viewers could fully immerse themselves in their world. The show was created by Addison. But despite producing the series and one of his acts, Jack Dee, being the host, he had a big job to persuade the BBC I was ready to carry the show as I was comparatively unknown.

The BBC were reluctant as they wanted big stars and more recognized up-and-coming talent. Far more established TV names, Jimmy Carr, Alan Carr, Sean Lock, Russell Howard and Frankie Boyle were booked. If I had been nominated or won the Perrier, maybe there would have been a case for my appearance but really I didn't deserve to be on the roster. None of that year's Perrier nominees or the winner were booked to appear, which is why it was a total shock to me when Addison called with the news.

'Michael. Addison. I've managed to convince the BBC to have you on *Live at the Apollo*.'

'*Live at the Apollo*? This year?' I asked, already starting to tremble, dislodging more plaster from the flimsy walls of my flat.

'They wanted you to share the show with another up-and-coming comic doing fifteen minutes each, but I pushed hard for you to do the whole show and I've just got them to agree. This is big for us. Just do what you did in Edinburgh.'

My prize at the Edinburgh Festival turned out to be the greatest prize of all, Addison's confidence. My own confidence had always been wafer thin. Anyone who knows me will testify to my endless panicking and need for reassurance. I got myself on a roll in Edinburgh. Everything seemed to click: my daily routine, the encouragement of my 5-star review in the *Scotsman*, the positive energy of my sold-out audience. But this was atypical of my normal behaviour. Usually before every show my mind filled with self-doubt: 'I can't do this.' 'I don't feel funny tonight.' 'I'm dizzy.' 'The audience don't look like my kind of people.' 'I need a banana.' 'That banana has made me feel weird.' After a show I'm even worse. 'Well, that was a disaster.' 'Was I too fast?' 'Did I seem like myself?' 'You don't think the audience seemed flat?' 'Was it better than last night?' 'Are you saying last night was terrible?'

The poor person who bore the brunt of this crazed behaviour was, and still to this day is, my friend, the comedian Paul Tonkinson. I first met Paul when we were both performing at the Glee Club in Cardiff in 2002. Paul, a northerner from Scarborough in North Yorkshire, was top of the bill and I was bottom. I knew Paul from the TV, he had hosted *The Sunday Show* and *The Big Breakfast* on Channel 4, so I admired him as a successful comic but mainly because he's hilarious. His gangly, goofy and high-energy physical style always rendered audiences helpless with laughter. When we first met I was inexperienced and clueless about stand-up. My gigs were more miss than hit. Following my set as the opening act at the Glee Club, I entered the dressing room after a lukewarm reaction from the Saturday night Welsh crowd to receive the customary round of polite but disingenuous recognition from the other acts on the bill. Nods and murmurs of 'Nice one.' 'Good gig.' 'Well done.' Paul, however, much to my surprise, leapt to his feet and erupted with praise.

'That was fantastic, mate, really strong, mate, some fabulous ideas in there, mate, so impressive, mate, how long you been going, mate? You're gonna be massive, mate.'

Paul's positivity, generosity and constant use of the word 'mate' is something to behold. He loves people, he's interested in people, he celebrates and supports people. As an example: when people ring my doorbell to sell things unsolicited I, like you, don't open the door. No thank you. Paul not only opens the door, he buys everything they're selling, invites them in for tea, finds out their life story and offers them a place to stay if ever they need it. Paul's home is like Christmas for cold-callers. Paul's always got a friend staying with him and his wife and three kids, or a friend of a friend who has fallen on hard times. He looks for the best in people. He's an amazing person, without whom I would have been lost so many times.

It was Paul who I called when I had an anxiety attack on the night of my *Live at the Apollo* performance. It was October 2007, just a few months after the disappointment of the Edinburgh Festival. I knew I was on the form of my life, but in Edinburgh I didn't have a chance to think or overthink due to the frequency of my shows – I was in the zone. This was entirely different. This was the biggest gig of my life so far, the biggest in terms of both the audience size and the stakes.

In Edinburgh I skipped through the streets with a Red Bull

before Franz Ferdinand launched me onto a stage that had become my second home. Now everything was new and unnerving. I had only ever been to the Hammersmith Apollo once before, when I stood at the back of a sold-out Billy Connolly concert. This was the big time. As my taxi swung around the Hammersmith roundabout, the vast frontage of the Apollo coming into view, I, like the BBC, decided I wasn't ready. The producer, Anthony Caveney, the loveliest and hairiest of men, met me at the stage door. I was in a terrible state. It took me a while to locate the door handle to exit the car. Caveney said hello several times before I answered him. I followed him to the stage for my sound check in a stupor. Seeing the colossal empty Apollo was a further shock to my system. This wasn't the Pleasance Above. I yearned to be in the Pleasance Above, I knew what I was doing there.

'Just say a few words to check the levels,' the sound man asked into his microphone from behind the sound desk at the back of the theatre. He seemed at least a mile away. I was speechless. I couldn't think of any words to say into my headset microphone. I forgot all the words in the English language. I was dumbstruck with fear.

'Just tell me what you had for breakfast,' the sound man prompted.

I was desperately trying to remember whether I had even eaten breakfast when Addison bounded onto the stage.

'Michael! How ya feeling?' Addison said so loud the sound man checked if he was also wearing a headset mic.

123

'I'm stressed, Addison. I feel really stressed about this. I don't feel good at all.' I was broadcasting my anxiety to all the crew and production team through my microphone, enabling the sound man to work out my sound levels while I had a meltdown.

'You've got your mic on. Take it off and let's have a chat in the dressin' room,' said a bemused Addison.

'Have you met Jo?' Addison then said as Jo Brand walked on the stage for her sound check.

Jack Dee was only hosting the first show of the third series with the remaining shows having guest hosts. Jo Brand was hosting my show. She was so kind and relaxed, and having heard me panicking into my microphone tried to put me at ease but I was in a semi-trance. None of this felt real. Jo Brand is a comedy legend. She was one of the pioneers of alternative British comedy in the eighties. It was suddenly all too much for me. I was way too far outside my comfort zone.

Addison gave me a pep talk in my dressing room, but it failed to have the desired effect. 'You've got this, right?' he asked at the doorway as he departed.

'Absolutely,' I lied.

Pre-show rituals are so important to find the right headspace. But the hustle and bustle of a TV recording limits the time available to focus on the job in hand. After I'd been to make-up and got myself suited up there was a constant stream of well-wishers knocking on my door: Danny, Big Fee Fay and others from Off The Kerb, Elaine and bigwigs from the BBC. I couldn't calm myself down. I looked at my watch: half an hour to go before Jo

Brand started the show and fifteen minutes after that, I would be on. My mind was spinning as I paced around my dressing room, now ignoring knocks on the door, talking my jokes through to myself.

I have to get out. I'm going to fuck this up.

I walked out of my dressing room and straight out the stage door at the rear of the Apollo.

'Do you need anything, Michael?' a runner in a headset asked as I whisked past her.

'No thanks,' I replied, resisting the urge to ask for a taxi home.

In the fresh air I marched past the enormous outside broadcast trucks, past security and round to the front of the theatre where I saw hundreds of people pouring in through the doors, leaping out of taxis and crossing the road from the tube station, like I had done myself when I came to see Billy Connolly. I walked among them, unrecognized. The audience for the Apollo never know who they are going to see perform. It could be any of the country's biggest comedy stars, but it was me, a comedian so unknown I was walking straight through the heart of them with not so much as a double take.

I was a nobody.

I circled the roundabout until I found a quiet spot down a side street and scrolled through As in the contacts of my phone until I reached 'Alright mate', Paul's traditional greeting whenever he picked up my call.

'Alright mate,' Paul predictably said on answering. 'You at the Apollo?'

'I'm on in half an hour. I had to get out for some fresh air. I'm really panicking. I don't know if I can do this. I'm freaking out. Properly,' I rambled despairingly.

'Just calm down, mate. Talk me through what jokes you're planning on doing.'

Paul's input went way beyond support and encouragement. He knew my jokes as well as I did. He has an extraordinary memory for my jokes, ideas, in fact pretty much everything I've ever said. We talked constantly about my routines and how to make them funnier with the right articulation, wordplay, pauses and physicality. We analysed everything. Paul was not only funny himself but he knew what made me funny. We would meet in cafes and giggle about ideas and sow the seeds of future stand-up routines. He was my wingman.

'I'm going to open with the tube stuff because we're in London, then all the Scottish stuff, the bodily malfunctions stuff, the baby stuff, the skipping routine and end on the snow bus story,' I explained.

'Mate . . .' Paul said with a dramatic pause, 'all those jokes are killer. The audience won't have seen anything as funny as that before. Just think, there's 3,000 people there who have never heard those jokes and they're all hilarious, mate. More people, more laughs, mate. It's gonna be wild. Just share all that great stuff with them. What an amazing position to be in, they don't know who you are, and you're the best. So exciting, mate. You're gonna blow them away, mate. I wish I was there to see it.'

I'll never forget how his words instantly washed away my nerves and fired me up. I crossed the road back towards the Apollo and joined the throng of people walking to the show once more, but my attitude was totally changed.

I was a nobody.

But not for long.

9

I deemed the Edinburgh Festival a failure but the nightly repetition had honed both my material and performance. I thought Edinburgh was a competition, but it was boot camp, it was training for *Live at the Apollo*. From the first big laugh I received from the Apollo audience I was in autopilot, not having to think as my words and actions flowed naturally, after night upon night of rehearsal. Paul's words resonated with me because although I was a mess in so many ways, the one thing I knew how to do inside out was tell those jokes. The difference between this night and all those before were the millions who would be watching at home.

'That's my boy!' barked Addison as he burst into the dressing room after the show, simultaneously ordering champagne from the same runner I nearly asked to get me a taxi home two hours earlier.

'You pleased?' he asked, but didn't wait for an answer. 'This is gonna be fantastic for selling tickets.'

Selling tickets was an obsession for Addison. He had been touring comedians in bigger and bigger venues for nearly two decades. He relished working his socks off to get a show sold out, then immediately put on an extra night. 'Shall we do one more? I think we can do it!' he would announce on hearing the news the extra night had sold out too. He loved the fight. He loved the challenge.

Addison had created different arms of his business empire that fed into one another. He represented comedians he found in comedy clubs and produced TV shows for them through his production company Open Mike. Television exposure would translate into demand to see their live tour, which Addison would also produce and promote through Off The Kerb. He was integral and instrumental in creating this well-oiled chain of success. People were critical of Addison's power in the industry, saying he had too much of a monopoly, but he wasn't taking advantage of situations, he was pioneering them. He was brilliant and passionate as an agent and as a TV producer and as a tour promoter. He could do it all, so he did it all. The greatest thing about the comedy business is that nobody undeserving can be a success – either the audience are laughing or not, either the TV ratings are high or not, either the tickets are sold or not.

Joe Norris was the man who organized the tours for Off The Kerb. Joe had been working with Addison for over twenty years and ran the business with him. They complemented each other perfectly as they were near total opposites. Joe is self-effacing and a total gentleman, endlessly apologizing for nothing, often accompanied by humble bowing. 'Don't mind me, Michael.' 'Sorry to interrupt, Michael.' 'I'll let you go, Michael, sorry to take up your time.' 'I'm sure you've got better things to do, Michael.' Whereas Addison liked wild nights out, Joe much preferred to watch cricket for five days solid whilst listening to Test Match Special on his headphones, apologizing to the whole ground if he had to get up from his seat. To say Joe is a creature of habit is a vast understatement. He has literally never been seen without his most trusted accessories, a copy of the *Guardian* newspaper in one hand and an umbrella in the other. There are few certainties in life, but I can guarantee you that Joe Norris will never vote Conservative or get caught in the rain. Addison loved Joe, and in keeping with his self-image of a Mafia boss, always referred to him as a 'Made man. He's untouchable.'

Depending on a comedian's pulling power Joe booked tours ranging from small local theatres of about 300–500 capacity, all the way to the largest theatres in the UK which tended to have around 2,000 seats, with the biggest being the Edinburgh Playhouse and the Hammersmith Apollo with over 3,000. But in 2002 Addison and Joe pushed the envelope further and booked the phenomenally popular Lee Evans into the 10,000-seat Wembley Arena. Addison loved the prestige of putting on a comedy show in a space traditionally reserved for the world's biggest bands and pop stars. In the following years Lee went on to break all sorts of sales records touring colossal venues across the land. Nothing excited Addison more than the mind-blowing scale of comedy in arenas.

'It's all about getting bums on seats,' Addison constantly said, mantra-like. Everything was geared to selling tickets for live shows. This was Addison's core business and where he started as a teenager promoting shows as the Entertainment Officer at Brighton Polytechnic.

How many seats I could get bums onto was the big question. I had sold out all my shows in Edinburgh, but the city then was filled with comedy-loving punters looking for shows to go and see. If I put on a solo show at an arts centre in Birmingham or Manchester, or a regional theatre in Exeter or Winchester, are people going to come?

Following my performance on *Live at the Apollo*, Joe started booking more and more venues for me to perform my own show. I had already done a few one-off shows around the country with varying success. A few months earlier I had performed a one-man show in Thirsk, North Yorkshire, at the Old Courthouse, which I confidently assume was once a courthouse but is now a small entertainment venue with a temporary stage and about eighty seats. I was thrilled to learn that the show had sold out.

'Thirsk loves me!' I exclaimed, when Joe told me the news on the phone.

With a smile on my face, I excitedly drove myself up the M1 for four hours only to be met with total disdain from the Thirsk audience.

'Ladies and gentlemen please welcome, Michael McIntyre.'

I pranced onto the stage in my shocking-pink shirt accompanied by barely a smattering of applause. Criminals would have

132

received a warmer welcome when the venue was still an actual courthouse.

'Hellooooo!' I said in my plummy camp London accent. That's all I said, one word. But that was enough for an elderly grizzled flat-cap-wearing Yorkshireman in the front row.

'Not for me,' he said as he stood up and walked straight out, soon followed by several others.

Entertainment options in Thirsk are limited so the majority of the audience came along for something to do and most seemed to regret that decision one word in. My career couldn't rely on locals taking a punt in remote locations. I needed fans of mine who had seen me perform live in a comedy club or on TV at the Royal Variety, on *Have I Got New for You* or hopefully, when I was at my best, on *Live at the Apollo.*

No more would I be driving myself, I was given my own tour manager, Terry. Off The Kerb used a stable of tour managers, from the cream of the crop Grazio Abela, a charming Maltese man of limited height and limited hair who had been touring with Jack Dee and Lee Evans for years, all the way down to Terry, who was actually an unemployed old school friend of Joe's. Terry was from Essex and his accent, like his waistline, was thick. I was very fond of Terry, but tour management really wasn't for him.

My first cause for concern with Terry was his eyes, both of which appeared to be lazy, and neither of which was looking at me when I first opened my front door to him. All I needed was for him to keep his eyes on the road, which by the look of him might require him driving while facing the passenger window.

It didn't take long before I felt incredibly unsafe with Terry. He seemed to suffer from extraordinary lapses in concentration, epitomized by a terrifying incident at Donington BP Services on our maiden voyage north to The Mart Theatre in Skipton. I had fallen asleep lying on the back seat of the car, my head resting on a pillow leaning against the back door. The car slowing and stopping at the petrol pump did not wake me from my slumber; what awoke me was so extraordinary I still to this day can't believe it happened. Terry got the petrol cap flap and back door of the car confused. Holding the petrol nozzle in one hand, he opened the back door of the car to find my sleeping head and not the petrol cap he anticipated. I opened my eyes to see the dripping nozzle inches from my face. I screamed. The shock of which prompted Terry to squirt a bit of unleaded onto my suit.

Terry was hugely remorseful, explaining that the car was new to him and now that he had his bearings would be filling the car itself with petrol in future, and not me. Terry was actually very shaken by the experience, so shaken in fact that he asked if he could light a cigarette to calm his nerves.

'Nooooo!' I screamed from the back seat of our petrol-reeking vehicle.

The Face Palm Emoji was invented for people like Terry.

Darkness fell and Terry, who refused to use the satnav owing to a half-baked conspiracy theory about being tracked by the government, still hadn't located the Mart Theatre. In fairness to

Terry, the theatre was remarkably remote. It looked like the opening titles of a horror movie as we drove through woodland on a single-lane dirt track. At long last, with the petrol odour still strong, we pulled up in a muddy field next to the least glamorous theatre I have ever and will ever perform in. It transpired that the Mart in the name of the theatre referred to the primary use of the venue as a cattle mart where farmers would buy and sell livestock. To supplement his income the local farmer decided to use the mart as an entertainment space. So instead of livestock being paraded on a central circular platform while farmers shouted their bids from behind metal railings, I now stood trying to make the same farmers and their wives laugh. As it happens the gig went pretty well. I made jokes about the absurdity of the venue, and apart from the occasional whisper of 'Can you smell petrol?' and 'I think the tractor might be leaking again', the show was a success. So much so that several farmers made bids to buy me at the end.

I'm pleased to report that after a ropey start things settled down with Terry. We drove up and down the country to most of the UK's smallest and least glamorous venues, many of which, like the Skipton Mart and Thirsk Courthouse, hadn't necessarily started life as a theatre. I played the Bristol Tobacco Factory, the Milton Keynes Stables and the Newbury Corn Exchange. In among these converted spaces were some beautiful little theatres of fewer than 500 seats where I always had my best shows, such as the Leeds City Varieties, the Lancaster Grand and the Winchester Theatre Royal.

A Funny Life

For shows closer to home I would save money by driving myself. Dispensing with Terry unfortunately didn't always lead to incident-free travel. Getting into my Seat following a run-of-the-mill show at the Soho Theatre in London, I paused before putting the key in the ignition as my trousers were digging uncomfortably into my expanding belly. Perhaps as a subconscious homage to my wife's pregnancy, I seemed to be gaining weight at the same rate as her. This was mainly owing to late-night scoffing after my shows. I tended to eat light before a performance but afterwards all bets were off. Lit only by the light of the fridge, I would stand in my 'galley' kitchen well past midnight and consume anything edible and in any combination, and if I didn't have a show the following night I'd wash it all down with red wine. The net result was that my trouser zip was starting to emulate my old Singapore suit and descend on its own. The relief of unbuttoning my ever-tightening trousers when I got home was increasing daily. On this occasion I couldn't wait until I got home and unbuttoned my trousers sitting at the wheel of my Seat. That's better. I then moved the car seat a few inches back for much needed additional space and set off for home (the fridge) while singing along to guilty pleasure power ballads on Magic FM.

I stopped at a red light on Tottenham Court Road with no other cars around and, with the volume on full and my eyes closed, belted out Foreigner's classic hit 'I Want to Know What Love Is'.

'I wanna know what love is, I want you to show me, I wanna feel what love is, I know you can show me.'

Just as I sang along with the backing singer in a high-pitched voice, 'Let's talk about love', I heard a deafeningly loud police siren.

My initial thought that this was a remix was immediately ruled out on seeing a police car in my rear-view mirror. I was so wrapped up in Foreigner's desperation to know and feel what love is that I had missed the green light. I accelerated away, hoping the police merely wanted to give me a nudge, but no such luck. The police continued to sound their siren as I drove across the Marylebone Road so I pulled over as did the police behind me, muting the siren but keeping the blue lights flashing.

It's a uniquely stressful moment when the police pull you over as you frantically try to remember whether you have been involved in any criminal activity. This was massively intensified by the shocking sight in my rear-view mirror. What resembled a SWAT team was approaching, four men wearing bullet-proof vests, masks and helmets and holding machine guns, actual machine guns. My mind raced. 'Am I an international drug dealer? No.' 'Are there holdalls of cash in the boot from a bank robbery? No.' 'Am I a radicalized Islamic terrorist? Surely not.' 'Am I playing *Call of Duty*? I don't think so.'

I silenced Magic FM and nervously waited for one of the heavily armed troopers to reach my car window. I activated the one-touch electric window (which came as standard in the Seat) and beamed my most unthreatening smile at the Robocop-style policeman.

A Funny Life

'What seems to be the problem, officer?' I remarked, hoping he was smiling behind his mask and goggles.

'Step out of the car, please,' he deadpanned.

I instantly obeyed his instruction. Meanwhile his three armed colleagues had caught up and all four aligned and faced me like a firing squad. As soon as I stood upright in the street, my unbuttoned trousers fell to my ankles. The four heads of the heavily armed counter-terrorist police dropped in unison and stared at my bare legs and pink cotton Marks and Spencer briefs.

I had been caught with my trousers down.

'Why have you exposed yourself, sir?' demanded one of the officers.

I quickly bent down and pulled up my trousers and tried to explain while struggling to do the button up.

'I'm so sorry, I just undid my button to be more comfortable because my trousers are too tight and I forgot so they, they fell down. Sorry.'

'You were sitting stationary at a green light,' said the first officer.

'What were you doing?' the second officer asked.

'With your trousers down?' added the third officer.

'And your eyes closed?' the fourth one chipped in.

'I was singing along to the radio and just didn't notice the lights had changed. I'm really sorry for losing concentration, but there was nobody else . . .' The first officer interrupted me.

'You're that comedian, aren't you? The skipping one?'

He was referring to jokes I made on *Live at the Apollo* about how skipping, although predominantly practised by little girls, is actually an incredibly effective mode of transport. And how people swing their arms when they walk and maybe if they swung their arms together they could propel themselves faster. I combined skipping with my double arm swing to create a new and more efficient method of travel, which I demonstrated up and down the stage.

'Yes, that's me,' I confirmed with a winning smile.

The other three members of the SWAT team were unfamiliar with my skipping routine so the officer tried to explain it to them before turning to me and instructing, 'You do it, it's your joke.'

I thought my shows at the Edinburgh Festival were make or break, then it was the Hammersmith Apollo, but it turned out my most important performance to date was a three-minute rendition of my skipping material for four counter-terrorism police just off the Tottenham Court Road. I'm pleased to say that three of them were amused; the other not so impressed. Can't please 'em all, he was probably from Thirsk. I escaped with a ticking-off about how in future I should sing along with my eyes open and my trouser button closed. Two of the armed officers then attempted my skip as they returned to their police car. It was my first experience of the power of celebrity. My brush with the law turned out to be quite an ego boost.

I had started to be recognized more and more. The venues I was playing were small, but I was selling them out. I had a small but growing fan base. On the circuit I had been making around £200 a gig, now every show was making me a few thousand pounds a time. The wonderful thing about the economics of touring is that people pay to be entertained by me, and me only. It's in my hands to build and sustain my audience and, by extension, income. My objective before every show was clear: give them such a good night that when I return with a new show, so do they.

Unfortunately I wasn't paid until the tour ended, so my desperation to buy our first home was on hold. House prices continued to rise faster than Kitty or my tummy. Kitty was struggling in our tiny flat with a tough pregnancy. Morning sickness is supposed to last the first few months, but it continued for her entire gestation, not only every morning but also every afternoon, evening and night. She was constantly nauseous.

'It's like feeling car-sick twenty-four hours a day,' she explained with a pained expression.

'That must be so awful, darling,' I would comfort. Resisting the temptation to relate it to being driven by Terry.

After nine months of me late-night eating after my shows and Kitty feeling sick, her waistline finally overtook mine. This signalled both the imminent birth of our second child and the end of Kitty and me sharing elasticated leggings.

Preparations were minimal this time around. All the baby stuff was hand-me-downs from Lucas. Our new baby was simply to step into Lucas's old life, a sort of newborn identity fraud. Our only planning was to have a name ready. We asked not to know the sex until he/she was born and settled on the names Maisy for a girl and Freddie for a boy.

Kitty's due date came and went with no sign of Maisy/Freddie. It was as if Maisy/Freddie overheard how close we were to being able to buy us a three-bedroom house and she/he decided to wait. The delay inspired jokes about trying to induce Kitty's labour. It transpired the most common advice to entice a baby's departure from the womb is to eat curry or have sex.

'No prizes for guessing who came up with these theories,' I began reciting in my show, before impersonating men in pubs saying, 'I can't believe we got away with that! I've had sex and curry all week. Last night I had a curry on her back while we were having sex.' 'Of course I tried it with my wife,' I said, 'before we were thrown out of the Raj King Restaurant in Muswell Hill.'

The truth is I was unable to test these theories in real life. Kitty said the thought of curry made her want to vomit, and when I mentioned sex she actually did vomit. Kitty had read that long walks can also induce labour and was more inclined to give that a try. So we strolled for an hour or so around Regent's Park and, seeing as Indian food wasn't an option, decided to stop for lunch at the Weng Wah Chinese restaurant on Haverstock Hill.

'It's happening!' Kitty shrieked, using a phrase I often shriek when the food is arriving.

My eyes darted around the restaurant expecting to see a Chinese waiter with a tray of crispy duck and pancakes approaching.

'No it isn't,' I said, disappointed.

'The baby! The baby's coming!' Kitty urgently announced.

It takes a lot for me to forgo a Chinese meal and you may think this was such an occasion. You would be wrong.

'Oh my God! We have to get to the hospital! I'll ask to get the food to go!' I responded.

Munching on a prawn cracker, I drove the Seat at breakneck speed to the Whittington Hospital in Archway. Kitty slipped into a Zen-like trance. She was determined not to repeat the agonizing and lengthy labour she experienced with Lucas. Everything was going to be different. Each contraction was handled with controlled breathing. Once in the hospital we were asked to wait in the maternity ward until a delivery room became free. The maternity ward was packed with crying babies and women in labour wailing through their contractions, only separated by flimsy plastic curtains. It was an animalistic and alarming scene. Even the Skipton farmers would have been rattled. But not Kitty, she was unfazed, deeply focused.

When we were taken to the delivery room Kitty's monastic silence continued. She refused all pain relief with a slow and deliberate shake of her head. Our midwife was an elderly West Indian lady whose frail demeanour belied her no-nonsense attitude.

'My name is Old Brown,' she announced like she was walking into a saloon bar in the Wild West, 'because I'm old . . . and I'm brown. Now let's get this baby outta ya!'

For the next few hours the only sound in the room was Old Brown instructing, 'Keep push'en, woman.' 'Dat's a good gurl.'

Then Old Brown suddenly turned and shouted at me, having not spoken to me once before.

'What time is it, man?' she bellowed.

I was startled. Had she somewhere else she needed to be? Was her car on a meter?

'Er . . . 3 . . . 25,' I stammered.

'Precisely, man?' Old Brown shouted even louder.

'3.27 and 10 seconds,' I replied, in fear of my life.

At that moment she held aloft our newborn baby.

'That is the time that your baby was born,' Old Brown announced.

'Quiet down now,' Old Brown said to our crying new baby.

Our son, covered in birthing fluid, was immediately silenced. Less than a minute old and he knew not to mess with Old Brown.

After I expertly cut the cord Old Brown swaddled him and placed him in Kitty's arms.

'Meet your mama,' she said, smiling for the first time.

'It's a boy!' Kitty said, her face flushed and beaming.

'He's beautiful,' I said with tears in my eyes.

'It's not Maisy then,' Kitty said.

'It's Ossie,' we both said, literally at the same time.

We had discussed the name Ossie only once before settling on Freddie, but as soon as we saw his face it was like we already knew him. His face was so rich with character and mischief that the name Ossie instantly seemed to fit.

On 13 April 2008, Oscar 'Ossie' McIntyre was born at 3.25, sorry, 3.27 p.m. and 10 seconds.

Our family was complete.

10

'You must go now,' ordered Old Brown within moments of Ossie's birth, opening the door and ushering us out to the corridor where we followed a queue of other women in labour that seemed to lead back to our car and beyond.

The whiff from the bags of leftover Chinese hit us as soon as I opened the Seat door. Now a dab hand, I strapped Ossie into Lucas's old car seat in record time. Kitty and I exhaled from exhaustion when we both got into the car. Kitty, who had exhibited supernatural powers throughout her labour, continued exhaling for about a minute, not dissimilar to the inmate in the film *The Green Mile*. We both turned to see Ossie sleeping snugly in the back. Welcome to the world. Not a care in his tiny innocent head. I envied him being able to sleep in the back of a car without fear of someone opening the door and squirting petrol on him.

'What a beautiful sight,' Kitty said.

'I know. I'm starving,' I said, only half joking about the Chinese food on the back seat.

Lucas was waiting for us at Alma Road with Kitty's sister, Claudia, who had been babysitting him. He was two and a half now and knew all about the baby in Mummy's tummy. At first he seemed excited to meet his brother. Sitting together on the Ikea sofa, Lucas stared at his newborn sibling with fascination, but when Kitty picked up Ossie and said, 'Come to Mummy' Lucas's face dropped, the realization he had a rival suddenly dawning on him.

'When is Ossie going?' asked Lucas. A question he then repeated hourly over the forthcoming months.

The real question was, 'When are we all going?' The addition of a baby made our flat even more pokey. When the neighbours' Friday night fornication woke Ossie up after we'd been trying for ages to get him to sleep, that was the final straw.

'That's it! We're moving out!' I yelled.

'Where to? We can't find anywhere,' said Kitty, directing Ossie to her breast, milk spraying in his eye before he latched on.

'Let's just rent again, rent a bigger place,' I suggested as the banging headboard of the neighbours' bed dislodged more plaster from our walls.

'Renting is such a waste of money, I'm sure we'll find our perfect place to buy. We just have to hang on, be patient,' Kitty insisted.

'I don't care. I'm away so much, I don't want to leave you here on your own with two kids. I know we have to be patient before we buy a place, but let's be patient somewhere nicer,' I implored.

Kitty remained steadfast in her sensible mindset, until we received what we decided was a 'sign', a loud crashing sound. 'What was that?' We leapt out of bed and headed to the living room where we found the blurry *Lovers* had finally given up their tenuous hold on the butchered wall and fallen, face down, to the floor. After my initial relief that I had not paid the extra money for a glass frame, Kitty announced she was finally sold on the idea of renting.

'You're right, it might be ages before we find somewhere. We can't stay here. Let's do it!' Kitty agreed.

So rather than the 'For sale' button on the website Rightmove, I clicked my old trusted friend, 'To rent'. To help determine our budget, I had a quick scroll through my diary beforehand, which was more packed than ever. For years I had been mainly gigging in clubs on the comedy circuit on Thursdays, Fridays and Saturdays; now I was busy most nights of the week until the end of the year. I had tour shows in all corners of the country and Big Fee Fay was booking me for plenty of corporates too. I was due to host the Pet Plan Awards, the Pub Food Awards, the Water Industry Awards, the Greeting Cards Awards, the Chemist and Druggist Awards – if you won an award in 2008 the chances are I handed it to you. I had also been booked to perform stand-up at events for big name companies such as Ford, Microsoft and Panasonic, as well as obscure ones like the Airport Operators Dinner and the Grain and Feed Trade Annual Dinner.

One of the more bizarre corporates was to entertain business-men on a golf day, not in the evening after their rounds, actually on the course between shots. I drove around the course on a buggy like a Ryder Cup captain, pulling up when I saw a group of players and attempting to amuse them. Beyond laddish innu-endo about threesomes, holding the shaft tight and shaving the hole, I struggled. The feedback to Big Fee Fay was that I was a 'nuisance'. But I got paid and headed on to the next one.

Another corporate event I thought would surely help my quest to become a homeowner was the Mortgage Awards, which I hosted at a venue called The Brewery in Central London. I joked all night about house prices and my struggles to get a foot on the property ladder. When Mark Benson, the winner of the main award of the night, 'Mortgage Advisor of the Year', was announced he triumphantly strode to the stage only for me to refuse to give him the trophy until he handed me his business card and a guarantee he would get me a home. He assumed I was joking but I phoned him at 9 a.m. the following morning. Having explained to him about the substantial income I would be earning over the forthcoming year the hungover Mortgage Advisor of 2008 said, 'Future self-employed income cannot be used to calculate borrowing. The mortgage is calculated on your last three years' earnings.'

This was the same shit they told me at my bank. Why was this guy so special? He ended the phone call by asking me if I enjoyed fishing and invited me to fish with him.

'I would love to go fishing with you,' I lied, before hanging up.

148

I was frustrated that the best mortgage advisor in the country's best offer was a fishing trip. So, flush with cash in the bank and more on the way from confirmed work, I clicked, for the first time in my life, 'High to Low' as the search criteria for the price of rentals on Rightmove. Forget flats, forget shared gardens and shared bathrooms, we're going all in. We soon found a house in Crouch End that was so idyllic Kitty burst into tears as soon as we walked in for a viewing, severely handicapping our negotiating position.

The house was on Barrington Road, a quiet residential street in the heart of Crouch End, by far our preferred location. Familiar Victorian terraced houses lined the road, but they were smart and hadn't been converted to flats. They were whole houses. Lovely family houses. The front door was newly painted duck-egg blue, Kitty's favourite colour. The interior was clean and light and newly refurbished. There were three double bedrooms for us all, a lovely bathroom with a full-size bath. It had a downstairs and an upstairs. Our whole life together, Kitty and I had only trod on communal stairs. The place was more than a step up; it was a whole staircase up. There was a downstairs loo, a large kitchen with our first dishwasher and French doors leading to a terrace and private garden that backed on to Priory Park, a picturesque little park with a playground for Lucas.

As we drove back to our comparative hovel on Alma Road, Kitty and I were deliriously excited, giggling as we took it in turns to do impressions of things we might say to each other if we lived there, things we had never been able to say to each other before like, 'I'll be up in a minute.' 'Have you locked the back door?' 'Don't forget to put the dishwasher on.' 'That reminds me, I need to cut the grass.' 'I might have a lie down . . . in the bath.' 'How many times have I told you to put the toilet seat down . . . in the downstairs loo?'

The house was genuinely beyond our wildest dreams; we would be more than happy to spend the rest of our lives there. To buy the house would have been well over our budget but, although it was pricey, we could certainly afford the rent for the next year.

Moving out of Alma Road I never even looked back. My attitude was good riddance. Kitty however reacted in the same way she had when we vacated all the horrendous flats we had rented before. She was devastated. She hates when anything comes to an end and nostalgically remembers all the good times, the important times, the special times in the story of our life together. Alma Road was where Lucas spent his first years, where he and Kitty spent so much time alone together while I was working. Times that are forever gone. I constantly look forward in life but Kitty always takes time to pause and mourn the end of any era.

On Lucas's second birthday when I said, 'I can't believe he's two already,' Kitty's eyes were full of tears.

'What's wrong, darling?' I asked.

'He's two,' she said through her tears, 'which means he's never going to be one again. That's gone. That person. One-year-old Lucas is gone forever.'

I love the way she sees the world. She savours every moment of our lives. Even if an old mug gets chipped we pretty much have to have a mini-funeral for it. So moving out of Alma Road was especially emotional for her.

'We can stay if you like?' I said, as she reminisced in the Seat, outside our flat for the last time, Lucas and Ossie strapped in the back and the boot (surprisingly spacious for a car in its class) packed with belongings.

'No thank you,' she laughed.

Lucas, who had only been saying 'When is Ossie going?' since his brother's birth, finally had something new to say.

'Can we leave Ossie here?' he asked, before I sped away to our upgraded life.

I will never forget the unbridled joy we all felt that first day we moved into Barrington Road, Kitty choosing where everything went in the new kitchen and Lucas tearing through all the rooms like he had been set free. Only two years prior we were in serious debt – now our lives had been transformed. We had two happy healthy boys, a beautiful family home and I was touring the country doing what I love, making people laugh. Kitty and I didn't feel like we were at the start of something, we thought that was it, game over, we are now living our perfect life. Well, renting our perfect life, but in time we'd be able to buy a similar house and live happily ever after. I had reached the summit of my ambitions. Addison, on the other hand, was doing what Addison does and thinking big, busily plotting success way beyond my own modest dreams. He phoned with his latest bombshell a few weeks after we'd moved in.

'Michael. Addison,' he said in his grumbling voice that always promised so much. 'Looks like I've got you a DVD deal with Universal to film later in the year.'

The DVD market for comedians was burgeoning. In 2008 there was no downloading or streaming – it was all about DVDs, and stand-up comedy DVDs had become big business especially at Christmas. Priced about £10 they were the perfect Christmas present and, although not the ideal shape, a popular stocking filler. Peter Kay and Lee Evans had sold enormous numbers of DVDs in the past few years. Again, as with my *Live at the Apollo* appearance, I didn't think I was yet at that stage. But this is what Addison did, he didn't pave a path, he bulldozed one.

'It's a pretty good deal for your first one. If it goes well I can get you a much bigger deal next time. Universal have predicted 50,000 sales,' Addison explained.

'That's a lot. Can I do that?' I replied, sitting at my new desk which I had set up in Ossie's nursery as he was still sleeping in our bed.

'Michael. You're going to have to get on TV and do some promoting but I think you can get there, otherwise I wouldn't have done the deal. Your ticket sales are going great.'

'Where will I record it?' I asked with excitement mixed with apprehension.

'At the Hammersmith Apollo, Joe's booked it for September 19th.'

'The Hammersmith Apollo? Just me. On my own.' I gulped.
'Michael. You've got to be one step ahead in this business.
We've got a few months to sell the tickets, if we can't shift them
all I can invite a whole load of people in for nothing. I've done
it before. It's gonna be tight. I'm just being honest with ya. But
it will look great to film it at the Apollo. Sends out a message
being at such a big venue.'

'Even if I don't sell it out?' I questioned.

'It's all about perception, my friend. Come on, let's go for it,'
Addison said. 'Do you want a boring life? Do you want to play
it safe?'

Of course my answer to this was probably yes. But that
wasn't an option with Addison.

'No!' I said, feigning confidence. 'Let's go for it!'

'That's my boy,' he barked.

There was a lot to digest after Addison's latest whirlwind of
a phone call. I was going to do my own show at the Hammersmith Apollo, the biggest theatre in the country, and record it for
a DVD. My smiling face would be on the shelves of supermar-
kets and on Amazon. Everything was now geared towards 19th
September, less than four months away. Every tour show was
now needed to build on and improve my jokes and keep finding
new ones.

I was happy with how the tour shows were going but the
content was a bit patchy, as I had lost a lot of my best material
on TV. Once you've broadcast a joke to millions of people, it's
dead. This is the annoying thing about comedy. When musicians

have a hit single it has the opposite effect, all the audience wants is to hear the hits. My life would have been so much easier if I could do my *Live at the Apollo* and Royal Variety sets until I'm old and grey, but the truth is nobody wants to hear a joke twice. The magic is gone. When a comedian does new material the audience is happy, when a musician does new material people go to the bar.

The Royal Variety act was only seven minutes long, but that was my best seven minutes at the time. *Live at the Apollo* was then my best twenty-five minutes. All those jokes were now kaput, never to be performed again. I still had half of the jokes from my Edinburgh show up my sleeve, but they weren't the best half otherwise I would have already used them on TV. My DVD had to be between eighty and ninety minutes long. That was in the contract. I had work to do.

Kitty and Lucas were the source of a lot of my new material, and Kitty had helpfully just given birth to more potential material too. My best new routine, however, was inspired by our now, thankfully, old flat in Alma Road. Just outside the 'galley' kitchen was a built-in dresser with two drawers. The bottom one was used for storing tablecloths and napkins. The top drawer belonged exclusively to me, and became known as my 'man drawer'. My ownership of the drawer was never discussed, I just laid claim to it over time, using it to store a combination of manly things and things I couldn't bring myself to throw away, like: batteries of indeterminate life, takeaway menus despite the fact that we always ordered the same thing anyway, light bulbs, foreign currency that was no longer in circulation, old mobile phones, radiator bleeding keys, keys from homes we no longer lived in, a tape measure, electronic cables whose function I didn't understand, instructions and guarantees for appliances – you get the idea.

I began describing the contents of my 'man drawer' onstage and it immediately resonated more than my other new material. I genuinely never know which ideas and thoughts are going to ignite an audience but from the first time I started riffing about my drawer, they were with me. Laughter is a message of encouragement, it's a green light to keep mining an idea. So night after night the jokes about my drawer grew. I would ask the audience what was in their drawers and added them to the routine. I soon began concocting a scenario whereby I would suddenly need all the hoarded contents of my drawer. Pretending to receive an anonymous phone call in the middle of the night instructing me to carry out various tasks.

'You must go to your old home via the side gate . . . Do you still have the Key? There will be an elderly man awaiting you, you must pay him . . . in Drachma . . . he will have with him an Argos toaster circa 1998, do you have any idea how it operates? . . . You must also bring with you nine triple A Batteries . . . that don't work . . . And then order a Chinese takeaway . . . on a Nokia 3210.'

I was relaxed and playful on tour. Sometimes new routines would just appear during the show, like the time I was chatting to a posh young man on the front row of a show in Oxford, who instead of saying he was drunk or pissed, said he was 'trolleyed' and then followed that up with 'absolutely rat-arsed'. I commented that posh people could probably use any word in the English language to describe themselves as being intoxicated and it would still sound acceptable: 'I'm lampshaded, I'm utterly gazeboed, I'm totally windscreen wipered.' The audience all started chipping in and we were in hysterics. I started repeating the idea every night until it became part of the show.

Whereas freedom to explore ideas onstage can lead to future routines, it can also lead to disaster. After a decent show at the Wolverhampton Civic Hall for a full house of just over a thousand people, I waited in the wings listening to see if there was an appetite for an encore. No matter the quality of a show, audiences tend to applaud when it's over. This may be due to gratitude or relief. After that initial applause dies down there is an excruciating pause when the audience either cheers for more or goes home. On this occasion the audience heartily cheered for my return. I pranced back onto the stage enjoying their rapturous reception, but instead of stopping centre stage I thought it would be funny to keep walking all the way through the stage and off the other side. When reaching the wings on the opposite side of the stage I then had the idea to sprint around the back of the curtain and reappear from the side I started on. Although I was there for comedy, I had become some sort of second-rate illusionist. The audience seemed to enjoy my playful antics, so when I reached the middle of the stage the second time I decided to do it again and carried on walking. I was intent on sprinting behind the curtain even faster this time; at this rate I would soon knock David Blaine off his perch, Penn and Teller would be history – forget Wolverhampton, I had a Vegas residency in my sights.

Unfortunately, when I heel-turned to begin my dash behind the curtain I lost my footing and fell backwards. I instinctively threw out my right arm to cushion the blow of my fall, which resulted in it being crushed under my body. Excruciating pain and a loud crunching sound confirmed something terrible had happened. I began screaming in pain just out of the audience's sight behind the curtain. The audience, assuming this was part my new magic act, kept laughing. The more I screamed for help, the more they laughed. The awkward reality was that these were the biggest laughs I got all night. My genuine agony seemed to be a highlight.

'This isn't a joke!' I cried from behind the curtain, cueing more laughs.

So many times during gigs when the audience weren't laughing I wanted to shout, 'This IS a joke.' Now they were laughing hysterically and it wasn't.

After a period of time that felt like hours, the laughter finally started to be replaced by concern. Waiting in the wings, on the side of the stage I had attempted to run back to, were the sound operator and Terry. Terry, of course, had seen the show many times before. The fact that I had never done this in any of my previous shows and was now screaming for help didn't seem to register as odd with him as he laughed along with the audience.

A Funny Life

The sound man however tentatively came to my aid and slowly walked across the stage, half the audience shouting that I might be genuinely hurt and the other half continuing to laugh. On reaching the other end of the stage the sound man dramatically pulled back the curtain to reveal me lying in pain on the floor.

'My arm! My arm! I can't move my arm,' I screamed.

The house lights were then turned on and everyone in the theatre collectively realized I had been seriously injured in an accident. I remember lying on the floor in horrific pain watching the audience's sympathetic faces file out at a ninety-degree angle.

I'm not sure if you've heard of the St John's Ambulance. I know I hadn't. The first time I became aware of them was lying on the floor of the Wolverhampton Civic Hall stage. The St John's Ambulance is an organization of volunteers trained in first aid who are on hand to offer medical assistance at crowded events. Two members of the St John's Ambulance were in attendance that night. It soon became apparent that the St John's Ambulance had no upper age limit when accepting kind-hearted volunteers, as these two were more than likely the oldest man and woman in Wolverhampton. The spotlight operator who had followed me throughout the show had positioned his beam of light directly at my anguished body. I looked up into the light to see the faces of the two volunteers hovering over me. My first thought was that I had died along with these pensioners and we were all together en route to the afterlife.

The gentleman volunteer, whose telegram from the Queen must have been imminent, then spoke to me.

'What is your name?' he asked, as his training kicked in.

Even through my torturous pain I found this question alarming. He was stationed to work that night at the *Michael McIntyre* show and then spent ninety minutes watching me at the back of the auditorium. Before I had a chance to reply, his colleague, who looked even more senior than him, answered his question instead.

'Brenda,' she said.

'Not you. Him,' he clarified.

'Michael. I'm Michael. My arm! My arm! Help me!' I yelled.

'Where does it hurt?' The geriatric St John's Ambulance man asked literally between me screaming, 'My arm!'

'It's my arm. I landed on my arm. I can't move it,' I shrieked.

'OK then,' Brenda said, taking control. 'Have you tried moving it?'

If I thought things couldn't get any worse, Terry then joined the scene by accidentally kicking my disabled arm as he walked past, triggering a level of pain that still makes me shudder to this day.

'Sorry, mate,' said Terry as he joined the faces staring at me in the spotlight. Then a fourth face came into view.

'Michael! Hi! I'm David, the theatre manager,' he said, like he was hosting a breakfast radio show in the Midlands. 'I'm the one who left you the fruit in your dressing room.' He then paused, waiting for me to respond.

'Thank . . . you . . . for . . . the . . . fruit,' I just about managed to reply. 'I think I've really hurt my arm. I can't move it.'

'OK, great.' He actually said the word 'great'. 'I've called an ambulance and they're on the way. Great show by the way, really funny stuff. I hope you'll come back to the theatre when you're back on your feet.'

Thankfully an actual ambulance soon arrived and hi-vis-wearing professionally trained medics took over. It was established that my shoulder had been totally dislocated and they were unable to relocate it on the stage so I needed to be transported to Wolverhampton General Hospital. My right arm was stretched wide and literally stuck in that position, meaning that when I was placed on the gurney I wouldn't be able to fit through the ambulance doors. This was explained to me and that the plan was to give me morphine so that I could tolerate the pain of bending my dislocated arm enough to squeeze me onto the ambulance.

Once the morphine kicked in, I have to say I felt a whole lot better about everything. I think I even booked in another show with David, the theatre manager, as I was suddenly super keen to return. The following hours are a bit hazy as I was put under a general anaesthetic at Wolverhampton General and woke up on a hospital bed with my shoulder slotted back in and moving fine.

'I need to phone Kitty. My phone is in my bag,' I groggily said to Terry who was waiting by my bedside.

Terry located my phone and helpfully asked if he could dial the number for me.

'Is it 9 for an outside line?' he inexplicably asked.

'No, Terry, it's a mobile,' I said.

'Don't worry, darling, I'm fine,' I said to Kitty when she picked up the phone in the early hours of the morning. I explained what had happened and that I would soon be on my way back home to Barrington Road.

The hospital gave me some X-rays of my shoulder that Terry put in the boot of the car and I tried to get comfortable in the back seat. The sun was rising when we finally made it home to find Kitty waiting in her dressing gown on the doorstep, overwhelmed with worry. Soon I was lying in bed recounting to her the story of how my misjudged encore ended in the local hospital. When I reached the end of the tale I realized I had left the X-rays in the boot of Terry's car and immediately phoned him. This led to a baffling conversation that still makes me laugh now while writing it.

'Hi Terry, I'm really sorry but I left my X-rays in the boot, please can you come back with them if you haven't gone too far?'

I was on Kitty's phone so he may not have recognized the number but still, his response beggars belief.

'Who is this?' he said.

The drugs and adrenaline meant that I slept fine and relatively pain free. But when I awoke the pain kicked in along with the reality that I was going to be out of action for a while. I had been starting every show by taking the stage doing the arm-swinging skip I had invented on *Live at the Apollo*, a favourite of both the audience and counter-terrorist police. It was becoming a bit of a trademark. Sometimes when people saw me in the street they would shout my name and then either do the skip themselves or ask for me to do it. I even heard a professional footballer had done my skip to celebrate a goal. The first thing I did when I got out of bed the day after my accident was attempt my skip down the corridor. What a pathetic sight I must have been, crying in pain as I struggled to fractionally raise my right arm.

In just a few weeks I had to record my show for DVD.

I was in a race against time to be back fit and skipping onto the stage at the Hammersmith Apollo.

11

I am accident-prone. I am also a hypochondriac. The net result of this is that there hasn't been a day I can recall when some part of my body isn't bothering me. You name it and I've either had it, suspected I've had it or have it right now. I am familiar with most specialists in North London hospitals, so it was no surprise that I already knew the doctor I was to see about my dislocated shoulder, as he had treated me for a knee injury I had not long before.

'Oh hello again,' I said on walking in. 'You saw me about my knee?'

'Yes. How is the knee?' the specialist asked, eyeing me over the top of his reading glasses.

'My knee is fine. But I've hurt my shoulder now. Am I in the wrong place?'

'No. I specialize in shoulders and knees,' said the specialist.

'And toes?' I suggested, playfully referencing the nursery rhyme 'Heads, Shoulders, Knees and Toes'.

I thought this might get a laugh, but unlike the bones of his patients, his lips failed to crack.

'No. Just shoulders and knees,' the specialist responded in a sincere tone.

After this awkward opening exchange he examined my shoulder and drew pictures of rehabilitation exercises I knew I would never do. I followed his advice and cancelled several immediate performances. Unfortunately, one commitment could not be cancelled or postponed. I was to host a pilot for a Saturday night game show called *Time of Your Life*. The BBC's Head of Entertainment Elaine Bedell (whose own head I had squirted with lemon juice) was still very much championing me, particularly with a view of me hosting Saturday night TV.

'Be careful, Michael,' Addison kept saying. 'Saturday night TV is the hardest thing to crack, it's a graveyard. The BBC will blow smoke up your arse until you're blue in the face, but then when you're in a shit show they'll turn their back on you. Seen it countless times before. I'm just being honest with ya.'

Addison loved a metaphor and wasn't afraid to mix them. My favourites were, 'We'll burn that bridge when we come to it', 'I'm like a bull at a china gate' and 'It's like two ships passing in a nightmare'. The point he was making about the BBC is that they had a problem finding hit shows on a Saturday night and were in the process of courting me as a potential Mr Saturday Night, but the nature of Saturday night telly is that if I hosted a flop it would be such a visible disaster my TV career could be over before it started. Addison always liked to test the water first on TV. *Live at the Apollo*, for example, was on BBC1 at 10.35 p.m. on a Monday night, probably the least glamorous slot of the week. Addison wanted that slot to see if the numbers grew before moving to a more prominent one. This cautious strategy did strike me as slightly at odds with his nature but he had been burnt in the past by overexposing his acts on primetime. So with Addison wary of throwing me straight onto Saturday nights, he wanted us to try and devise a show specifically for me, and not just take one that the BBC offered.

I had begun spending days at Open Mike, Addison's production company in Soho, trying to come up with TV show ideas. I had experience of 'development' (as it's called in TV) having worked as a lowly runner for the production company Tiger Aspect when I was in my twenties. The job of a runner is basically to make tea and coffee for producers and deliver stuff around Soho. Please don't have an image of me as a hotshot young wannabe destined for the top. I was the laziest of runners. I spent most of my time either making mistakes or locked in the loo playing the game Snake on my Nokia 3210 mobile phone.

The head of the entertainment department at Tiger Aspect was Mark Linsey, a friendly faced chap who I had never engaged with until once he asked for some croissants at a meeting after I dropped off a tray of coffees. I seized the moment to hand him an idea I had written up for a TV show called 'TV Licence Evaders'. A game show where the contestants were students who hadn't paid their TV licence, and all the questions were ironically about television programmes that they were illegally watching. The winner won a brand-new television and their TV licence fee paid for a year, and the losers were handed over to the authorities to face criminal charges. Mark summoned me to his office soon after and said he loved the idea but legal problems meant it wasn't possible. He was kind and encouraging to someone at the bottom of the pile. I hoped he'd immediately promote me and have me working on his team but instead he asked for a coffee, and said he never got the croissants in the meeting last week and that simply can't happen again. I then went to the loo to play Snake (that sounds rude, but isn't).

So I brainstormed for ideas for my own Saturday night TV show while guzzling tea and eating entire packets of Jaffa Cakes in the time it would take an average person to eat one. The result was a game show called *Time of Your Life*, which the BBC liked enough to commission a pilot, due to be filmed the week after my dislocated shoulder in Wolverhampton. I would love to share the format of *Time of Your Life* with you, but genuinely can't remember, as it was such a disaster my mind has deleted it. I know it had something to do with people competing with each other who were all at the same time in their lives, who were engaged, having a baby, taking their driving test, etc. I remember Tony Blackburn and Craig Revel Horwood taking part. I remember Addison insisted on me wearing a suit that was so sparkly, epileptic viewers would have needed a warning. But the main thing I remember is that the recording went on so long that the entire audience, every single one of the 462 people in Studio 1 of the London Studios, had left by the time the show reached the final round. One by one they filed out during the course of the four-hour record until not a soul remained, just rows and rows of empty seats.

'Congratulations to our winners. Thank you for watching and good night,' I said at the end of the show, even though nobody was there watching and, as a non-broadcast pilot, nobody ever would.

Plenty of excuses were made by the producers as to why 462 people left the studio. 'Don't forget the last train is at 11.30 p.m.' 'It's a weekday so people have work and school in the morning.' But the truth was that if the show was remotely exciting and entertaining, surely at least one person would have stayed until the end.

'What about Elaine from the BBC? Did she like it?' I asked the producer.

'She had to leave, unfortunately,' came the reply.

The good news was my shoulder didn't hurt once during the filming. Before the recording Addison kept saying, 'Dr Showbiz will sort you out', which is an expression that means the adrenaline produced in response to having to perform will mask any pain. Having not heard this before I thought an actual doctor was going to see me, some kind of celebrity doctor. I said to Danny that I didn't think I should be treated by another doctor without consulting my GP. When he stopped laughing he explained that Dr Showbiz wasn't a real person. My shoulder pain returned the following morning but I now felt confident about being pain free for my DVD recording, even if decidedly unconfident about being the BBC's new Mr Saturday Night.

The best news of all was that the Hammersmith Apollo was sold out. My worries about having to give away tickets to fill the seats were unfounded. Dr Showbiz paid me several visits before my warm-up shows leading up to that all-important night. As with my *Live at the Apollo* gig the year before, this was the culmination of months of hard work creating and polishing my material. The advice my wingman Paul 'Alright mate' Tonkinson gave me then, still held. As the biggest show on my tour, there's no reason why it shouldn't be the best.

The DVD was recorded on a Friday night in my home town. No need for a long journey with Terry at the wheel. I had even lost a bit of weight, so if the police did stop me en route my trousers would at least stay up. Rather than stressing out at having to sit in the make-up chair and greet pre-show well-wishers, I embraced the whole occasion. Thankfully, it was just one of those days that I felt on form. As soon as I arrived Danny and Addison burst into my dressing room and rather than ramp up my tension, I started joking about my journey there, as it was a Friday, and how people always stress about traffic being a nightmare on a Friday.

Addison and Danny were laughing away as I did impressions of people having actual nightmares about traffic on a Friday. I felt good, and soon I was onstage opening with all the very same jokes I had just made up in the dressing room. I had never said any of this before but it was natural and, seeing as the whole audience had just negotiated the stresses of travel on a Friday, funny. I had other jokes about traffic that I just flowed into from there. Jokes about enjoying seeing people stuck in traffic on the other side of the motorway, when there's no traffic in your direction. 'You hope the traffic goes on forever.' And jokes about farm traffic in the countryside when you get stuck behind a tractor and can't cope with the pressure to overtake as a queue of cars forms behind you. 'You have to risk your life by driving into oncoming traffic.' Eventually a man in a black BMW overtakes all of you at once and a small part of you can't help but want them to crash.

What I love about recalling jokes is that I always remember when the idea first popped into my head before they were built into routines over countless shows. I remember being on the M4 revelling in the misfortune of people stuck in traffic as I sailed past. I remember staying with Kitty's parents, Simon and Alexandra, in their home in Somerset after a gig in Taunton and, when I got back late, joking over red wine and food they'd saved me from dinner, and making them laugh about how I got stuck behind a tractor on my way back. As they were laughing I was already thinking this could be material. And so it was on the night of my DVD, with me in the dressing room making two people laugh and then making 3,000 people laugh with the same ideas. What's funny in the car, at dinner or in the dressing room, is funny full stop. My show that night was a collection of hundreds of little ideas that made me laugh and I joyously shared them, free from anxiety and self-doubt.

I watched the edit of the DVD and felt relieved and excited. Addison called once he had watched it too.

'Michael. Addison. Just watched the DVD on my own with all the lights off. I fucking loved it. I think we got a great product here. Now we gotta get it out there and push it hard!'

We decided to call the DVD *Live & Laughing* and began the process of flogging it. Universal predicted 50,000 sales in total. The pre-sales are always regarded as a good indicator and they weren't great, with less than 2,000. I never understood pre-sales of DVDs. Who is that organized? Do people that organized have much of a sense of humour? But I loved those 2,000 people who had pre-ordered, my biggest fans. So the outlook didn't suggest anything monumental in terms of sales. But Addison had been fired up and went into promotional overdrive. He bought whole page ads in national newspapers and even put me on a billboard on the Westway in White City so all the BBC execs could see it on their way in to work. Well, it depended on their timing, as it was on one of those changing billboards that rotated every few seconds. I drove my mum down to see it and, after driving around the Westway roundabout several times, had only seen adverts for HSBC, Nike and the new Audi A5 over and over again.

'I love that car,' my mum enthusiastically exclaimed.

'We're not here to see that car. I'm supposed to be on that billboard,' I replied, frustrated.

The fourth time driving around I saw the advert for my DVD start to appear and slammed on the brakes, nearly getting rear-ended by a very angry white-van driver who was wildly hooting and swearing at us.

'That's my son!' my mum proudly yelled to him, pointing at the huge billboard, as he hurled abuse at her.

'Behind you! That's my son!'

The aggressive white-van driver did look around but unfortunately the billboard had rotated again and was now an athletic girl posing in new Nike trainers.

Appearing on, and being funny on, TV shows was the best way to push the DVD. I had never appeared before on any of the traditional shows used for promoting, so with Addison's advice of 'The more you do, the more you'll sell!' ringing in my ears, I agreed to do all of them: *The One Show*, *This Morning*, *Richard and Judy*, *The Big Fat Quiz of the Year* and *The Graham Norton Show*. All these shows certainly helped get the word out there, but there were three shows where I was able to do stand-up and showcase what I did best, that really made the difference.

The first was hosting *Live at the Apollo*, which Addison said he wanted to be 'show one', meaning the first of the series to be broadcast, usually the one that gets the highest ratings. The second was a special celebration for Prince Charles's sixtieth birthday called *We Are Most Amused* at the Wimbledon Theatre, to be broadcast on ITV. And the third was back at the Royal Variety, this time at the London Palladium, also in the presence of Prince Charles. I think it reflects on how busy I was promoting myself that the future King of England was seeing me twice in the space of a few weeks. I had to do about fifteen minutes' material on the *Apollo* and seven minutes on both the Royal Variety and *We Are Most Amused*. Obviously all the material had to be different in case viewers saw more than one and thought I was a one-trick pony, and also there was the Prince Charles situation; I couldn't risk him shouting out, 'Heard it' at the Royal Variety or 'I am less amused the second time' at *We Are Most Amused*.

I had a few jokes that I'd edited out of *Live & Laughing* but really I had to take the majority of the material from the DVD. The way I saw it, it was like when musicians release a single as a taster to encourage you to buy the album. Although following this analogy, I was releasing three singles at once, but it was a calculated decision for maximum exposure. I divvied up my material over the three performances, saving the 'man drawer' for the Royal Variety. On *Live at the Apollo*, I hosted and introduced Rich Hall and Rhod Gilbert onto a stage that was starting to feel like home. The notoriously stuffy Royal Variety audience didn't laugh once when I opened with all my traffic jokes. Not once. Maybe they hadn't ever been in traffic. I know that the Royals have a police escort but I assumed the audience might have experienced a bit of nose to tail. Thankfully all the traffic stuff was edited out and the audience found the generosity to titter a bit once I got into their man drawers.

My two Prince Charles shows were pretty glamorous affairs. At the Royal Variety I met Peter Kay for the first time, who was charming, encouraging and naturally hilarious. But *We Are Most Amused* was like a who's who of comedy legends. In the afternoon all the performers took the stage together to rehearse the finale and the meeting of birthday boy Prince Charles and Prince Harry who was accompanying him. I was starstruck and dumbstruck standing next to the likes of Rowan Atkinson, Bill Bailey, John Cleese and Joan Rivers. This was just an afternoon run-through, not the main event, so nobody was in performance mode. Save that for tonight. But there was another comedian there who showed that he is just that, a natural born comedian. A man who seemed to have comedy running so much through his veins there was no turning it on and off. He was just on. As soon as he joined us onstage he had everyone in hysterics. They may have been legendary contemporaries, but for him they were just a group of people, another audience to entertain. That man was Robin Williams, and I'll never forget it. Everything that caught his eye became fodder for laughs. He was creating characters, doing voices, poking fun, grabbing whatever he could to use as props. He was a marvel. I never got a sense he was showing off or laying down a marker to remind everyone he was the best; I just felt he saw funny all around him and revelled in sharing it. Rather than being intimidated I found the whole day exhilarating. There's nothing better as a comedian than knowing your jokes work, and after all my tour shows and my DVD recording, I was bristling with confidence. I remember hearing John Cleese laughing loudly behind the curtain during my performance. It was a dizzying night.

Despite the glittering array of stars on display for Prince Charles, one special guest appearance sent the crowd wild. Andrew Sachs playing Manuel re-enacted scenes from *Fawlty*

Towers that under normal circumstances would have been well received, but this was the time of the infamous 'Sachsgate' scandal, so the audience were even more full of goodwill. The scandal involved Jonathan Ross and Russell Brand who got caught up in a media storm, the details of which there's no need for me to rehash. The reason I mention it is because it had a knock-on effect that benefited my DVD sales and career.

Live at the Apollo was getting under 3 million viewers in its safe Monday late-night slot on BBC1. But the BBC suspended Jonathan Ross following the controversy with Andrew Sachs, resulting in the cancelling of *Friday Night with Jonathan Ross* and a devastating blow for my former neighbours' sex life. Their loss was my gain as the BBC scrambled around looking for another show to fill Jonathan's plum Friday night slot. Addison, who represented Jonathan and was the executive producer of the chat show, pushed hard for another of his shows to fill the gap: *Live at the Apollo*. The series was in the can and ready to be broadcast and I was the host of the first show. So rather than be broadcast on Monday night with little fanfare, the new series of *Live at the Apollo* replaced *Friday Night with Jonathan Ross* and received significant media attention. People who had never seen *Live at the Apollo* watched, people who had never seen stand-up comedy watched, and lots of people who had never seen me watched. The ratings rocketed to 4.5 million, pretty much the same as Jonathan Ross was averaging. As a result the BBC became even more excited about the draw of stand-up on TV, and more excited about me.

All of these shows, and the unexpectedly high-profile nature of *Live at the Apollo*, created the perfect storm for the selling of my DVD. On the day of the release in mid-November 2008, I drove to shops all over London to see *Live & Laughing* hit the shelves of HMV, Virgin and WHSmith, as well as all the major super-markets. If my grinning face wasn't visible enough to shoppers, I would shamelessly move stacks of my DVDs to a more prom-inent position.

I had no idea how *Live & Laughing* would sell. The Universal predicted figure of 50,000 total sales was my only indicator. Sell-ing more than that would obviously be a win. In only the first week *Live & Laughing* sold 40,000 copies. Addison called me with the news and was more pumped up than ever. He smelt blood.

'Michael! Addison! Strap in, my friend, here we go,' he announced with relish. 'Forty thousand in week one is fantastic. I think you might have broken some kind of record. If you haven't we'll find one. I'll call you back.'

This was classic Addison. He wanted to make a song and dance about how well the DVD had done in its first week. Get some positive press. Keep driving sales. But was there a record I could claim? It wasn't the highest sales in the first week of a comedy DVD as Lee Evans sold 250,000 copies that week alone with his latest DVD. But was it the highest-selling 'debut' comedy DVD in week one? Unfortunately not, as both Ali G and *Little Britain Live* had sold more. But after many phone calls and fact checks, Addison finally found an official record, albeit a long-winded one. He called me to proudly announce the record I had broken, not a record anyone had previously laid claim to, but a record nevertheless.

'Michael! Addison! Fantastic news. Your DVD is the "Fastest-selling debut stand-up DVD",' and then he added for good measure, 'of all time. I've got that on a press release that's going out first thing tomorrow morning. You just let me do my thing. I know what I'm doing.'

'Will I be able to buy a house now?' I asked.

'I'll buy you a house tomorrow if you want, you can pay me back,' he offered, and meant it.

There had been many highs in my career so far, but this felt different. I rushed to the off-licence and asked for a bottle of their most expensive champagne, then I asked for their second most expensive instead, then the third, before buying the fourth. Popping the cork in the kitchen at Barrington Road, Kitty and I didn't feel like this might be the start of something, we knew that it was.

Live & Laughing sold nearly 500,000 copies that Christmas. It was the second highest-selling comedy DVD of the year behind Lee Evans and the twelfth highest-selling of all DVD releases.

After all the years in comedy clubs, all the years of Edinburgh Festival heartache, the thousands of miles of driving around the country trying to make people laugh everywhere from cattle marts to golf courses.

I was, finally, an overnight success.

12

With my profile rising, Addison went into overdrive, firstly hiring a publicist for me. Addison worried a lot about the press and the power they wield. He had just been through a nightmare with Jonathan Ross and wanted his clients to have the best protection. His escalating fear of the press during the Sachsgate scandal did lead to a funny story, when his lovely wife Shelley, 'Shell' as he called her, started using the fashion website Net-a-Porter that delivers designer clothes to your door. When the doorbell rang to drop off something fabulous for Shelley, Addison saw the shadow of a man behind the plate glass of his front door.

'Hello. Who is it?' Addison barked.

'Net-a-Porter,' came the reply.

'A reporter?' Addison said, flustered. 'You can fuck off, get away from my house.'

'Net-a-Porter,' the poor chap repeated.

'I've got nothing to say to any reporters. Now you better fuck off or you'll regret it,' Addison threatened.

'I've got a purse for you,' the Net-a-Porter delivery man said.

'A purse?' said Addison. 'What is this? A fucking boxing match? I don't want your money, I don't take bribes. I've got enough money. I got nuffin to say. Now fuck off.'

Later in the day Addison opened the front door to go to his Pilates class (I know, I couldn't believe it either, but he loved Pilates), and found a beautiful Chanel purse on the doorstep and immediately took it to his wife.

'Shell! You won't believe this, but a reporter has just left a Chanel purse on the doorstep. It's quite nice as it happens,' Addison said before Shelley explained that she had ordered the purse herself from the Net-a-Porter website.

'Oh shit,' said Addison. 'You better call them and apologize. I wasn't particularly welcoming to their driver.'

So Addison hired Gary Farrow, who he kept referring to as 'the Legendary Gary Farrow', to be my publicist. Addison introduced me to 'the Legendary Gary Farrow', who then introduced himself as 'the Legendary Gary Farrow', over lunch at the Japanese restaurant Roka on Charlotte Street. I thought there was only one Addison, but Gary seemed very much cut from the same cloth. His character was at least as big as the celebrities he represented, and there were some huge names among them: Elton John, George Michael, Gordon Ramsay, Jeremy Clarkson, Ozzy and Sharon Osbourne. Addison and Gary regaled each other with showbiz stories at top volume while I quietly ate sushi rolls.

Gary was so well connected it had become a bit of a party trick. 'Name any famous person in the world,' he kept asking me. Whoever I picked he would invariably reply, 'I've known him for twenty years.' And then proceed to tell a hilarious and borderline incriminating story about them, immediately followed by Addison, who also claimed to have known them for twenty years, trying to top it, all the while chopsticks were flailing and bits of rice flying around the table. They were both so loud all the other diners were tutting and rolling their eyes, not that Addison and Gary noticed or cared. It was a blessed relief to the whole restaurant when the bill finally came after two hours of bravado and Addison finally uttered the words I'd been waiting for, 'I'll end on this.'

Show business is a dog-eat-dog world. These two were survivors. Heavyweights. Winners. Titans. I knew I would be well looked after with them in my corner. I also knew that I would avoid ever having lunch with them both together again.

In order to get as famous as the Legendary Gary Farrow's other clients and warrant my hiring him, we had to find the right TV show for me. The BBC had paid for a pilot of *Time of Your Life*, which resulted in a time in my, and the audience's life, that we all wanted to forget. They were well aware of the success of my DVD *Live & Laughing*, mainly because Addison sent them daily updates that they certainly hadn't asked for. Addison, wildly building up his act's success, was relentless, firing off emails in the early hours of the morning to all and sundry with news of the latest DVD charts and extra tour dates being added. Anything positive that happened, everyone was going to know about it.

My champion Elaine Bedell had just left the BBC to work alongside Peter Fincham, the head of ITV. The television industry, like politics, is a bit of a merry-go-round, with the major players hopping from job to job and channel to channel. The adage of making sure you're nice to everyone as you never know where they're going to be down the line is especially pertinent in broadcasting. Peter Fincham used to be the controller of BBC1. Peter and Addison were extremely close and had a long history. I too had a history with Peter as he had given me my break at the 2006 Royal Variety. Peter and Elaine being fans of mine and running ITV was 'good news for us' Addison said; he loved flirting with ITV and using them as a stalking horse to keep the BBC on their toes. Replacing Elaine as Head of Entertainment at the BBC was Mark Linsey. The very same Mark Linsey who had been so supportive of me and my 'TV Licence Evaders' idea when I was a runner at Tiger Aspect. Now he would be offering me coffee and croissants and trying to sign me up to host shows for TV licence fee payers on the BBC. An ironic twist of fate I greatly enjoyed.

So a meeting was scheduled with Mark and the controller of BBC1, Jay Hunt, another sign that things had moved to the next level. I thought the agenda was the disastrous pilot, *Time of Your Life*, but Jay, who is fiercely intelligent and fast-talking, quickly and thankfully dismissed the possibility of filming another one and focused on the success of *Live at the Apollo*.

'I want you to become the regular host of *Live at the Apollo*,' Jay announced.

'We thought you were a brilliant host. It will be your show

like when Jack Dee hosted. Michael McIntyre's *Live at the Apollo,*' Mark added.

'Shut up, Mark, and get me a croissant,' I snapped.

No I didn't! But it would have been funny.

'That would be amazing,' I said, honestly.

The key for me had always been doing stand-up. That's what I had been working on for so long. Stand-up comedy is my vocation, what I'm best at. My struggling on panel shows didn't impress anyone. Hosting the game show pilot in a sparkly suit resulted in the whole audience leaving. Everything positive that was happening to me was because of stand-up. Hosting *Live at the Apollo* was my dream job. But there was still a question about material. If I was going to host six *Live at the Apollos*, that's about fifteen minutes per show, which means I'll need an hour and a half's worth of material. Plus another DVD deal was very much in the works for the next Christmas; that's another eighty minutes, and there's no way any of that material can overlap; nobody is going to buy a DVD with the same jokes they've just watched on TV. So, as much as this was my dream job, I didn't think I could come up with nearly three hours of jokes in a year, it was just too much of a stretch.

'What about taking the show on the road?' I suggested.

The only way I could think of creating that much material was to use local jokes. I had been gigging all over the country for years and always came up with jokes specific to the place I was in that I used to break the ice, just as I had done in Edinburgh. I had loads of Welsh jokes, Geordie jokes, Northern jokes, Irish

181

jokes. If we could film *Live at the Apollo* from a different city each week I would not only have a ready-made angle for my jokes, I already had most of them written. I thought it was a great idea, but the BBC were reluctant.

'*Live at the Apollo* is a brand now. Not only is the "Apollo" in the name, but in order to get the biggest comics it's probably better to be in London,' Jay correctly pointed out.

Never one to miss an opportunity to produce more shows and make more money, Addison of course had the solution.

'So let's make another show, a stand-up show on the road with Michael hostin',' he suggested.

Loving the idea I picked up the baton. 'I know all the comedians on the circuit and there are so many who have a brilliant ten minutes that they've perfected over the years. Let's put them on the show. They're funny. Also, they're totally match fit as they perform their sets every night, often multiple times a night.'

'We can hand-pick the most beautiful theatres in major cities across the UK,' said Addison, tag-teaming with me to get it over the line. 'I tell you, those audiences are going to lap it up. When do major TV shows ever come to them? We can get local celebrities in the audience, book local comics too.'

'Let's do it,' Jay and Mark agreed together.

'And we'll keep the Apollo with guest hosts?' Addison confirmed, clarifying he would be leaving with another show on the BBC.

'Yes, of course. This will be Michael's show and the Apollo continues. And I'd like to put Michael's show on Saturday nights.

You know how much we want him there. What shall we call it?' asked Jay.

Without pausing for thought, Addison leaned back in his chair and spread his arms wide.

'*Michael McIntyre's Comedy Roadshow,*' Addison declared.

And just like that my own TV show was commissioned. Doing what I love and do best on BBC1, on a Saturday night, and I already had most of the jokes oven-ready.

Now you're probably wondering what impact this sudden rush of success was having on our finances. Well, it was having a tremendous impact. I sold the Seat Altea, and when Kitty stopped crying about all the wonderful times we'd spent in the car, even turning Lucas's vomiting over that poor Scottish estate agent into a nostalgic memory, I bought us both a car. Not new, I still wasn't prepared to lose the amount of money cars depreciate. I bought a year-old Mercedes C-Class Sports Coupe for myself and a year-old BMW X5 for Kitty, the winner of Used Car of the Year at the corporate I had hosted a couple of years before. But the main benefit of my corporate hosting was of course meeting Mortgage Advisor of 2008, Mark Benson. With our deposit growing exponentially, Kitty and I were viewing more and more expensive homes to buy every week. Everything was moving so fast.

'You gotta get something with gates, Michael,' Addison advised on the phone while I was pushing Ossie on the baby swing in Regent's Park. 'Don't get something too small cos you'll regret it and have to move. Get something nice for a few million.'

'A few million? I don't have a few million, Addison,' I objected.

'Get a big mortgage out with that mortgage man you keep going on about, because you're gonna easily pay it off next year,' Addison insisted.

'You don't know that for sure. I can't overextend myself, Addison.'

'I've been talking to Joe and looking at all your DVD sales. We see no reason why you can't sell out arenas. So you know me, my friend. I say we go for it, at the end of this year. Put an arena tour on sale.'

'Oww!' I screamed, so lost in Addison's latest wild idea that I let Ossie's swing hit me.

'An arena tour? I've only just done the Hammersmith Apollo, I'm not Lee Evans,' I said.

'Michael, listen to me, you sold half a million DVDs, half a fucking million people bought your DVD. You're gonna have your own show on BBC1 for six Saturday nights. I think we can do it. You're red hot. You know me, I like a challenge, and when you sell out these arenas, and I think you will, that's when you make the real money. Buy two fucking houses.'

What was I supposed to say? Addison had been right about everything else.

'OK. If you think I can do it,' I replied.

So, with Addison's words ringing in our ears, Kitty and I started to look at houses in Hampstead, a place we'd always dreamt of living. As fate would have it we viewed a terraced house just off Hampstead High Street, on the very same road where we'd once viewed the flat with no bathroom. But this was a whole house and newly refurbished. It was a similar size to the house we were renting in Crouch End, but the location made it astronomically expensive.

'It's lovely, but it's still a bit small, maybe we should be living further out,' Kitty said to me outside after we'd seen it.

'I've got something down the road,' the eavesdropping estate agent said. 'It's more expensive, but from everything you say, I think you'd love it.'

So we allowed him to take us to a house that was well over our budget, and of course we instantly fell in love with it. It was a substantial, homely, six-bedroom Edwardian proper Hampstead house. Could this beautiful house really be our first home? What first-time buyer buys a house like this? Kitty and I felt like we'd won the lottery.

I spoke to Mark Benson, who set about securing the substantial finance. Borrowing millions of pounds is as big a risk as it sounds. The ever-optimistic Addison, however, felt we should be buying an even bigger house. 'No gates? You'll have to move again in a couple of years.'

But I was terrified I was overborrowing. Show business is notoriously precarious, and everything could come crashing down in an instant.

As I was about to find out.

13

I was invited to present an award at the 2009 BAFTAs. The BAFTAs is the most prestigious night on the Television Awards calendar. It was an honour to be asked and also another sign that I was being inducted into the glitterati. Kitty and I always enjoyed the BAFTAs on TV every year, tucked up in bed watching the celebs swan down the red carpet. Now we would be joining them. We went to Selfridges where a camp Brazilian personal shopper selected designer dresses for Kitty to try on in a private dressing room between sips of champagne. While she was on cloud nine I was on internet banking, seeing if we could afford the dress or whether I'd have to take out another mortgage. I even treated myself to a new suit. My new publicist to the stars Gary Farrow sent me off to David Beckham's tailor to get kitted out.

On the night of the BAFTAs a chauffeur-driven car came to take us to the ceremony at the Royal Festival Hall. Kitty looked spectacular in her new designer dress as we crossed Barrington

Road in the warm spring evening sunshine. Our neighbours' curtains twitched as we climbed into the big black Mercedes feeling like celebrities.

Presenting an award should be relatively simple. You make a quick joke or reference to the award and then open an envelope and read the winner. I was co-presenting with Tess Daly and the award was for Best Sitcom. I wrote a little dialogue for us whereby she asked me questions and all my answers were the titles of well-known sitcoms.

Something like . . .

'Good evening, Michael.'

' 'Allo 'Allo.'

'You're looking well.'

'Cheers.'

'Who are you here with?'

'Friends.'

'Things are going well for you at the moment, aren't they?'

'The Good Life.'

I knew it was silly but I thought it was funny. The BAFTA producers said they thought it was funny, Addison thought it was funny, Tess Daly thought it was funny and told me that Vernon Kay thought it was funny. Kitty thought it wasn't funny. Kitty was worried and said I should think of something else. This was probably the first and last time I didn't listen to my wife. My thinking was that even if it wasn't funny it didn't matter, it was playful, it was fun and my back-up plan was to shout 'Taxi', in reference to the seventies American sitcom.

We arrived at by far the most prestigious event we had ever attended. The stars were out: Helen Mirren, French and Saunders, Harry Hill, Ant and Dec, Alan Sugar, Stephen Fry. I was nervous in such company. This was certainly a step up from the Kitchen and Bathroom or Customer Service Awards. Once inside I had a quick rehearsal with Tess on the stage, where I recognized the studio director who had worked on my DVD.

'Do you think that joke was funny?' I asked him, as Tess and I were ushered offstage.

'This audience is notoriously stuffy,' he ominously said.

What did that mean? He didn't answer my question. I wasn't asking about the audience. There was nothing I could do about the joke now, it was in the autocue. I felt sick with worry as Kitty and I took our seats, surrounded by an array of glamorously dressed TV stars. Graham Norton was hosting. I had met him once when I appeared on the Christmas edition of his show a few months earlier. I'm a big fan of his, I loved all his shows on Channel 4 and now the BBC. His opening monologue was typically sharp although the audience did seem quiet, the loudest laughs coming when Graham was at his bitchy best. As the show went on I became more and more apprehensive. The studio director was right, this was a stuffy affair. The room was polite but flat, and the evening seemed to be going on forever.

Five minutes before I was due to present my award I was fetched from my seat and taken backstage. I desperately needed to pee and rushed quickly to the loo, passing Patsy Kensit in the corridor. Whilst peeing I had an idea. At the end of the first half of my tour show I did a little routine about how desperate the audience must be to pee. I assumed that some of the BAFTA attendees must also be in that state as the ceremony had gone on for hours already. This was perfect, I thought. I'll take this flat room and bring it to life. I'm used to playing to audiences every night, I'll inject some laughs into the proceedings.

'I'm going to do this little joke first about peeing,' I said to Tess.

'Peeing? What? Peeing?' Tess replied, puzzled.

The error I was making was mistaking this theatre full of television stars, producers, directors and writers for an audience of people who had paid to see me.

Graham introduced me as the next big thing in comedy. Tess and I strode out with big smiles on our faces. I was clutching the extremely heavy BAFTA. The autocue with our sitcom banter was visible in front of us but I ignored it.

'Just by way of applause, who is desperate to pee?' I asked jovially.

Hardly anyone responded. My view from the stage was a sea of famous or important people looking confused as I continued.

'Who could pee?' I asked. Again nobody responded.

'Who does not need a pee?' When nobody reacted to this either, I realized I was in serious trouble and the finale to this had to be good. But it required the audience for that, and they weren't playing with me. I carried on the joke regardless. I couldn't just leave it there, like I was doing some kind of urination survey.

'Who during these questions has had their peeing status elevated from "does not need a pee" to "could pee"?' Nobody responded. I saw Rob Brydon grimacing near the front, empathizing with my plight. Dawn French was just looking down at the floor.

'Who has now pissed themselves?' I asked.

At this point in my show there is normally much laughter and then we have an interval, but now just a deathly silence, not even tumbleweed. What was I doing? I was standing onstage at the BAFTAs, the classiest most dignified event of the year, talking about peeing.

Just when I thought things couldn't get any worse, Tess Daly, who I had forgotten was standing next to me, started reading the appalling script I had written from the autocue.

'Hello, Michael?'

' 'Allo 'Allo,' I had to say, with again no response whatsoever. It was excruciating, hell on earth. It wasn't just celebs and the audience at home who were witnessing this death, but it was also my employers, the bosses at the BBC who had just commissioned my own series as well as all the bigwigs from all the other channels. The whole entertainment industry was seeing me be the least entertaining person in the room. I saw Michael Grade and Melvyn Bragg slowly shaking their heads as I continued.

'You're looking well,' Tess grinned.

'Cheers,' I said, my mouth drying out from the tension.

I looked for my wife in the audience. Now, I wasn't aware of this but at major televised award ceremonies, when someone leaves their seat to collect an award, present an award or just go to the loo, their seat is taken by a 'seat filler' so that the audience always looks full on camera. These 'seat fillers' tend to be young good-looking aspiring actors. I kept mentioning sitcom titles to the audience who were either embarrassed for me or revelling in the failure of the bright young thing who couldn't hack it, whilst desperately scanning the audience for Kitty. I needed her support in this most painful moment, a friendly face in the crowd. Finally I spotted her and she was sitting next to some hunk. Who the hell is that bloke? I'm midway through dying on my arse and she's already replaced me with some younger better-looking heart-throb.

I cut short the 'joke' and Tess announced the winner. I had blown it big time. My night was a disaster. This was to be beamed into people's homes across the land. My only hope was that maybe it didn't look so bad on TV. I felt so exposed. It was such a bad performance that I was worried Graham Norton would reference it. After Tess and I performed our primary function of handing the trophy to the producers and stars of the deserving winners, *The IT Crowd*, I left the stage and was nearly out of earshot when I heard Graham say, '*One Foot in the Grave*', which received a massive laugh at my expense.

I have to admit that Graham's joke was funny. I had left a bad smell in the room and he brought it back to life with a very clever line that used my own joke to crucify me. What had been very bad was now horrific. I was mortified. The show wasn't quite 'live', there was a delay of about an hour. I may have humiliated myself in front of the great and the good of the television industry but there was a small hope the damage could be limited for the millions watching at home. To die on my arse is one thing, but to be expertly and publicly ridiculed by Graham Norton on national TV was the nail in the coffin. Nobody was more aware of this than Addison. As soon as Graham delivered his damning line, Addison leapt out of his seat and sprang into action, shuffling along his row: 'Excuse me, excuse me, sorry,' before leaving the auditorium to try and call the producers to see if anything could be quickly edited out before it was broadcast.

Surely my night couldn't get any worse. I returned to my seat to find Kitty as mortified as me, but she couldn't help reminding me she never thought the joke was right and, with her head in her hands, kept whispering, 'Why did you do that peeing thing? What was that?' Rob Brydon presented an award and showed me how it was supposed to be done. Short, concise and funny. Everybody laughed and I realized just how badly I had got it wrong. I was on edge for the remainder of the ceremony, terrified that somebody else would reference my catastrophic appearance.

'To present the next award, ladies and gentlemen please welcome Chris Moyles and Davina McCall,' introduced my career-slayer Graham Norton.

'Go on, Chris, do it!' egged on *Big Brother* host Davina when they reached the podium.

'No, I'm not,' resisted Radio 1 DJ Chris.

'Go on,' Davina repeated.

Nobody had any idea what they were talking about. Kitty and I were still sitting in fear – surely this had nothing to do with me.

'OK then,' said Chris Moyles. 'Who needs to pee? Does anyone need to pee? Who could pee?'

He was doing an impression of me. If a train had been passing I would have thrown myself under it. The cameraman thrust his camera in my face for my reaction.

'Just smile, keep smiling,' Kitty whispered to me.

A bad reaction from me would only make things worse, if that was possible. I smiled and laughed as if I could take a joke, but the joke, again, was on me. Addison, whose bottom had only just touched back down on his seat after trying to get Graham Norton's quip edited out, immediately sprang back to his feet to call the producers again.

'Shall we go?' I said to Kitty.

I wanted to walk out, go home, I couldn't hack this. It was too much. I was being humiliated and rejected by the industry I was trying to break into. I had the cheek to think I belonged and they were kicking me out. I felt sick to my stomach.

'We can't go,' Kitty said, 'it will look like you've just stormed off in a huff. We have to stay, you have to take it. I told you not to do that joke. And what was that peeing thing? I still don't understand it.'

The ceremony ended and I found Addison and Gary Farrow. If ever I needed them, it was now. Their faces were white as sheets. It was bad.

'I think it's gone,' Addison said.

'What's gone?' I asked, assuming he meant my career.

'The Norton joke and the Moyles impression, I think they edited them out, but I'm not sure.'

I felt like everyone was staring at me, whispering, pointing. I needed some air. I nipped outside and called my mother and told her what happened in advance of her watching it on TV. My mum and my stepfather Steve had followed my whole career to date, glued to the screen, proud of me. She photographed the TV when I was on it and displayed the photos all over her house, she even photographed my name when it was on the SKY TV Guide: '*Have I Got News for You* with guests Michael McIntyre and Krishnan Guru-Murthy' was framed in the downstairs loo. And now they were about to see me fail.

'Call me and tell me if the Graham Norton joke about me is in and the Chris Moyles impression,' I said.

'My God, Michael, what's happened there tonight?' my mother worried.

'Just call me and tell me, OK?' I said.

I hung up and headed back to find my table for the traditional dinner after the ceremony. I located Kitty sitting with the BBC executives who had commissioned my *Comedy Roadshow*, Jay Hunt the controller of BBC1 and the new Head of Entertainment, Mark Linsey. I couldn't face them, I wanted to cry, but as soon as they saw me they rallied around me, supporting me, telling me how much they believed in me. The whole thing was so embarrassing, having to be consoled when all I had to do was hand a trophy to *The IT Crowd*.

During dinner my mum called. There was nothing rude from Graham Norton and Chris Moyles on the TV. Addison had worked his magic and limited the damage.

'How did my bit look?' I asked tentatively.

'Terrible, Michael, it was really bad. I'm sorry, I have to be honest with you, darling. What on earth were you doing? What was that peeing thing all about?'

Kitty and I were desperate to leave but couldn't just bail on Jay and Mark, who had become very important people in my life. My mortgage depended on them. So we tried our best to shake it off while guzzling wine. Polite conversation at dinner had thankfully moved on when Addison and Gary came over to our table. Addison was still upset about the whole occasion and had obviously been drinking at least as heavily as us. He was wild-eyed, fidgety, up for a fight.

'I can't fucken believe it. Graham shouldn't have done that. It's disrespectful,' he slurred, taking the night's events personally.

Addison always went a bit gangster when he had a drink and the last thing he ominously said before Kitty and I headed home was, 'Graham Norton might have a little accident tonight. Don't be surprised if he falls down the stairs.'

Kitty and I had a serious discussion in the car about whether I should carry on in TV. I had a live following now, why not just keep touring and stay out of this cut-throat world? I cited examples of Billy Connolly and Lee Evans who are pure stand-ups and avoid too much telly. It had been a tough night.

The next morning I typed my name into Google and saw the *Sun* report that I walked onstage as a comedian and left as Tess Daly's straight man. I searched the word BAFTA to see what else had been written about the night and was shocked to see the main news headline on BBC News. The room started spinning, I couldn't believe my eyes.

'GRAHAM NORTON FALLS DOWN THE STAIRS AND BREAKS HIS RIBS AFTER BAFTAS'

What's Addison done? Was my sitcom name joke with Tess Daly so unfunny that it set off a chain of events that would lead to Addison's arrest?

I immediately called Addison but it went straight to voicemail. So I called Gary Farrow.

'Have you seen the news?' I asked frantically.

'No, I just got up, what is it?' Gary asked.

'Do you remember what Addison said last night about Graham Norton falling down the stairs? Well look, look on BBC News.'

'Holy shit!' screeched Gary when he saw the headline. 'I've known Ad a long time, twenty years, I can't believe he would have done anything like that. I'll do some digging. But I must admit, it doesn't look good.'

It didn't. A frantic few hours followed of trying to get hold of Addison, thinking he might have done something terrible. But the hilarious truth was that Graham Norton had actually just fallen down the stairs, possibly after a few drinks himself, and Addison was at home sleeping off a hangover.

Addison and I laughed about the coincidental misunderstanding when we finally spoke, but the night had taken its toll on both of us.

'Forget about it now, Michael. We've got a lot to do and you've got a lot to look forward to. That was just a blip. Fuck 'em. You've learnt your lesson.'

This was easier said than done; I was battered and bruised by the experience. It was a rude awakening.

'The whole atmosphere last night seemed so nasty, Addison,' I whined.

'Michael. Who said this would be easy? This is a battle, my friend, and I don't know about you but I'm here to win. Let last night go. We've got to make your *Comedy Roadshow* now and I need you on the form of your life. Wouldn't it be nice if next year you stuck it to them all and won a BAFTA,' Addison said, like a corner man geeing up a losing fighter.

Let's face it, everybody in TV dreams of winning a BAFTA, but my experience that night began an obsession.

Everyone at the BAFTAs laughed at me, certainly not with me. If I hadn't had Addison I'd have spent the day in bed feeling sorry for myself, contemplating retirement and some kind of self-imposed witness protection programme with a new identity.

But I did have Addison, so instead I felt like the Terminator.

I'll be back.

14

Kitty and I decided we couldn't afford the house in Hampstead. The BAFTAs were a sign that things can slip very easily. The stress of owing so much money was too much. So I called mortgage man Mark Benson, who had far more success than me at awards ceremonies. I hoped he hadn't watched the BAFTAs but no such luck.

'Home Improvement,' he said when he picked up the phone.

'What?' I replied, not understanding.

'The sitcom *Home Improvement*, because I'm your mortgage advisor. I'm doing your joke from last night. Tough crowd. Don't worry about it. You were very funny at last year's Mortgage Awards. Anyway, I've got good news. The bank's agreed to the mortgage so you can make an offer on that house.'

'Cancel it,' I said. 'I think it's too much to borrow.'

'You're the boss. Wasn't that a sitcom too? No, it was *Who's the Boss?* I'm good at this though. Maybe I should have given out the award,' said the uncharacteristically perky Mark Benson.

I wish he had.

Despite my new-found determination to win a BAFTA I hadn't actually made any television shows yet, so it was currently a pretty long shot, unless 'Worst Presenting at an Awards Show' became a category. Luckily filming of my *Comedy Roadshow* was about to start. The production team was the same as *Live at the Apollo* so I was in safe hands, everyone knew exactly what they were doing. We settled on Manchester, Brighton, Belfast, Birmingham, Swansea and, of course, Edinburgh as the six cities to host the shows. I met with Addison and producer Anthony Caveney to discuss who we should book for the series. The format would be for me to introduce three acts and a headliner. The headliner would be a recognizable and successful comic, but the other three would be lesser known or indeed unknown. This was obviously a huge opportunity for up-and-coming new comedians. An opportunity that didn't really exist before. The *Comedy Roadshow* would be potentially giving eighteen comedians their big break. But these spots were by no means just reserved for young talent, they were for anyone of any age and experience who wasn't well known but had a funny ten minutes. We booked headliners like Rhod Gilbert, Jason Manford, Sean Lock and Al Murray. We booked new talent like Sarah Millican, who was already starting to make a name for herself, and Micky Flanagan, although it was a bit later that things really took off for him. But there are two comics who credit the *Comedy Roadshow* for launching their careers. John Bishop, who stormed the Manchester show, and young Scot Kevin Bridges, making his TV debut, who blew the roof off the Edinburgh Playhouse. Full details of how things went from there can be found in their own autobiographies.

Hosting the *Comedy Roadshow* was stress-free for me, a rare state of mind. I had plenty of jokes about each city already and always travelled up a few days early hunting for more. The theory that the audiences would be extra enthusiastic because we had made the effort to go to them was more than borne out. Also, the tickets were free as it was a TV recording, adding even more feel-good vibes. The atmosphere, especially in Edinburgh, Swansea and Manchester, was electric. I felt confident that if the audience were having this much fun, the BBC1 viewers would too.

Simon Cowell reigned supreme as the king of Saturday nights on ITV, with *Britain's Got Talent* in the spring and *The X Factor* in the autumn. Any BBC show other than *Strictly Come Dancing* would be destroyed in the ratings by these juggernauts. Thankfully the *Comedy Roadshow* was launched in June against a new sitcom on ITV that wasn't a hit. We decided the first to be broadcast would be the Edinburgh show. I kicked it off by skipping onto the stage and truthfully telling the audience this was my 'favourite city of them all', then launched into two big local routines about Scottish patriotism and kilts that I had been perfecting for years. Buoyed by the response of the local crowd in Edinburgh when I told them they were my favourite city, I shamelessly told all the cities they were my favourites hoping it would become a playful catchphrase.

Kitty and I watched the first *Comedy Roadshow* on 6 June 2009 in the living room at Barrington Road. The blurry *Lovers*, who were no longer blurry after I discovered the protective film when we moved, hung proudly above the fireplace on a perfectly smooth wall next to our new plasma TV. Everything in our life seemed new.

'Look, it's Daddy on the TV,' Kitty said to Lucas as he charged up and down the wooden floors demanding to watch *Power Rangers* instead.

Kitty had seen the show several times as I showed her different cuts of the edit but watching it broadcast on TV was thrilling. I tried to see into the front rooms of the neighbours opposite. Were they watching BBC1? It's an amazing experience to have your own show on TV. To be the thing that is on the telly right now. I was more excited than nervous. I was doing stand-up. This is what I was becoming known for. This was my comfort zone. Plus, although my name was in the title, I was very much sharing the show with the other comics. The pressure was diluted. After the end credits rolled, Kitty and I opened a bottle of champagne as congratulatory texts flew in and Lucas finally got to watch what he wanted.

At precisely 9.36 a.m. the morning after a TV show is broadcast, the ratings come out. Ultimately this is the only result that matters. Positive or negative feedback from friends, family, the BBC, the press or the internet is relatively meaningless. The all-important thing is a number you are given the morning after when either the celebration or inquest begins. Word of mouth can of course impact on the number, but the number itself is the result. Having had no experience of ratings for my own show I slept well and woke up still on a high from the night before. The BBC and Addison on the other hand were experiencing mounting apprehension as their bedside clocks ticked towards 9.36 a.m. Now we would find out if people did want to watch stand-up in primetime, and if people did want to watch me on a Saturday night.

At 9.37 a.m. my phone rang with an unrecognized number. In the past I didn't pick up unknown numbers but now that I was debt-free and everything was so new, I went for it.

'Hello?' I said, in a formal voice reserved for when I don't know who I'm speaking to.

'It's Jay Hunt,' came the reply. It was the controller of BBC1 herself. When things go badly people don't call, when things go well they call on your mobile on a Sunday morning.

'Michael, so many congratulations! The show got 5.1 million viewers last night. That's just huge for a new show, huge for any show and huge for this time of year.'

It had worked. I couldn't see from my living room window, but plenty of the front rooms on Barrington Road must have been watching. And just like that, I had a hit TV show. No need for any high-concept format or scripting, just comedians doing what we've been doing every weekend for years. The BAFTA audience may be filled with all the movers and shakers of the TV business, and the awards themselves are decided by a panel of them, but it's not them who decide who makes a show a success, it's the viewers, and 5.1 million of them just watched mine.

'Hello?' Mark Benson said into his mobile phone, showcasing his own voice for when he doesn't recognize a phone number.

'It's Michael McIntyre, sorry to bother you on a Sunday, but I just wanted to say I would like that mortgage after all. Is the mortgage offer still valid?' I asked.

'It should be. I'll check in the morning when I'm back in the office. *The Office*! That's another sitcom. Hahaha. I'm fishing at the moment, such a beautiful day for it. You still haven't sent me the dates when you can join me.'

'I will,' I lied.

The banking system was collapsing and house prices were plummeting. This was wonderful news for me as the Hampstead house was owned by an American banker desperate to sell up and move back to the States. So my low offer, compared to what he'd paid at the height of the market, was accepted. At last Kitty and I were on the ladder, just as the ladder was starting to burn and people were falling off it. What was certain was that we weren't on the bottom rung. The extraordinary Addison-catalysed events of the past two years meant that we had bypassed several rungs and found ourselves pretty much at the top. Kitty and I barely had a chance to catch our breath. Everything that was happening seemed to be happening to us and no longer because of us. We were being swept away by my success. I had strived for success but had no way of knowing what success actually meant. Success was just a word, an ambition, a dream: now it was really happening. Just a year before we were still living in a tiny rented flat and now we were moving into this huge Hampstead house of our own. The *Daily Mail* printed a photo of the front of the house with the headline 'The house that jokes built'. Gary Farrow called to apologize for the press invading my privacy, but I kind of loved it.

After only a year in Barrington Road, in what we thought was the house of our dreams, we were moving up again. That house had witnessed so many dramatic changes of fortune in our lives. When I look back I always remember it being sunny there: sunny when I parked outside in my new Mercedes, sunny when I carried Ossie through the front door returning from a trip to the park, sunny when I threw open the curtains in our bedroom in the morning, sunny in our small garden with Lucas heading up and down his little plastic slide. I just googled historical meteorological records and the hours of sunshine per day were actually below average that year, but that's not how I remembered it.

So this time when we left one home to move to another, I joined Kitty in feeling emotional. Kitty, Lucas and Ossie moved into our big new house and officially I lived there too, but the rest of the year I was flat-out working. Addison and Joe booking an arena tour after my DVD sales seemed terrifyingly optimistic but turned out to be a masterstroke. Ticket sales were flying and extra dates were being added wherever they were available. My first ambition as a stand-up had been to play The Comedy Store in London. I remember thinking that if I could get booked for weekends there then I would have well and truly made it. The trajectory since I achieved that goal was now becoming absurd. Selling out the Hammersmith Apollo was wild, but now I was embarking on a tour that included a record-breaking six nights at the 10,000-seat Wembley Arena, more than anyone had played before in its history. My four nights at the Birmingham NIA arena were also a record and I sold out the O2 Arena, which with 15,000 seats is the biggest in Europe. Michael Jackson had booked out the O2 that autumn for a comeback tour that never was when he died at the end of June. I ended up taking three of the dates that he would have played and selling them all out. The O2 Arena is in fact so big that it's visible from space. Although I'm sure Terry would still have struggled to find it. Thankfully I now had a new tour manager, the vastly experienced Grazio Abela who knew every venue in the land inside out, as well as where the petrol cap was on all modern vehicles. Together, Grazio and I embarked on a warm-up tour around the country to build material for the main tour and ultimately for my new DVD to be filmed at Wembley and released for Christmas.

I performed around eighty warm-up shows to get the material in shape for the arenas. My final warm-up date was at the Eastbourne Congress. Addison hadn't seen any of my new jokes and said he was coming to see the show as he had a house in nearby Brighton. It was a big night for me to get his approval. Addison was not just my agent but had become my friend. He was fiercely loyal and protective and there for me no matter what. He always made the point of saying, 'Michael, call me any time, whatever it is and I'll sort it out. Three o'clock in the morning, I'm there for ya.' He mentioned I could call him at three o'clock in the morning so many times I thought maybe it was actually a more convenient time for him to chat. It was amazing having someone in my life to look out for me, to look after me. Any problem I was having, personal or professional, he would always know what to do.

Addison came to Eastbourne with one of his best mates, the former British heavyweight champion boxer Scott Welch. Addison adored Scott. He most likely wanted to be him. He loved boxing. Addison's great-great-grandfather was the bare-knuckle boxing champion Tom Sayers. I'd known him for years now, but he hadn't once mentioned any family member to me other than Tom Sayers, who he mentioned all the time. He was especially proud to have come from bare-knuckle fighting stock. Personally I had zero idea who Tom Sayers was; my knowledge of boxing didn't stretch back to the mid-nineteenth century. I just acted impressed every time he mentioned it, which tended to be when he'd been drinking.

Addison didn't drink often, maybe once a month. He would actually schedule it in. He felt he needed to decompress, but instead of a spa day he would go on a bender, often letting me know in advance: 'I'm going off the grid for a couple of days. I'm havin' a bit of a night out. I need to let my hair down.' When Addison was 'on one' he became a totally different person, morphing into an alter ego that was basically an East End gangster.

He was getting into gangster mode after the BAFTAs when he said Graham Norton might fall down the stairs, which turned out to be more of a premonition than a threat. There was a whole alternative and surely fictional world that would come to the fore after Addison had a few drinks. Early signs were when he started talking closer and closer to your face until he was literally millimetres away. Then he would start reeling off stories of his imagined gangster lifestyle. I started to listen out for key words and phrases to know where he and the night were heading, taking them as my cue to scarper as quickly as possible. One was when he said, 'cos you know I'm related to Tom Sayers the bare-knuckle fighter'; another was when he used the word 'shooter' as a slang word for gun. He would say something like, 'Things were getting pretty fuckin' heavy when he got a shooter out and I didn't have my shooter.' I would literally have no idea what he was talking about. Ten minutes earlier, while we were waiting for the wine to arrive, we would be debating which was the most beautiful Matcham theatre or whether I should use an interior designer for my new house, and then suddenly I'm in a scene from *Lock, Stock and Two Smoking Barrels*. Addison wasn't a gangster, he didn't fraternize with gangsters or carry a gun. He was a show business agent, I'm sure of it.

Addison would also twist my life into his gangster plot. The first time we ever spoke on the phone I told him about how my previous agent was going to sue me for money I owed him after my first Edinburgh festival in 2003. I subsequently told him a while later that I paid off the agent by selling the gold cufflinks

I inherited from my grandfather to a jeweller in the West End's Burlington Arcade. This story resonated with Addison and I was touched about how upset it made him. 'I'm going to find those cufflinks, Michael, and buy them back for you,' sober Addison sweetly said. But every time he'd had a drink he would bring up the story, blaming my old agent, whose name – Duddridge – he always got wrong.

'Me and the boys are gonna get some shooters and pay Birdridge a visit for what he did to you,' Addison would slur while spitting on my face.

'Who? What are you talking about?' I would ask.

'Bumbridge. That's who. He knows what's coming to him. Breaks my heart to think of you pawning your grandfather's cufflinks. That's all you had of him,' Addison continued, romanticizing the story. The truth is he was my step-grandfather and we weren't that close. The cufflinks were quite hideous, held little sentimental value and actually came in really useful as I got about £400 for them.

'Addison, it's fine. It really wasn't a big deal. Just forget about it. OK?' I would plead.

'Do you know I'm related to Tom Sayers?' he would reply, his eyeball touching mine. 'I tell you, Fuddleridge doesn't want to mess with me.'

Primarily Addison and heavyweight boxer Scott Welch were buddies but there's no denying that Addison loved having Scott by his side. It was a bit like Cersei Lannister and 'the Mountain' in *Game of Thrones*. If ever there was any trouble, Addison would

say, 'I could send Scott round?' like he was Tony Soprano, but it
would be over such trivial things. I once told him about a mean
kid at Lucas's nursery.

'Do you want me to send Scott round?' was Addison's genuine response.

'To the nursery? He's three years old, Addison.'

'No, I mean have a word with the dad. Would soon shut
him up.'

Bearing in mind Addison's regular tendency to sensationally
embellish I doubt this one is true, but it's certainly a funny image.
I once asked Addison if he'd ever needed to 'send Scott round'
and he told me about a time when he got involved in a flaming
row with some scaffolders working on his Brighton house. So
Scott came round and proceeded to shake the scaffolding until
they all fell off like apples from a tree.

I saw Addison and Scott arrive in the ex-champ's Bentley
from the window of my dressing room at the Eastbourne Congress Theatre. I was naturally nervous. If Addison didn't like the
show there was really no time to fix it before the arena tour
started the following week. My best new joke was a joke about
the jars of herbs and spices that never get used in the kitchen
cupboard. I don't think I have ever had a routine that evolved so
slowly over all of my warm-ups before finally becoming one of
my best. The joke started out as a sort of rambling chat about
why some things in life become the leaders in their field. Like A4
paper being so much more successful than the other paper sizes,
or HB pencils winning out over the alternative leads, or salt and

pepper being the top two spices. For so many gigs these jokes struggled to raise a laugh but I kept persevering. I knew there was something in it. After a while I started to get good laughs riffing on salt and pepper and the jealousy the other herbs and spices must feel looking at them proudly waiting on the dining table ready for action, while they remained unused in the cupboard. I had the cumin saying he had been out of the cupboard only once in his life for a Bolognese experiment recipe in 1992, I had the sage saying he used to live in the family's old house and moved from the cupboard there to the one in the new house and still had never been used. The paprika said she fell out of the cupboard once and was put back in the wrong way round, seven years she had been like that: 'I've still got the plastic on my head. Why the fuck did they buy me?' The joke culminated in my impersonation of a 'Chinese five spice' jar, who arrogantly claimed to be five times better than all the other spices, but still had never been out of the cupboard.

Everything in the Eastbourne show went well but the herbs and spices routine was the strongest. Addison and Scott burst into my dressing room afterwards. Scott was full of uplifting praise but Addison just stood in the doorway, his head and shoulders ducking and weaving like he was in a boxing ring.

'John West tuna,' he said with a big grin on his face.

'What?' I asked.

'That herbs and spices joke was fucking brilliant but there's more there. I think you should have John West tuna at the back of the cupboard. Trust me. I'm just being honest with ya.'

A Funny Life

Addison helped me with so much in my life, but this was the one and only time he helped me with a joke. Little changes can make a routine so much funnier and with that final tweak after months of perfecting, that joke and the whole show was done. Ready for the arenas.

'I got to say, Michael, I thought the show was really fantastic. This calls for a celebration. Shall we all have a drink?'

'NO!' Scott and I said in unison.

15

The experience of playing arenas will always be the most mind-blowing of my life. I don't know how pop stars feel when they play arenas or even stadiums, but having an event that size all for me and a bunch of jokes about my life will stay with me forever. I appreciated every aspect of those arena nights. I knew what was happening was special. I knew I was one of very few people to achieve anything like this and I wasn't going to take any second for granted. Maybe if I was younger and riding a wave of new-found success or if I was a rock star on drugs, the enormity might have escaped me and I would look back and regret not being wholly present. But not me, I appreciated every moment.

Like in Edinburgh my days were spent readying myself to peak at 8 p.m. I spent the morning walking around whatever city I was in, looking for potential jokes, sitting in cafes with a pen and paper and running through my set, adding bits here and there. In the afternoon I had my customary nap at the hotel or, for my London shows, at home. I was suddenly not only staying in the best hotels but the best rooms the hotel had to offer. In Manchester I stayed at the Lowry Hotel. My suite had a grand piano and was at least twice the size of all the flats I had rented over the years. Although I do remember complaining that there was no shampoo in the bathroom: 'Who wants a grand piano but no shampoo?' I complained to reception.

'Billy Joel?' came the witty reply from the Mancunian on duty.

In Birmingham I stayed in the Presidential suite at the Hyatt Regency. It was on the top floor and had views of the whole of Birmingham (which actually made the room more expensive, if you can believe it). The windows were floor-to-ceiling glass and when the manager first showed me around he told me that when Luciano Pavarotti stayed in the suite he insisted they had the glass toughened in case he leaned against it and plunged to his death on Birmingham's New Street. For my entire stay all I could think about was how Pavarotti slept in this bed, looked in this mirror, sat on this loo. My Pavarotti room also had a huge Pavarotti-sized Jacuzzi. Between shows I was bubbling away in the Jacuzzi singing 'Nessun Dorma'. This was the high life. Unfortunately this particular Jacuzzi developed a fault and started up on its own when I was fast asleep in the middle of the night. A Jacuzzi is loud enough when there's water in it (I always feel it spoils the romance when you have to scream sweet nothings because you can hear sweet FA), but when the Jacuzzi is empty and the jets are activated it makes the loudest and most horrible mechanical noise imaginable. I dreamt someone was power drilling my skull before I woke up and frantically tried to work out what was happening. In the midst of the horrendous noise I lost my bearings and, rather than running into the bathroom, ran straight into the floor-to-ceiling windows. So, thank God Luciano Pavarotti had them toughened and I survived to tell the tale.

When staying in the best hotel rooms available it's commonplace that other celebrities have stayed in the room before you and the hotel staff always loved telling me who. When I played the Newcastle Arena I stayed in a seaside town called Seaham. It soon became apparent I was only the second celebrity to stay at the hotel, and for some reason the staff seemed to think all celebrities would behave in exactly the same way.

'Lionel Richie stayed here too,' the receptionist said within moments of my arrival (it's important when you read the name Lionel Richie you do it in a thick Geordie accent. I'll give you time to master it. Good).

A porter tried to take my bag and I said I'd be fine carrying it.

'Oh no. Lionel Richie wanted me to carry his bag,' the porter said as he ripped the bag from my grasp.

'This was Lionel Richie's suite,' the porter said as he opened the door.

The room was bitterly cold with all the windows wide open and a howling gale billowing the curtains off the ground.

'It's freezing in here,' I said, shivering.

'Lionel Richie said he liked the breeze,' replied the porter.

'When was he here?' I asked.

'A couple of summers ago,' the porter said.

'It's November,' I said, closing the windows.

This is how it continued for my whole stay. When I complained there was no still water in the room the receptionist said, 'But Lionel Richie preferred sparkling.' I ordered room service and sat waiting for it at the small dining table in the corner but the lady who brought it carried the food straight past me, put it on the bed and put the TV on: 'Lionel Richie ate his lunch over here, with the telly on.' And when I checked out and the manager asked if I'd enjoyed my stay, I told him that the plug kept getting stuck in the bath, to which, looking astonished, he replied, 'Lionel Richie seemed fine with it.'

In Sheffield I stayed in a hotel recognized as the best in the city. I was famished after the show so I called room service after midnight to be greeted by surely the grumpiest northerner in the long history of grumpy northerners. He actually said, 'What?' when he picked up the phone. Well, technically he said, 'Wa.'

'Is that room service?' I asked.

'I suppose,' he said.

'Well is it?' I asked again.

'I'm the night porter so it's not a full menu,' he drawled.

'OK, well what do you have, please?' I asked.

'Let me go and have a look in the fridge.'

After a few minutes he returned.

'There's cheese,' he said dolefully.

'And?' I asked, hopefully.

'That's pretty much it. There's a bit of bread.'

'Well this sounds like there's some cheese sandwich potential here,' I said, trying to inject an ounce of joviality. 'Can I have that then, please?'

'Help yourself,' he said and meant it.

'Are you going to bring it up?' I asked.

'No,' he said as if I'd asked him an outrageous question.

'But it's room service,' I said, hoping the name itself would help him understand.

'Yes,' he said, 'which means you can have it in your room. But if you want it, you can come and get it.'

This extraordinary exchange actually worked out very well as I was able to recount it onstage for the 13,000 people who came to see me the next night at the Sheffield Arena. In fact I also gained some more free material that night from a man working security at the venue. I had popped outside the back of the arena to make a call as the phone reception in my dressing room was bad. When I re-entered the venue via one of the back doors a security guard stopped me.

'Have you got a pass?' he asked.

Initially I thought I would enjoy this encounter as he obviously didn't yet realize it was me, the person whose show it was, the person whose face is on the front of the pass, and the person whose face was on the front of the pass that was currently around his neck.

'No, I don't, it's my show,' I said smiling, pointing at my face matching the one on his own pass.

'If you don't have a pass you can't come in. Those are the rules,' he said.

'This is my show. Surely I can just use my face as a pass to get in?' I asked once more.

His response to this was, I have to say, as logical as it was quick witted.

'The Queen's face is on money,' he said, 'but she can't use her face as a tenner, can she? Get a pass or you're not coming in.'

When I was finally let in after a phone call to my tour manager I went straight onstage and shared the story with the audience, who loved it along with the room service tale.

I've got another little hotel story here that I feel I must squeeze in as it always makes me laugh. Although it is rude, so brace yourself. Undoubtedly one of the finest hotels I stayed in on the tour was Chewton Glen in Hampshire when I was performing at the Bournemouth International Centre. I was walking around the substantial and picturesque hotel grounds when I stumbled upon a building site. When the general manager of the hotel introduced himself in the hotel restaurant later that day, I asked him what they were building.

'Luxurious treehouses,' he announced in his frightfully posh accent. 'You must come to stay when they're completed. We're building them all on stilts overlooking the river. They will be magnificent. Slight snag though, management want to name them each after types of willow trees as the forest here is full of all sorts of willows, but I've strongly objected.'

'Why is that?' I enquired, only making polite conversation.

'Well, there are five in all. No probs with the first three, White, Weeping and Peachleaf. They sound rather lovely, don't you think? The problem is the last two . . .' He then paused for dramatic effect, 'Crack and Pussy.'

I burst out laughing.

'You're kidding. The hotel wants to name the treehouses crack and pussy?'

'Yes, and they're interconnecting. It's madness, isn't it? Guests are going to call up and ask if we have any rooms and we'll have to say things like, "We have the pussy and the crack available",' he said, giggling and seemingly getting posher. 'I'm sure you'll be very happy in the pussy, if not, you're welcome to try the crack.' He carried on, determined to take it too far.

The O2 Arena was the pinnacle of the tour. You may remember this was originally the Millennium Dome, a venue purpose-built for a purpose nobody understood. So, soon after the turn of the century the government sold it to a global events company who seamlessly converted it into the biggest arena in Europe, with Prince the first to play there. The O2 is the cream of the crop as it is vast and newly built, with shops and restaurants, corporate boxes and lounges. Next to my dressing room there was a bookcase that you pushed to reveal a secret 'rock star room' which had a full bar, pool table, air hockey, foosball, video games, big comfy sofas and huge TVs. None of the other arenas had books, let alone books hiding secret rooms.

Like the Skipton Cattle Mart or the Thirsk Courthouse of yesteryear, some venues were originally built for a very different purpose and converted to accommodate large crowds. The Nottingham, Sheffield, Belfast and Newcastle Arenas are all ice arenas, hosting ice hockey matches. I had no idea ice hockey was even played in this country. There are big scoreboards hanging from the middle of the roof and metal railings in gaudy colours to pen in crowds at the sides, who all have to sit on uncomfortable plastic bucket seats. The floor seats are actually over the ice with rows and rows of makeshift chairs that don't always match, like a school play in the gym. The ice is, of course, covered up. It's bad, but not that bad. People aren't sliding around on their chairs and slipping as they find their seats. When the audience try to leave quickly at the end of the show to beat the rush and say, 'Come on, get your skates on', they don't mean it for real. But covering the ice doesn't stop it from being properly chilly. Also, the trapped ice would evaporate (apparently this is actually called sublimation, but I thought if I wrote 'sublimate' you would have a false idea of my intelligence), forming a cloud of fog floating throughout the bottom half of the arena. 'Don't worry, that'll clear when all the bodies come in and it'll warm right up in here,' the venue staff always said in their huge duffel coats, blowing into their hands to keep warm, their eyebrows frozen like Leonardo DiCaprio in *The Revenant.* The audience thought they were there for comedy, but for the venue staff they were there to emit their collective body heat.

The fact is, audiences in Sheffield, Newcastle, Belfast and Nottingham are as warm hearted as they are warm bodied. London audiences are traditionally tougher; the theory is that they are spoilt by being in the capital with the world at their feet. Whereas when it's ice that's at people's feet it actually makes them more up for a good time. I loved those shows as much as the O2, but for different reasons. The O2 just felt so glamorous. I also loved being at home and not in a hotel. Living life in hotels on the road made performing in such huge venues less surreal. But being at home all day doing normal stuff, knowing that I was playing the O2 that night for 15,000 people seemed even more unreal. I'd pick up Lucas from nursery or push Ossie around the supermarket (Waitrose now, naturally) in the shopping trolley while Kitty picked dishwasher tablets and a few hours later I was a superstar. I found myself shamelessly telling everyone I encountered, 'I'm playing the O2 tonight, my own show, just me.' I would tell the butcher at the Waitrose meat counter, the chap stacking shelves, the lady at the checkout, the security guard, the drunk man begging at the cashpoint, you get the idea.

My routine for the arena shows was to arrive at the venue around 6 p.m. and head straight to the stage, where I would stand alone, checking the sound and visualizing the show. I always had nervous energy to burn. On my first ever night at the O2 I was so hyped up I sprinted up and down the aisles as fast as I could. Looking back, that was weird, but I just had to try to expel some of the adrenaline that was overflowing. There was a lot of pacing. Pacing on the empty stage, pacing in my dressing room and pacing to and from my dressing room to the stage. I always liked to peek my head around the impossibly large drapes behind the stage before the show, marvelling at all the people amassing. These sights I will never forget. Thousands of people piling in, my people, my fans, holding plastic bags with my name on it full of merchandise inspired by my jokes, like a radiator-bleeding key with 'I live in the man drawer' inscribed on it, or a wallet for Scottish money with 'legal tender' written on it. It was a mind-boggling view.

We filmed a silly intro of me at home in my show suit and head mic realizing I was running late and doing my skip all the way to the venue, stopping at traffic lights and setting off speed cameras along the way before skipping onto the stage at the start of the show as if it was in real time. The sound an audience makes in an arena is very different to a theatre. It's not that it's significantly louder, it's that it comes at you in waves as it takes time to travel from the back. It took some getting used to as my timing was slightly disrupted. I'd be starting the next joke with laughs from the previous one still arriving. When you factor in the echo as well, I was never really sure what the audience were laughing at. Also, the audience weren't always looking at me; in the main they were watching me on three huge screens behind and either side of the stage. 'People at the back are thinking, "We should have just bought the DVD",' I always said near the top of the show.

Well, it turned out many of them bought the DVD too. *Hello Wembley*, recorded at Wembley Arena, sold over a million copies before Christmas and was the Christmas 'Number 1' – *Harry Potter* was number 2. *Hello Wembley* was also the highest-selling DVD of the year on Amazon of all titles. My tour ended up selling over half a million tickets and I won the British Comedy Award for Best Stand-up.

The essence of my life as a comedian was the same as it always had been. I'd find something funny, scribble it down and build it into a routine. I just kept doing that while my audience grew and grew and grew. In just two years I'd gone from performing to eighty reluctant locals in Thirsk, North Yorkshire, to millions either live or at home on DVD.

It was a wildly exciting and wonderful time. I couldn't stop smiling and Kitty couldn't stop shopping.

I was living the dream.

16

I loved being famous. There's a scene in the film *The King of Comedy* when Jerry Lewis walks through the streets of New York and every passer-by beams when they see him. 'Hey, Jerry!' they all say. I always wanted to be like that, to leave the house and the world lights up for you. I love people, I love chatting and making them laugh, it's why I got into comedy. Before I was famous I would leave the house and be surrounded by strangers busy in their own little bubbles. Fame burst all those bubbles and suddenly everyone knew me and was excited to meet me. Addison told me to start wearing a cap, 'You don't want to get mobbed.' I did want to get mobbed. Screaming people telling me they love me. Yes please. Obviously I preferred talking to people to posing for selfies. Some people, dare I say older people, can really struggle with selfies. It can take a while to find the camera on their phone and then invariably they press 'video' rather than 'photo'. I've starred in thousands of short films with old ladies, always with the same dialogue. 'I think you're filming this?' I say, and they say, 'Am I? Sorry. I've pushed the wrong button.'

Some people can get confused with the concept of selfies. I once met two gentlemen in Ireland who stopped me in the street. One asked me if he could take a selfie. When I agreed he then handed his phone to his friend and said, 'Can you take a selfie please?'

'Why do you want a selfie of me?' his friend replied in his Irish tongue, while taking a photo of himself.

'I don't. I want a selfie with Michael McIntyre.'

'A selfie is when you take the photo of yourself, yourself,' I interrupted.

'That makes a lot of sense now that you spell it out,' he said before correctly holding his phone up in front of the both of us grinning.

Unfortunately, the camera was facing away towards his friend and not towards us in selfie mode. He then took the picture of his friend. His two attempts to have a photo with me had resulted in two photos of his friend, and none of me, or him.

With fame came fortune, opening up a whole world of fun and extraordinary privilege. I paid off our mortgage on the Hampstead house in full in less than a year and, no sooner had the Seat Altea been replaced by a BMW and Mercedes, Kitty bought a Porsche Cayenne and I was practically given a brand-new convertible Jaguar XKR on their VIP deal, the theory being that I would be photographed driving around in it and gain them some publicity. This actually worked out well for

Jaguar but not for me. Within a week of owning the car I pulled up outside Lucas's school at pick-up time and spotted a place right outside the school gates. I could sense the other parents and kids staring at me, the famous comedian in his expensive growling sports car. I felt supercool. That is until I opened my door into oncoming traffic. A terrifyingly loud crunching sound followed and my door was taken clean off the car. I still tried to look cool as I stepped out of the now door-less car, but I'm not sure I managed it. It turned out one of the mums at Lucas's school was driving the other car involved.

'That was your fault, you opened the door straight into my car. What were you doing?' she rightly said. 'All the mums are witnesses,' she added as she pointed to a group of mothers gawping at us at the school gates.

'Well I think you were driving too close to my car. That dad is a witness,' I replied, pointing at the one dad surrounded by all the mums at the gates. It was a joke that didn't go down so well.

Someone took a photo of my now one-door sports car that ended up in the *Sun* newspaper and Jaguar were thrilled at the free publicity.

We started going on extravagant family holidays in every school holiday, the first one being to the island of Mauritius, where we fulfilled another life goal and flew First Class. Regardless of the luxury, comfort and gourmet food, just the fact that you've made it to First Class makes you feel fabulous for the whole flight. I loved looking around at the other people in First Class. We are the First Class people. Often there are other celebrities on board too. A few years ago I noticed Superman, Henry Cavill, sitting behind me on an Emirates flight back from Dubai.

'Not flying yourself, Soop?' I asked as I pretended to be walking to the loo, but really just got up to make that joke. 'Says a lot for Emirates that you've chosen them to fly you.'

'Is it a bird? Is it a plane? It's Superman, on a plane, eating a bird,' I said, pointing to his food as I walked back past after my fake use of the loo.

'It's steak,' Henry Cavill said, possibly starting to get annoyed.

'Don't ruin it,' I said.

This continued throughout the flight as I made a series of bad jokes every time I walked past him. After the plane landed my family and I raced him to customs at Heathrow. 'Come on, kids, we must beat Superman.'

The hotel in Mauritius was stunning. I naturally spent most of the holiday complaining about the prices. There was an over-water sushi restaurant where you could see fish swimming around your feet as you ate their dead relatives with soy sauce and slices of ginger.

'These fish are laughing at you,' I said to the manager, pointing to the fish swimming below. 'How can you charge so much money for what is just swimming around us for free? You don't even cook them! I can't afford this every day, for lunch tomorrow I'm taking my family snorkelling with chopsticks.'

A few weeks before the trip, Lucas had recovered from a very mild case of chickenpox. When I say mild, he literally had one spot. Unknown to us until halfway through our exotic holiday, Ossie, who was now one and a half years old, had contracted the disease.

'Uh-oh,' Kitty exclaimed as she was smearing Factor 50 over Ossie's back. 'I hope that isn't what I think it is.' She had spotted a single red blister on his shoulder.

'Even if it is chickenpox,' I said, 'hopefully it'll just be one spot like Lucas.'

That turned out to be wishful thinking as Ossie broke out in the severest of cases, his entire face and body covered in nasty red spots. It was a horror story. There were more spots than skin on his poor little body. I began furiously googling what to do and read numerous anecdotal reports on the website Mumsnet that having a bath in oatmeal was incredibly soothing and would stop the incessant itching that was causing Ossie a lot of distress. The hotel were very helpful and provided us with a small baby bath and plenty of oatmeal, after I tried to convince Kitty to wait until breakfast, as breakfast was included in our meal plan and the oatmeal would be free, especially as we had been to the sushi restaurant for lunch again that day.

Placing Ossie into the oatmeal bath was a wonderful moment that gave him immediate respite. Seeing him calm and itch-free was a huge relief for all of us. We then sat on the balcony and watched the sunset over the Indian Ocean. Kitty, Lucas and I, all with healthy-looking suntans, wrapped in each other's arms on the comfy white-cushioned outdoor sofa with spotty Ossie by our feet happily splashing around in porridge. Eventually we had to take him out of his bath, and thankfully he remained content as we tightly wrapped him in a fluffy white baby dressing gown that I was destined to 'accidentally' pack. Without thinking, I hurled the used oat bath over the balcony onto the rocks below us but instead of hearing a splash, I heard screams. Looking over the balcony I saw a young couple, almost certainly newlyweds as the hotel was heaving with honeymooners, covered in used chickenpox-infused oatmeal, yelling in what I think was Russian. I hid from view and fortunately nothing came of it, although we did see them around the resort for the remainder of our holiday. 'Hide! The chickenpox porridge people are coming,' we would say as we cowered behind a pedalo or a stack of sunbeds.

The process of noting ideas whenever they came and building them into routines I'd then try out in small venues continued constantly so that I had new material for my next tour, for the second series of the *Comedy Roadshow* and for when I became the youngest-ever host of the Royal Variety Performance in 2010. Focusing on stand-up was the safest way for me to stay on top. But the day after I hosted the Royal Variety, at the London Palladium, Addison called me with his latest thunderbolt.

'Michael. Addison. Where are you?'

'I'm at home,' I said.

'Can you get to Holland Park by 1 p.m.?' Addison mysteriously asked.

'Yes. Why?' I said.

'I need you to go to Simon Cowell's house. He wants to meet you. I've been working on this for a while with Peter Fincham at

230

ITV and I think I got you the job as a judge on *Britain's Got Talent*. Peter has been pushing you to Simon really hard but he's never met you. So get down to his house for 1 p.m. I'll text you his address.'

This literally came out of the blue. *The X Factor* and *Britain's Got Talent* were truly TV titans. They were national events rather than television shows. The ratings for the 2009 *BGT* final, when Diversity beat Susan Boyle, peaked at over 19 million, making it one of the most watched TV shows in history. I was totally and utterly seduced by the prospect of being a judge. I immediately assumed I would become the nation's sweetheart like Cheryl Cole had on *The X Factor*. Simon Cowell's success and popularity was sky high, he was the god of entertainment television and I had to be at his house by 1 p.m. In essence I was going for an audition with Simon Cowell. As I drove there I worried he would raise his hand when I was mid-sentence to say something like, 'Can I just stop you there? You're not ready for this. I think you'd be better suited to cruise ships. It's a no.'

After speaking to Addison I forgot everything I'd learnt about sticking to what I did best. I struggled on panel shows, I struggled to host a game show, I struggled to give out awards, but I suddenly believed I would be a tremendous talent judge. Addison too was very excited by the prospect of me becoming a judge. He was prepared to break his own rule of keeping as much control as possible for Simon Cowell. The magnitude of the exposure *BGT* would give me outweighed everything else.

I hope I'm not betraying Simon's privacy by describing his

house, which is readily available to view online. He lives in a beautiful and befitting double-fronted mansion and had a black Ferrari and a black Bentley in the driveway. I checked my flies and tucked in my shirt as I walked up the stairs to the grand entrance before ringing the doorbell. Would he answer the door himself? Would he have a butler? Maybe it would be Louis Walsh or Sinitta, covered in leaves, who greeted me.

'Hello,' came a low female voice over the intercom.

'It's Michael McIntyre for Simon . . . Cowell,' I said.

A few minutes later the door slowly opened on its own. I wasn't expecting an automatic door, especially in such a grand Georgian manor.

'Hello?' I called out before stepping into the reception hall. It was then I noticed that the door hadn't opened by itself but had been opened by a very small Asian housekeeper.

'Come in. Take seat. Mr Simon coming,' she said as she led me to a huge L-shaped sofa in an informal living room off the hall. It was just after Christmas and I spotted a splendid Christmas tree in another reception room opposite, where a maid was picking up pine needles on her hands and knees like a human hoover. At that moment the man himself bounded in, super relaxed and drinking green juice through a straw.

'Hi Michael. Do you want one of these?' Simon asked, gesturing to his juice.

'What is it?' I asked.

'It's full of great stuff,' he said, before reeling off a list of things I usually made a point of avoiding, 'kale, spinach, broccoli, celery.'

'Yes please,' I said to my surprise.

It was so surreal sitting with him. We had never met and yet I felt like I knew him so well having watched people singing to him for years. I was just about to belt out 'I'm Not Going' from *Dreamgirls*, when he thankfully took the lead. He explained that he wasn't going to judge *BGT* until the live shows as he was making the US version of *The X Factor*, so he had hired David Hasselhoff to judge with Amanda Holden, leaving a spare seat on the panel that Peter Fincham was very keen for me to fill. He didn't know anything about me, he said he didn't watch comedy and preferred cartoons, but we got on well. I liked him immensely but I knew I would; I was a big fan and massively admired him. After about fifteen minutes he stopped talking and stared at me.

This was the moment.

I'd seen it a thousand times on *BGT* and *The X Factor*: he was about to judge me. My face went the colour of the juice I was still holding but had no intention of sipping.

'You're very confident. I like that. I like you. I'm going to call Peter and tell him I want you to be the new judge,' he said. It wasn't four yeses but it was the one that always mattered most.

I got the job. No boot camp. No 'come back next year'. Straight in. I tried to play it cool but I was elated. I wanted to jump up and down crying and tell him I wouldn't let him down. More than anything else I wanted to run into the open arms of Dermot O'Leary.

'Nice cars,' I said to Simon as we stood on his porch to say our goodbyes.

'Don't like that one. Love that one,' he said, judging his cars like he judges wannabes on a Saturday night.

As I lay in bed with Kitty that night I told her that being a judge on *BGT* was almost certainly a mistake but I just had to do it. I couldn't say no to Simon Cowell. Also Addison got me good money for what was certainly going to be a fun ride.

The most positive thing I can say about my experience as a judge on *Britain's Got Talent* in 2011 was that nobody remembers it. I'm sure you, the reader, didn't either. *BGT* is a talent show, it's about unearthing new talent. It's not about me. The show isn't designed or edited to make me look good and nor should it. I never considered this. Every week the show was broadcast to at least 8 million people and most of the jokes I remembered making in the auditions weren't there. The show had to be edited around the best and the worst auditions and not around my best jokes. Also, every time I was critical of an act, especially in Glasgow I recall, I was loudly booed by the audience. Being booed on TV was never my plan.

When Simon joined us for the live shows that were on every night leading up to the live final, everything went up a notch. The problem for me was that I didn't really know Simon. Amanda and David had known him for years but having not had a chance to get to know him over the auditions, all the confidence I had built up disappeared and I was too in awe of him. I was very much the main man at my arena shows and on my *Comedy*

Roadshow, but there was no doubt who the main man was now. Also, Simon's trigger-happy history of firing people certainly doesn't promote a relaxed environment.

Despite everything, I was keen to do the show again. I felt I was getting into my stride and would improve. It was just such a cushty job to do in conjunction with my own shows. *BGT* is the biggest show on TV, being a judge cements me as a household name, and it's done and dusted after a few weeks' filming leaving the rest of the year to do other stuff. Of course I wanted to do it again. I had put another arena tour on sale for the autumn of 2012 and tickets were already shifting fast.

After the final I composed a text to Simon thanking him for hiring me, telling him how much I enjoyed the experience and how much I was looking forward to the next series. I tried to edit down the text, but it was a pretty long one, probably too long. I re-read and re-edited it several times before pressing send. I hoped for a similarly lengthy and gushing reply but received the single word 'Ditto'.

'Did Simon text back?' Kitty asked.

'Yes,' I answered.

'That's good. What did he say?'

I then proceeded to read the text I sent him back to her as if he had written it, as I was too embarrassed about my one-word reply and technically that is what ditto means.

'Wow. He loves you,' Kitty said, before I explained that he actually just replied 'ditto' to my text.

'Well, that's a bit different I suppose.'

Months later I started reading press reports that Simon wasn't happy and wanted to replace the judging panel, but Peter Fincham kept insisting to Addison that my seat was safe. Then in September when Kitty and I were on the Eurostar for a romantic trip to Paris, Addison broke his sequence of exciting positive phone calls.

'Michael. Addison. You're out. Peter just called. Simon Cowell won't budge, he wants you gone.'

'Oh no,' I said. I felt rejected and upset. It was a kick in the teeth.

'But he said he loved me being a judge and it was an experience he'll never forget . . .' I said, but really I was just reciting the 'ditto' text again.

The train went into the tunnel under the Channel and the phone lost signal. For twenty minutes Kitty and I focused on the many positives, particularly the number of dates being added to my tour, but adding my name to the list of people Simon Cowell had fired was a blow to my ego. I felt foolish for taking the job in the first place, my gut having told me this was always the odds-on outcome.

When the train emerged in France I called Addison back, he told me not to worry and that Gary Farrow had already released a statement saying I'd quit the show to concentrate on my tour, and that became the narrative. I jumped before I was pushed. Not out of the train, it wasn't that bad. My tour wasn't until the autumn of the following year, 2012, and ended in December; *BGT* films in January and February so I could have easily done it, but nobody seemed to question that. The press loved any stories about Simon Cowell and would have enjoyed reporting his putting me to the sword, but luckily I came out of it unscathed and thankfully Simon didn't feel the need to correct the reports of my quitting. I resisted sending Simon a rude message as I knew 'Ditto' would be his response. Peter Fincham also called me while I was on the train and apologized. He said he wanted me back but there was no changing Simon's mind.

Addison's reaction was always to fight, to use setbacks as fuel to win another day and it was rubbing off on me. To be honest, so many extraordinary things had happened to me that I needed these mini-vendettas to keep my motivation high. After my BAFTA experience I was desperate to win one and often fantasized about that moment (normally on my own while listening to loud music in my car), and now I wanted to show Simon Cowell that I wasn't someone to dismiss. I totally respected Simon's decision, 'That's Showbiz' after all; not only is it his show but history proved he made the right call as *BGT* went from strength to strength without me. What I'm saying is that in life, use what you can to drive you, and even though it was an absurdly long shot, my new fantasy became coming up with a show that would beat Simon Cowell in the ratings.

When I was a kid my favourite boxer was Lennox Lewis. Lennox became the undisputed heavyweight champion of the world. He had forty-four fights in his career and lost twice. Losing is part of life. All the clichés about defeat making you stronger are true. Those losses would have inspired many of his future wins. What I always love about Lennox Lewis is that he avenged both those defeats. He fought both those men again and beat them, easily. Erasing those two blots showed character and made for a better story, a better journey than just being undefeated.

After several mini-bottles of red wine on the Eurostar I sent an extremely embarrassing text to Peter Fincham and told him that ITV needed to watch out, as I would now be creating an entertainment show to topple *BGT* or *The X Factor*. I'm not even sure I meant it. Deep down I knew it was a pipe dream. Simon Cowell is the king, a once-in-a-generation TV powerhouse; I should probably just go back to stand-up and forget about it, but I needed to feel I was on a mission, and of course I was drunk.

He didn't text back.

17

The *Comedy Roadshow* had run for two series and the feeling was we had pretty much exhausted the number of great comedians and major cities. So, instead, Addison and I decided to bring the roadshow home, back to London to make a one-off Christmas Special to be filmed at the iconic Theatre Royal, Drury Lane. The show was to be broadcast on Christmas Day itself, the most coveted slot of the year. Bruised by my *BGT* experience I was determined to produce our best show yet. Booking the show had been a nightmare as we knew the line-up had to be sensational to warrant such a plum slot. Addison and I worked our socks off to convince the right guests to appear. Obviously this was the job of the booker, but Addison was so well connected and I thought if I personally reached out it might help. All the hard work and stress paid off as we ended up with a strong line-up of James Corden, Miranda Hart, Rob Brydon, Jack Dee, Sean Lock,

Rhod Gilbert and David Mitchell, and Kylie Minogue to sing us out with 'Let It Snow'.

A lot was riding on the show and as ever Addison was there with me every step of the way. We were speaking constantly about the production as I had various new ideas to make the Christmas Special extra special. What I did not know was that Addison was double-booked that night. There was only one date available for us to film at the Theatre Royal and it happened to be on the same night as the filming of the Jonathan Ross Christmas show. Addison knew that I would freak out if he told me he wasn't going to be at my recording. After all the difficulties we had booking the show, could I not even book my own manager and producer. But Addison was in exactly the same boat with Jonathan. He was his manager and the producer of his show. Addison isn't a man of split loyalties – he gives one hundred per cent to all his clients. There was no way Addison could let either Jonathan or myself down. But how could he be in two places at once?

So, without telling me, he came up with a plan to have a taxi bike at his disposal throughout the night. A taxi bike is a motorbike that you sit on the back of, while the rider weaves and speeds in and out of traffic to race people around London in record time. *The Jonathan Ross Show* filmed at the London Studios, which was conveniently only a five-minute ride away over Waterloo Bridge. While I was performing my opening fifteen minutes of stand-up at the Theatre Royal, unbeknownst to me, Addison was at the London Studios for a pre-show chat with Jonathan in the make-up room.

'Have a great show tonight,' Addison hollered as he slipped out of the door before sprinting down the corridor while strapping his helmet on, leaping up the stairs two at a time to reception, then rushing out of the door and onto the back of the motorbike.

'Fucking go!' he yelled as he clung onto the faceless human courier.

Meanwhile, I was on the Theatre Royal stage. 'Ladies and gentlemen, what a treat we have for you now, the legend that is, Jack Dee!' I announced to thunderous applause.

While Jack and I were shaking hands, Addison's head was still bobbing up and down on the back of the bike on Waterloo Bridge. But by the time I came offstage, and was just about to ask where Addison was, he came bounding towards me in the wings of the theatre.

'That was fantastic, Michael, you're on fire tonight, great crowd. I've got them to change the lighting, I want the audience to look a bit warmer but you're on top form. Perfect start. I've just got to see how they're getting on in the truck,' Addison said, referring to the outside broadcast lorry.

But of course he didn't go to the truck, he leapt back on the taxi bike, 'Fucking go!' and whooshed back across Waterloo Bridge and straight into the TV gallery, to where he could watch Jonathan's show and communicate with him in his ear while he was interviewing Tom Cruise.

A Funny Life

'Dynamite so far, Jonathan, fuckin' funny,' Addison said. And with that, it was helmet back on and away he went to catch me coming offstage again, following my introduction of Sean Lock.

'They're in the palm of your hand tonight, Michael. What a show! Keep at it. I couldn't be more proud of you,' Addison said, concealing his motorbike helmet behind his back.

Addison, of course, actually had no idea how each show was going as he was riding pillion through traffic most of the time, but I genuinely remember him being with me whenever I needed him. He must have crossed Waterloo Bridge more than ten times, making sure he was there for his clients, his acts, his boys: that's what mattered most to Addison. Other than being slightly confused by his being out of breath all night and wearing a leather jacket for the first time ever, I had no idea.

The *Christmas Comedy Roadshow* did end up being the best show we had made and the most successful. The overnight rating was 6.5 million, the consolidated rating, after catch-up on iPlayer, was over 8 million, and a few weeks later, in January 2012, it won the National Television Award for Best Entertainment Programme. A great start to the momentous year of 2012. The Queen's Jubilee and the London Olympics made it a huge year for the whole nation and coincided with my enormous record-breaking tour, *Showtime*. My ten sold-out nights at the O2 beat Rihanna's record and overall the tour sold more than 640,000 tickets, officially making me the biggest-selling comedian in the world.

'What now, Michael?' Addison said to me in the conservatory

of his home in Islington when the tour had finally ended just before Christmas.

Together we had reached the summit. We were a formidable team. Addison always said to me, 'You just let me do what I do' and on the flip side he let me do what I did, and the result was I was now the biggest live comedian on earth.

'Michael, you probably won't have to work another day in your life now with the money from the tour. Maybe take a break for a bit. Spend some time with the family,' Addison suggested.

I was desperate to spend more time at home. I missed a lot of my boys' growing up while on tour. I had done over 150 shows that year, mostly staying away in hotels, and when I was home I was tired and preoccupied. There was a life-size cardboard cut-out of me at one of the arenas that I had nicked and put in Ossie's bedroom, and the truth is I was barely more of a father than that cardboard cut-out. I had been absent for too long. I suggested to Kitty I should take a year off but her immediate reaction was that would be a disaster and I would not only go mad myself, but drive her mad. I always need a project, a focus, a goal.

'I really need to be doing something, Addison. When I'm not working I do go a bit weird. Kitty says I need to keep busy.'

'I'm the same, Michael, but sometimes in life and in this business taking a breather is the right thing to do. You can't do another tour for at least three years. I think the *Comedy Roadshow* has run its course. I'm just being honest with ya.'

'I want to break America,' I said, slightly taking myself by surprise. 'I'm the biggest-selling comedian in the world, Americans will love that. Let's go now while it's still true.'

But Addison swiftly talked me out of it.

'Americans blow smoke up your arse until you're blue in the face but it's all bullshit over there. They promise the earth but nothing happens. And what if it does? You wanna move to America? I think it's a terrible idea,' Addison said in no uncertain terms.

Having seen how much appearing on TV impacts ticket sales I was keen to be visible on the box to keep my profile high, and for that to be on our own terms after the *BGT* debacle. But if we weren't going to do any more *Roadshows*, what could I do?

'Then how about I do a chat show?' I blurted, thinking aloud.

A chat show had long been a natural progression for comedians, especially the greats in America like Jay Leno and David Letterman. Addison produced not only the Jonathan Ross chat show but also the excellent Alan Carr's *Chatty Man*, a huge hit show on Channel 4. He knew how to make successful chat shows as much as anyone. I expected him to light up and say, 'I thought you'd never ask!' But instead, without hesitation he said, 'I think that would be completely the wrong thing for you to do, Michael. I'm just being honest with ya. You're not a chat show host. To be a good chat show host you need to be interested in other people, Michael, it's about the guests, it's not about you. You like to be the centre of attention. I can't see it working.'

For the first time in our relationship I ignored the instincts of a man whose instincts, I would tell anyone who would listen, were second to none. I told Addison I thought I could do it and, while mumbling about how he didn't agree, he said that if that's what I wanted he would make it happen.

Within weeks it was all agreed. The now controller of BBC1 Danny Cohen and Head of Entertainment Mark Linsey commissioned *The Michael McIntyre Chat Show* for BBC1. The plan was to film the series in February 2014, giving us a whole year to prepare, leaving plenty of time for me to be home and to take my family abroad every school holiday, including a big trip to Disney World at Easter that the boys were wildly looking forward to. By making *The Michael McIntyre Chat Show*, Addison would be the executive producer of three major chat shows on all three major channels, ITV, Channel 4 and the BBC, with us all competing for the same guests. Oh, and then there was the BBC's flagship chat show too, and most successful of them all, *The Graham Norton Show* which always got the best guests anyway. We weren't exactly filling a gap in the market.

The BBC wanted to go big and put my show on a Saturday night but Addison insisted it was scheduled in his tried and tested Monday night 10.35 p.m. slot where he'd started *Live at the Apollo*.

'We'll do six low-key episodes on a Monday night and if it doesn't work, we can get out with minimum damage. And if it does work we can move it to primetime,' Addison cautiously explained.

Addison was aware that my show needed to be different to

the others. It couldn't just follow the conventional chat show formula. It had to reflect me and showcase me. He was very worried about whether we could make it work but we had time to perfect our ideas and for me to learn the ropes. RADA studios, a theatre space belonging to the famous drama school, was booked for several dry runs over the summer of 2013. An audience of around a hundred came to see our first run-through with Bruno Tonioli, Stacey Solomon and Nigel Havers booked for me to interview. The set-up was classic chat show with me behind a desk talking to guests on the other side. As it was only a run-through I didn't really give it much thought, nor did I research or prepare for the interviews, but I loved it. I loved being in front of such an intimate audience after all my arena shows. I loved being spontaneous and improvisational and I loved having things to play with, the swivelling office chair I was sitting on, the desk, the cameramen, the audience, and of course the guests, who were so much fun and certainly in the case of Bruno, wild. Honestly, it was riotous and hilarious.

'The road to Damascus, my friend,' Addison barked as he burst into my student dressing room afterwards with Mark Linsey from the BBC. I had no idea what that meant, but he kept repeating it over and over again.

'Michael, I couldn't see it until today. I really didn't think this was going to work but I think this show is going to be fantastic. We've got to rip up the rule book, break the third wall.'

'Fourth wall,' Mark corrected.

'I don't care, break all the fuckin' walls. It's anarchy we want, unpredictability, off the rails. Michael freewheeling, going against convention, an alternative chat show, and these are the types of guest we should have, Bruno Tonioli and Nigel Havers, people like David Dickinson, people you can have fun with who don't take themselves too seriously. Let Graham Norton have the stuffy Hollywood stars, we'll be having more fun.'

And then he said the words that I had learnt so many times to trust, words that always led to success.

'Michael. Leave it with me. I know what I'm doing.' Before one final, 'The road to Damascus.'

It became apparent that my taxi driver home had also never heard the expression 'The road to Damascus', because when I asked him he typed it into his satnav. So I googled it and found out it was a moment of insight that leads to a dramatic change of attitude, coming from the Bible when Jesus converted the Apostle Paul to Christianity. So in this instance Addison was the apostle, Jesus was my chat show and Christianity was Addison thinking it was actually going to work.

Addison had a vision, it emerged in an unconventional way, but he was suddenly more excited about the chat show than I'd ever seen him about anything we'd done before. Up until that RADA run-through I'd begun to share his doubts about whether this was the right thing to do. I was struggling with the collaborative nature of producing a TV show. The *Roadshow* was just an extension of everything I'd done before, stand-up comedy and editing. Now I was working with a whole team of producers and researchers, who by simply doing their jobs were annoying and confusing me. They wanted everything meticulously planned, as they should, whereas I just wanted to create a show that would allow me to be funny in the moment. In the run-through I basically ignored everything that was scripted and had a laugh. But all my worries had now evaporated. I now had a super-excited Addison who, via the road to Damascus, was fully charged and in charge. I'm not a TV producer, he is. Trusting Addison had brought me everything, so I just relaxed about the show. I've got the greatest weapon in show business, a passionate Addison. All I had to do was whatever he told me.

One of the things Addison told me was to enjoy my success, and 2013 was the first stress-free year in my career for as long as I could remember. It took becoming the highest-selling comedian in the world for me to finally relax about my finances. I've always loved cars and started purchasing them for the people I loved. I bought my mum an Audi A5, the car she admired from the advertising screen my *Live & Laughing* DVD poster shared when we nearly crashed on the Westway roundabout. I bought my wingman Paul Tonkinson, who had once bailed me out in a petrol station when I was so broke all my bank cards were rejected, a Mercedes. And one breakfast I said to our house-keeper and nanny Lorraine, a remarkably brilliant person who had looked after Kitty when she herself was a child, that if she could throw a tea bag into a mug from a short distance, I'd buy her a car too. I had never seen her so focused as she scrunched up the circular Tetley Extra Strong bag to increase its aero-dynamics. Her eyes narrowed on the mug like a professional

On my 'ill-fated' chat show –
most likely trying to phone a taxi!

Playing it cool with
superfan Kate at the
2014 Royal Variety
Performance.

The stage is where I'm happiest and it was nice to have this reminder on my 2015 *Happy & Glorious* arena tour.

Playing Send to All on the *Big Show* with a (soon to be very embarrassed) American celebrity.

Trying to rescue the situation when my surprise for
firefighter Andy didn't go to plan.

Hairdresser Natasha gets the biggest surprise of her life.

The exceptionally brilliant producer Dan Baldwin and me winning a Rose d'Or (I generously let him keep the box).

Joe (*centre*, concealing his *Guardian* and umbrella behind me), Danny and me being given the key (and spare key) to the O2.

Paul Tonkinson and me onstage at the Spark Arena in Auckland, New Zealand.

Performing at the O2 having let myself in using the key shown opposite.

Beloved Joe with his umbrella and *Guardian* – 'Don't mind me, Michael.'

Love this photo taken by Kitty, who came to see
my show at the Radio City Music Hall in New York.

At home in Hampstead recovering from yet another injury.
Also a glimpse of my 'upside down' legs!

The love of my life.

darts player looks at the triple twenty. She sent it flying through the air, it caught the rim but landed safely home and we spent the rest of the day at Cargiant where she chose herself a Mini Countryman.

We had our Disney trip, as well as holidays in the Maldives, Italy and Dubai. We bought a country house in Wiltshire called Breach House, full of everything fun I could think of, a swimming pool, sauna, tennis court, table tennis table, pool table, air hockey, trampoline, croquet, darts, arcade machine, full-size football goal, even a room in the house with two mini goals just for football. Of course the kids still mainly played on the Xbox while I shouted about making the most of the house, but that's modern life. Kitty and I owned Breach House officially, our names were on the deeds, but in truth we co-owned it with a lot of animals who tried to force us out. The problem lay with us only spending weekends there. On weekdays various creatures moved in, so that when we arrived on Friday nights after spending two hours on the motorway after school pick-up, we never knew what to expect. The house became a sort of wildlife park for vermin. Our gravel driveway turned out to be a killing ground and toilet, with dead birds and other unidentifiable deceased species scattered around fox and rabbit poo. The first time I took the rubbish out and lifted the bin lid I was greeted by thousands of maggots crawling up towards me. Cluster flies literally took over the whole top floor of the house. We discovered this when Kitty went to store some linen up there and then came running downstairs screaming, with flies spewing out of her mouth like that character in *The*

Mummy. Seeing that the top floor was occupied, the wasps chose to nest in the guest room on the first floor and the hornets settled for the boot room. We thought things were picking up when a heatwave coincided with a Bank Holiday weekend. It was a wonderful moment when we all jumped in the swimming pool as if we were in a Mediterranean villa and not twenty minutes from Junction 15 of the M4. But soon, having already learnt so much about insects from the maggots, cluster flies, wasps and hornets that I was considering pitching a nature programme to the BBC if the chat show didn't work out, we were introduced to the horseflies. If you aren't familiar with horseflies let me fill you in. They are big ugly flies that land on you and then they bite you, hard and painfully. They are attracted to shiny things apparently, and Kitty, the boys and I splashing around in the pool on a sunny day became so shiny that a plague of them headed our way. Shooing doesn't really work as they keep buzzing back trying to bite you. So the best course of action is to slap them and kill them, prompting a chorus of 'Got you! You little shit,' from Kitty and me, and inappropriately repeated by eight-year-old Lucas and five-year-old Ossie. Not only would Kitty and I slap ourselves, we also slapped the flies landing on the children, be it on their body or face. The dream we had of our life in the country when we saw the idyllic swimming pool in the estate agent's brochure amounted to Kitty, the boys and myself all screaming, swearing and slapping each other.

Probably the worst weekend was when there was a leak in the pipe to the septic tank. Now, as a city person I was unaware of septic tanks. A septic tank is a private treatment plant on site for human waste. You know when people move houses and say, 'The previous owners left all their shit behind', well with country houses that is often precisely the case. The leak meant that the entire terrace was covered in faeces and, just to complete the scene, a family of rats eating it. The terrace covered in shit was the rat equivalent of our trip to Disney World. They were thrilled. The result of the cluster flies, wasps, hornets, horseflies and rats was that Jason from Pest Control became a close family friend and was at the house more than we were. Jason put down rat-catching boxes full of poison only to find a snake in one of them the following week. Dream houses aren't always that; in hindsight even Bear Grylls would have thought twice about buying Breach House.

Meanwhile, Addison was having better luck building a dream house of his own. He had long wanted to live in Lonsdale Square, less than ten minutes' walk from his current Islington home, but houses there rarely came onto the market. In typical Addison style he knocked on the door of his favourite one and made them an offer they couldn't refuse. For the past few years he had been applying for various planning permissions and renovating his new house while he and Shelley continued to live in their old one. Addison was so excited and keen to show it off, particularly the enormous and extravagant fishpond he was constructing in the garden. Addison, a big fish himself, loved fish. He now also loved dogs, having recently got two. You would naturally expect him to have a Rottweiler or a pit bull and take them for walks with his heavyweight boxer best mate. But no, he had two little 'teddy bear' dogs, a Shih Tzu, Bichon Frise cross, normally the dog of choice for ladies who lunch. He did look a bit hilarious with those two little dogs, although his self-image was still very much of a man living life on the edge. He had recently become addicted to a new television series, *Ray Donovan*, about a 'fixer' who solved the problems of his celebrity clients in LA, usually in criminal ways with bribes, threats and violence.

'It's like lookin' in the mirror, Michael. I am Ray Donovan. Call me Ray,' he kept saying.

Kitty and I hadn't had a chance to see Addison's work-in-progress dream house yet, despite him always mentioning that we must. We finally got to see it in December. The night before, I hosted my annual Christmas show at the Hammersmith Apollo. Having seen how much money can be generated selling tickets for live comedy I had hosted *Michael McIntyre's Christmas Charity Show* for the last three years, calling in favours from other comics and singers to perform for free to raise money for children's charities. Addison was doing the same thing on a much bigger scale with his annual *Comedy Gala* at the O2 Arena, with the profits building a brand-new wing at Great Ormond Street Hospital.

The atmosphere at my charity show was very relaxed. Kitty came for a rare stress-free night out when I was gigging and the bill was full of comedians just having fun and giving something back. Jack Whitehall, Russell Howard, Rob Brydon and Josh Widdicombe performed and Katherine Jenkins and Tom Odell sang. Addison was there and as always on great form, in his element, chewing people's ears off with his latest gossip.

'Have you seen *Ray Donovan*?' I kept hearing him say whenever I was in his vicinity.

Tom Odell sang his hit 'Another Love' to close the show and as soon as he came offstage Addison grabbed him and started telling him the entire history of the Hammersmith Apollo.

'Darling,' Kitty said to me in the green room afterwards, 'Addison really wants us to see his new house, he says it's nearly done. Would be nice to go before Christmas. He'd love that.'

I looked round to see Addison two inches from the face of a terrified-looking Tom Odell and could just about hear him saying, 'It's probably going to be the biggest garden pond in London . . .'

'He's so excited about it. It would mean a lot to him,' Kitty reiterated.

'Yes, we definitely should. I was going to pop round to see him at the office tomorrow to give him his Christmas presents. Maybe you can come and then we can see his new house after, apparently it's like five minutes away.'

So the following day that was the plan. Addison was always amazingly generous with his Christmas presents, which tended to be expensive works of art. I always knew they were expensive as Addison never failed to tell me, normally with the phrase, 'I'd get that insured if I were you', and then he would reveal the actual price: 'Tell the insurers it cost eight grand.' I had bought him three presents. I had a set of mugs made for the office on which I had printed all of his classic phrases. The top of the mug read 'Addisonisms' and then a list including, 'We'll burn that bridge when we come to it', 'I could send Scott round', 'It's like two ships passing in a nightmare', 'I'm just being honest with ya', 'Do you know I'm related to Tom Sayers', 'I know what I'm doing', and the last one of course being, 'I'll end on this.'

Kitty and I sat with Addison and Shelley in the living room of their current home in front of a small Christmas tree and a roaring fire. Addison at home always looked a bit strange to me, wearing jeans and a cardigan and not his shiny blue suit, his uniform. His reaction to the mug was hilarious. He put his glasses on and read all of his most well-worn phrases aloud and then looked at me with total confusion.

'Michael? What is this?' he asked, genuinely puzzled.

'They're Addisonisms. All the things you say. On mugs. For the office.' I smiled. 'A bit of fun. Classic Addison.'

He had no idea what I was talking about and denied using any of the phrases ever. Luckily the awkwardness was broken by my two other presents, which he went nuts for. Shelley had let me steal his dogs for a professional photo shoot that I had framed, and I had a Ray Donovan poster made with Addison's face superimposed over the face of Liev Schreiber, the actor who plays him, with the very appropriate actual strapline on the poster, 'Hire Power'. To say he loved it is an understatement.

'I am Ray Donovan,' he repeated.

Then we all walked together to Addison and Shelley's new house in Lonsdale Square. It was one of those cold, crisp and sunny winter's days. Addison kept telling us over and over again that this was the route he walked the dogs. He was over the moon to be showing us his dog route. He stopped at just about every tree along the way. I thought he was expecting one of us to pee against it, but it was to tell us more history about the buildings and the area.

'I always look up. I always look up at buildings. It's fascinating,' he said, using another sentence that could have made it onto the mug.

His new house was magnificent. Addison and Shelley showed us around with so much pride. There is something so special in sharing a life with someone and then building your perfect home together, perfectly suited to your needs, a private world created for the rest of your lives. A forever home. The house was nearly finished. It had taken years of meticulous planning and to see it coming to fruition made Addison as happy as Kitty and I had ever seen him. He was already working out where his Ray Donovan picture would go. 'Maybe instead of the bathroom mirror,' he said.

We all hugged goodbye outside his soon-to-be front door in the winter sunshine. Merry Christmas.

But that would never be his front door.

And I would never see him again.

18

We were spending Christmas in our country house with just Kitty, the boys and her mother Alexandra. I was getting dressed upstairs in the little dressing room off our bedroom, while Kitty and her mother were chatting over breakfast in the kitchen and the boys were in the TV room in their pyjamas playing each other at FIFA on the Xbox. I saw Joe's number pop up on my mobile phone and didn't think anything of it. Although he didn't call often, I assumed he just wanted to wish us a Merry Christmas and thank us for the present I left for him in the office when I visited Addison a few days before.

'Hi Joe' I said, casually.

'Ad's dead,' he said.

People talk about how hard it is when someone who has been ill for a long time dies, that the end is still such a shock even though they knew it was coming. When the news comes out of nowhere with no warning whatsoever it hits you like a thunderbolt, instantly turning your world upside down. Joe explained that Addison had had a heart attack at home. Shelley called an ambulance but they couldn't save him. His heart stopped. He's dead. I couldn't speak. 'I'm so sorry, Joe,' was all I could manage before I hung up.

I rushed downstairs in a daze. There was my life, the life I was living just moments before the phone rang, still going on. I passed the boys bantering, with their Xbox controllers in their hands, and reached the kitchen where Kitty and her mother were, the log fire ablaze and the smell of warm croissants in the air. This life, this absurdly idyllic life that we were living, was a life Addison had made possible for us.

'Addison died,' I blurted out in the doorway of the kitchen.

Kitty and her mother screamed in shock as I tried to explain the little I knew. We went into the TV room where the boys were playing and paused their game while Kitty told them that something bad had happened. I sat between them and started to cry. Lucas was eight years old and Ossie only five. They were the ones who cried in life, when they grazed a knee or banged their head, not me, not their dad. They had never seen me cry before. Still to this day it's the only time they have seen me cry. It didn't cross my mind how shocking that would be for them, but their reaction was so sweet and kind that I cry all over again when I remember it. They instantly understood. In the middle of bickering and playing FIFA they were suddenly cuddling and consoling me, looking after me.

I spoke to Shelley, who described the brutal horror of the

night before. My heart broke for her. How could Addison die? He's stronger than all of us put together. It didn't seem possible. It didn't seem real. I phoned some of Addison's other clients and quickly learnt how the special relationship I had with him was identically reflected in the special relationship he had with us all. I remembered him bobbing up and down on the back of a motor- cycle on Waterloo Bridge to be there for me and Jonathan Ross on the same night. That was a metaphor for every day of his life. He gave his all, to all of us. Some of his acts had been with him for over twenty years and others were just a few months into the astonish- ing ride of having him as an agent, but he loved us all equally.

He was my agent for seven years. Only seven years did I know him, and what he did for me is astounding. The saddest part of that whole horrible Christmas was that whenever I needed help in any aspect of my life, from a leaking washing machine to a family problem, I would call Addison and he would always, absolutely always, know what to do. That's when I really felt it. The pain and confusion I was feeling made me want to call the only person who could help, the only person who would have the answers, Addison himself. My gut reflex reaction was always to turn to him. I relied on him so much. Three weeks earlier I had a meeting scheduled with Addison and the produ- cers of my chat show about how things were progressing, as we were due to start filming the series in February. For the first time ever Addison didn't show up. I tried calling him but his phone was switched off. Without Addison I deemed the meeting totally pointless and barely paid attention or contributed. This was

A Funny Life

Addison's show. We're all going to do what he says. I had no idea about chat shows, and the producers, as with everyone I had met in this business, paled in comparison to Addison.

I emailed him that night, and below are our messages.

> Hi Addison,
> Are you ok?
>> Nobody told me you weren't coming to the meeting today.
>>> Michael x

Two days later, he replied.

> Dear Michael,
> Took a few days off as I needed to let off some steam as the whole business was starting to get to me. Sorry not to be there on Thursday but my head wasn't right so Shelley wanted me to shut off for the rest of the week.
>> Hope you understand as it had nothing to do with you.
>>> Addison x

I replied to him with an email I will forever be happy I sent. Telling him, reminding him, of his genius and how much I depended on him.

Michael McIntyre

Sorry you had a bad week Addison.
If it's worth anything, I think you are an
extraordinary, wonderful and brilliant man . . .
and much like the plot of festive favourite 'It's a
Wonderful Life' . . . without you, we'd all be fucked!!
    You and me are about to make the best show on
TV . . . Exciting times are coming . . . Type
Damascus into your satnav!!
    Michael xx

A few hours later he replied.

Dear Michael
About to call you as I've recharged and feel good
about life and the business again although I've put
my back out with all the stress but will sort that out
today as my shoulders are 2 inches higher than they
should be!
    Love you for the message and yes it will be the
best fucking chat show ever.
    Bring it on!
    Addison x

I suppose it follows that a man who carried the weight of his
clients' lives on his shoulders would do his back in. He lived a
complicated and stressful life, one that I don't know the half of.
What I know is what he meant to me and I'm so glad I had a

chance to tell him before I lost him. On the off chance you haven't seen *It's a Wonderful Life*, it's about an angel who shows a man what the world would have been like if he had never been born, and in doing so how he had influenced so many lives for the better. My life without Addison would have been very different.

The cause of his death was sketchy but it did seem that the night after Kitty and I had seen him last at his new house he had gone to the Off The Kerb Christmas party, which led to one of his infamous nights out. He was a fit man and extremely health-conscious and terrified of illness and death. He was going out less and less and knew that lifestyle had to end. Recently, whenever he went for a night out he would say afterwards he was going to stop, that would be the last time. And now, in the worst possible way, it had been.

A few weeks later Kitty and I went to Addison's funeral at the Golders Green Crematorium. Outside in the drizzle we spotted Danny and Joe and Fay and Ann from the office, comedians like Dara Ó'Briain, Adam Hills, Jack Dee and Lee Evans, Addison's brother and mother and Shelley, all starting to gather. Of course the mood was sombre but I had no experience of being anything but upbeat in this company so I felt relatively normal beforehand and when I took my seat in the chapel. But when the service started and the pall-bearers walked in carrying the coffin, it hit me so hard. Addison was in there. In that box. Dead in that box. He's not a person anymore. I had never in my life felt more sad. When my father died I was seventeen and devastated, but the circumstances were different. We were living apart. He was in America and I was in London. The pain came in waves and at unpredictable times. But that single moment when I saw Addison's coffin was immensely harrowing for me. I broke down and cried uncontrollably through the whole service.

Addison was a one-off. I knew I would never meet anyone like him again and nobody else could possibly have such an impact on my life. He wanted to look after me and, although I didn't know it until he was gone, I needed to be looked after. He made me feel safe like nobody in my life had before. He was such a force of nature and character that I could always hear him in my head for hours after we'd spoken and I wanted so much to keep hold of that, to keep hold of him and his crazy voice guiding me. We were a team. Every victory was a victory shared. We had taken on the comedy world and won. He was irreplaceable.

How could I carry on without him?

I've always been acutely aware of the precarious nature of show business. Every single TV or film star who slipped out of favour had a winning streak before where it looked like they could do no wrong. Of course they did, that's why they became famous. When I decided I wanted a chat show the BBC fell over backwards to give me what I wanted because I was, in their view, a good bet. The *Comedy Roadshow* was an award-winning hit. I was hot. But a few wrong moves and that can quickly change. Not only did I have to make the chat show a success, I had to make it immediately. Kitty and I discussed whether I should pull out and cancel, but we concluded that it was probably better to throw myself into work as a distraction. There was also the feeling that Addison was so excited about the show and had so much faith after his road to Damascus moment that, with him always being right, the show would surely be a success. The problem, however, was that I never got around to asking Addison what his vision for the show actually was. I was clueless.

To help myself feel more confident I brought in my friend and wingman Paul Tonkinson to join the production team Addison had assembled. Paul's job being the one he had been doing for free since we met, to help me be funny. Also, to help perk me up and because life's too short, I bought myself a black convertible Ferrari to arrive at the studio in style. I'd had lots of ideas for the show over the last year, some good, some not. I had an idea called 'Can I come?' where I would meet people randomly in the street, ask what they were doing and then say, 'Can I come?' We thought this would lead to hilarious bits of TV that we could drop in the show between me interviewing guests, but that didn't turn out to be the case. Roaming around the aisles of the DIY shop B&Q I met a gentleman who said he was buying paint to decorate his son's room. 'Can I come?' I asked, and then spent the afternoon at this house in Battersea painting his son's room while the boy was at school. After some mildly amusing banter the homeowner left me to finish the job on my own, with my camera crew literally just filming me painting. We edited down the footage and the result was not only as boring as watching paint dry, watching the paint dry was actually one of the more entertaining moments. But there was one idea I had that everyone loved and I was surprised hadn't been done before: 'Send to All'. The idea was that I take someone's phone from the audience, send an embarrassing message to all of their contacts and then leave the phone on my desk and, between interviewing guests, keep coming back to it throughout the show to read out funny replies.

I also had the idea of booking a well-known chat show host as my first guest to teach me the ropes; Sir Terry Wogan agreed to be my first guest, with Lily Allen and Sir Alan Sugar also on the show. Two knights of the realm to kick off the series that was broadcast in the Addison-selected slot of 10.35 p.m. on a Monday night. I tried to be loose and spontaneous like I had been in the run-through that so excited Addison, but I found so much of the format inhibiting and restricting. An essential part of stand-up is standing up; now I was sitting down, and behind a desk like an office worker. The guests were way too far away from me, it was more like a job interview than a comedy interview. I was incredibly relaxed in the run-throughs at RADA because I wasn't taking anything particularly seriously and neither were the guests, but now this was a proper TV show and everyone was a bit more guarded and on edge. My natural instinct was to treat everything as fodder for jokes but guests aren't comfortable with that, they worry the joke is on them. Addison's first reaction had been that I would struggle, as a chat show should be about the guests and not about me. I found the first recording confusing and uncomfortable. The Send to All segment was strong and undeniably funny, but I hadn't enjoyed the interviews. I was out of my depth.

I didn't know the language or the mechanics of a chat show and I had no original spin on it either.

In the dressing room after the first recording I ripped off my tie but still felt strangled. Mark Linsey from the BBC was there, along with Danny, who was now my main agent, and Paul looking and feeling awkward with a notepad. Where was Addison? I needed Addison.

I was acting like a prima donna, ranting about how bad I thought the show was and looking for scapegoats and excuses. Everyone was full of praise but I knew their words were more in hope than expectation. You always get a sense of how good a TV recording is by the way people talk about the subsequent edit. If a show goes well everyone says, 'How on earth are we going to cut that down?' but after my first chat show people were saying things like, 'That'll edit up really well. A few extra laughs, get rid of all the awkward bits.' 'We were filming for two and half hours and we only need forty-five minutes. It'll be great. You'll see.' 'After the edit, the show will be unrecognizable.' There was a lot of wishful thinking in that dressing room.

When the chat show aired I realized just how desperate the press are for things to fail. The truth is, it's a much better story. I was to be given no time at all to learn the ropes, I had to hit the ground running or I would be destroyed. The show rated well at 2.3 million, which for a late Monday night slot was well above the average, but the reviews were simply dreadful. The show and my lack of skills as an interviewer were ridiculed and trashed. It was an assassination and I still had five more shows to make. I was in the middle of a nightmare. The Monday night slot that Addison had asked the BBC for was being referred to by the press as 'the graveyard slot', the narrative being that the BBC were so ashamed of the show it had been hidden away to die. The ratings dipped to 1.9 million for the second show. A drop-off is expected after a show launches and the 1.9 million was still way above the average for the 'graveyard' slot but the headlines were now about the 400,000 people who had switched off. After only two shows, two shows! Mark Lawson in the *Guardian* wrote an article entitled, 'The Michael McIntyre Chat Show. Where did it all go wrong?' I read it and felt sick to my core. I was ruining everything.

The whole production team remained positive – what else could they do? – but I was broken. I just couldn't handle the abuse. I was drowning and didn't know how to save myself. I needed Addison to save me. Probably the lowest point, and a moment that sums up my whole experience, was when Paul and I headed into the studio to film the second show. I was driving my new Ferrari, the sun was shining, and Paul was doing his utmost to turn my mood around. I was actually starting to buy into his motivational speech.

'Fuck the press mate, this is nothing new. Just remember they're not picking on only you, they pick on everyone mate. All sorts of brilliant shows took a battering from the press. You can get through this. You will get through this. Come on, mate. Get this in perspective. You're fine. You're the one in the Ferrari,' he said as we stopped at a red light in Holborn.

Buoyed by Paul's words and the blue skies above, I decided to push the 'Open Roof' button on the dashboard of my convertible Italian sports car. The mechanism takes around thirty seconds. A flap behind us lifted up and the whole roof slowly folded away, gradually revealing Paul and me in the open air. The roof retracted with a final clunk, and a beep confirmed it to be fully open. At that precise moment, a man crossing the road looked over his shoulder and shouted, 'Oi, McIntyre, your new show is shit!' prompting me to immediately push the 'Close Roof' button, reversing the entire process. The roof slowly raised back over our heads as the man continued to hurl abuse, 'Worst show I've ever seen', with me red faced and Paul mumbling, 'I'm so sorry, mate, tough times.'

The series was deemed a bona fide disaster, its lowest point surely being my having to do a serious interview with my friend Nigella Lawson. This was her first interview after her marriage break-up and I was stuck between a rock and a hard place. What I wanted was for us to have a giggle while she grilled something in the studio – what I didn't want was to grill her. Booking Nigella was a coup, an exclusive. I had to do some kind of Oprah impression otherwise face further media massacre. I remember driving to the studio that day (roof up, obvs) and wondering just how I had got myself into such a mess. Nigella was dignified and rightly guarded and my attempts at being a serious interviewer were cringeworthy.

In the six weeks from the first to the last episode, I felt I had already destroyed everything. Whatever Addison envisaged in his road to Damascus moment, it certainly wasn't the show we had made. A stroke of luck, however, meant that the controller of BBC1, Danny Cohen, had missed most of the series as he was on holiday in the Maldives.

'Michael! Hi! It's Danny Cohen. I'm back,' he said to me on the phone soon after the series ended. 'I've been on an island resort where they have a "No Shoes No News" policy so I've been completely shut off. How did the show go?'

Boy, did I wish I had a 'no news' policy too. I had unfortunately read every single savage sentence written about my chat show but, amazingly, Danny Cohen hadn't read a thing.

'Great!' I said, lying through my teeth. 'The series went great. Really well received.'

It turned out the BBC still had faith in me as a chat show host, but I didn't. My confidence was so low I had decided the only opinion that mattered was the man abusing me at the traffic lights when I put my Ferrari roof down for the first, and possibly last, time.

It had been only three months since I wrote Addison that email saying that like in the film *It's a Wonderful Life*, without him I'd be fucked.

Now he was gone.

And I was.

19

Money in the bank. Two houses. A Ferrari. I should probably have taken a break. Grieved the loss of Addison. Taken stock. Unfortunately that's not my nature. I went into full panic mode, my catastrophic thinking in overdrive.

'What am I going to do? I can't afford to make another mistake like this. The BBC are backing me now but one more disaster and their belief will wane. People will go off me. I'll sell fewer and fewer tickets. I'll be back on the comedy circuit. I was a judge on *Britain's Got Talent*, now I might have to go on it and audition. I'll probably get four "nos" from the judges, or three nos and a "ditto" from Simon. We'll have to move back into our half bath flat in Alma Road. Maybe Mark Linsey will give me my old job back as a runner, I do still have my Nokia 3210 in my man drawer to play Snake on the loo,' I ranted to myself, aloud and often.

Tour. I had to put a tour on sale. Get back on the road. Do what I do best. I met with Danny and Joe and decided to book an arena tour starting in the autumn of the following year, 2015. Good. That's security. I have a plan. I can be doing warm-up shows until then. Build the material. Keep busy. But I have to keep my profile high. I have a lot of tickets to sell. I need to be on TV. I need to be funny on TV. I need to begin to erase the memory of my chat show, or as it had now been renamed in the press, 'ill-fated chat show' or 'much-maligned chat show'. The BBC wanted me to do a second series and I was hesitant to pull the plug. Without Addison as a buffer, bigging me up, I felt nervous that the chat show was all that was on the table for me and didn't want to lose the only thing I had. Maybe I could turn it around? Also, I didn't have any other ideas for TV shows I could host anyway. And, as ever, there was another new controller of BBC1, Charlotte Moore. Danny Cohen had 'gone upstairs', presumably barefoot and hopefully still thinking my chat show received glowing reviews. Charlotte was now my fourth controller at BBC1. First there was Peter Fincham who gave me my big break at the Royal Variety, he was now running ITV. Then there was Jay Hunt who commissioned the *Comedy Roadshow*, she was now running Channel 4. Then there was Danny Cohen who was promoted to some all-powerful role at the BBC called 'Head of Television'. I don't know what that exactly meant, but I'm sure when he was at home nobody would dare take the remote control away from him.

Now Charlotte Moore was in charge of BBC1 and the ever lovely and supportive Mark Linsey was still Head of Entertainment. I had never met Charlotte. The words 'background in documentaries' worried me. What if she wasn't a fan of mine? What if she wanted to just make documentaries? Or a documentary about how the once most successful comedian in the world threw it all away? If Addison was alive he would be making sure Charlotte knew I was the most exciting talent at the channel, bombarding her with my tour sales records, DVD charts and threats to take me to ITV. He'd call me up and tell me we're having lunch with the new controller at the Ivy or the Dorchester. He'd arrive late and begin his hypnotizing playbook. I often called Addison 'The Captain'. It was a nickname he loved. He was in charge. Without him, it was just me, low on confidence, bruised and confused.

I met with Charlotte and Mark at the BBC. I may have hated doing the chat show, and the perception was certainly that everyone else hated watching it, but the ratings had held up at around 2 million and by the last episode had regained all the 400,000 viewers lost after the first show, although the press would never report that of course. The BBC liked the idea of keeping my chat show on a Monday night, an irreverent alternative to Graham Norton on a Friday night. They felt the show deserved another outing to find its feet, to establish itself from what was, according to the ratings, a decent foundation. I didn't want to express anything negative in the meeting, under strict instructions from Kitty who was very worried I would burst into tears sobbing, 'They were all mean to me.'

So I told Charlotte and Mark I loved making the show, I couldn't wait to do more and agreed to film another series and keep it on a Monday night. I had to. If the BBC didn't want to cancel the show, why should I? Who cancels their own show? But deep down I knew I couldn't really do it. I was stalling. I had to come up with another plan.

The prize for winning *Britain's Got Talent* is to perform on the Royal Variety. That of course was my prize in 2006, courtesy of Peter Fincham who then made me a judge on *Britain's Got Talent* but Simon Cowell fired me. You know all this. Now that Peter Fincham was in charge of ITV he rightly felt it would be a good idea for the Royal Variety to be on the same channel as *Britain's Got Talent*, so he bought the rights and (I'm going to use abbreviations from now on, I think) the RVP moved from the BBC to ITV because of *BGT*. So, with the world turning full circle, Danny called me to tell me that ITV wanted me to host the RVP. This was the perfect plan to start to banish the memory of the chat show. The answer to all the lows in my career has always been stand-up. I struggled adapting to panel shows, a game show, giving out awards, TV judging and chat show interviewing, but stand-up was always my saviour.

The new darlings of the royal family, Kate and Wills, would be in attendance and not Prince Charles, who had already seen me at three RVPs and also his sixtieth birthday. Not that he remembered, however. I had recently hosted a dinner for the Prince's Trust and before the dinner there was a line-up for him to shake the hands of some celebrity ambassadors and some ex-offenders who had been rehabilitated and helped by the charity. So myself, Gary Lineker, Cheryl Cole and Phillip Schofield stood in a line with the men and women whose lives had been turned around by the Prince's Trust. Prince Charles was thrilled to chat to his old mate Cheryl but unfortunately when he reached me he asked, 'So tell me how the Prince's Trust has helped you?'

'No, I'm hosting tonight,' I said, smiling and hoping my face would ring a bell, the memory one, not the one he rings when he needs a servant.

'That's wonderful. It's amazing what can be achieved when you put your mind to it,' he said before spotting Gary Lineker.

'Gary, how good to see you,' HRH said, moving along the line.

I was really pleased that William and Kate were going to be at the Royal Variety. Surely I could be a bit cheeky with them and take a few more risks. They were a young couple who had recently had a baby, there was a lot for me to work with. Kate and Wills were fresh royal meat. I bounded onto the stage at the Palladium fully loaded with bespoke jokes for them. I congratulated the royal couple on the birth of Prince George and shouted 'Who's the daddy?' to William which I certainly hadn't planned on, but they were so relaxed and laughing along that I immediately felt loose. I did an impression of William reading George a bedtime story: 'And then the Prince and the Princess kissed on the lawn of the magnificent palace and lived happily ever after . . . Anyway, enough about my day, what book are we going to read?' And I did an impression of them feeding their baby using the classic technique of pretending the spoon is an aeroplane, except in their house they have nine Red Arrow pilots holding little red plastic spoons, who do a fly-by first.

The show felt like a comeback gig. For the first time since I lost Addison, I felt back in control and happy. I asked to have a look at my bits in the edit before the show was broadcast. The Royal Variety was being edited at ITV itself and the morning I was due to drop in I read an article about ITV bringing back *Sunday Night at the London Palladium* and Peter Kay turning down the chance to host.

'Why haven't they asked me?' I said to Kitty, showing her the article on my phone at breakfast.

'I don't know. Probably because you're with the BBC, I suppose. It's an ITV show, isn't it?' Kitty suggested.

'But it's just the kind of show I should be doing. It's perfect for me. It's what I'm best at. I love the Palladium. I was just there. *Sunday Night at the London Palladium* is a legendary TV show, the whole country used to watch it,' I said.

I was drawn to the security of hosting a show that already had such a huge identity, a ready-made and loved format. I felt so qualified for this job. *Sunday Night at the London Palladium* was my show to host, regardless of what channel it was on. Being a chat show host was not my strongest suit. This *was* my strongest suit and without Addison I had to play safe. After years of observing Addison using ITV as a pawn and an ace up his sleeve (yes, I've gone for the double there, both chess and cards, Addison was that cunning), now there was a show on ITV I could genuinely see myself doing. There was nothing similar on the

BBC. As I drove to ITV to view the edit of the Royal Variety I couldn't get the idea of hosting *Sunday Night at the London Palladium* out of my head.

I was given a space in the underground car park at ITV. As I pushed the button on my key fob to lock the doors of my Ferrari I heard the roar of another sports car driving down the ramp. Which ITV star could this be? Ant? Dec? Schofe? Bradley Walsh? Lorraine Kelly in a Lamborghini? I caught a glimpse of the car as it prowled the rows. It was a black Bentley Continental. Classy. The engine stopped and the car door opened.

'Peter,' I called out. It was the head of ITV himself, Peter Fincham.

'Michael. Good to see you. Very well done the other night,' he said, bleeping his own car locked.

Suddenly this felt like fate. Without thinking, I just blurted it out.

'I heard you're remaking *Sunday Night at the London Palladium*. I want to host it.'

'Do you always conduct cloak and dagger meetings in car parks?' he asked quizzically. 'Have you been waiting down here for me?'

'No. I just arrived to go to the edit and I saw you. But I do agree it's a bit Deep Throat,' I said, referring to journalists meeting a secret informant in a car park during the Watergate scandal, which I immediately felt I should clarify.

'Like Watergate. Not the seventies porno. I don't want to do the job that badly,' I said.

'OK, leave it with me. We'd definitely be interested. Let me talk to the entertainment heads and get back to you. What about the BBC?' Peter asked.

This felt exciting. I was going it alone. I was now my own Addison so I thought I should throw in a few Addisonisms.

'We'll burn that bridge when we come to it. I'm just being honest with ya,' I said, before he walked away to the dimly lit stairwell.

'I'm like a bull at a china gate. Do you want me to send Scott round?' I then illogically added, but thankfully he was out of earshot.

Things moved quickly and everything was agreed within a fortnight. I was to be the new host of *Sunday Night at the London Palladium*. I knew it was the right decision. I would film it in the spring of 2015 and then go on another tour in the autumn. I had taken control of my own destiny. I arranged to meet Mark Linsey from the BBC in the restaurant of the Langham Hotel to break the news. I told him that I was going to host *Sunday Night at the London Palladium* on ITV as it was the right show for me and that the chat show wasn't. I was finally able to be honest about how uncomfortable the chat show made me now that I had another option on the table. I expected the meeting to be a polite formality. Goodbye and good luck. Hopefully work together again in the future. Mark's reaction genuinely surprised me. He immediately said, 'Why not make a variety show in a theatre for the BBC?'

This was a remarkable turn of events. I had inadvertently followed Addison's own playbook. Addison was always bluffing about going to ITV. I wasn't bluffing, but it amounted to the same thing. I was going to get what I wanted, even though I hadn't known what I wanted until I read about the Palladium show and met Peter Fincham in an underground car park. I was an accidental agent. Mark quickly gathered the troops and the following morning I was at the BBC having an emergency meeting with Mark, the new controller of BBC1 Charlotte Moore, and the head of everything Danny Cohen.

Charlotte said, 'Michael. We believe in you. If you want to make a variety show in a theatre, then let's do that.'

And all the while Charlotte was talking, Mark Linsey was playfully chanting, 'Do it. Do it. Do it. Do it.'

I would never have had the gumption to dictate to the BBC the show I wanted to make. That's not what I do, that's what Addison does. 'I know what I'm doing,' he said so many times. Well I didn't, but thankfully I'd ended up at the right place. I instantly agreed to make the show for the BBC. The chat show was dead. Monday night at 10.35 p.m. was the graveyard slot after all. RIP. I called Peter Fincham and profusely apologized for stringing him along and he totally understood, saying he never thought the BBC would let me go. My self-esteem had been so low that I just felt lucky to have a job offer from either.

Now this was my chance. My chance to take everything I had learnt and make a defining TV show of my own that properly played to my strengths. But who could I make this show with? How could I find a TV producer to replace the irreplaceable Addison?

The producers who worked on the *Comedy Roadshow* and the chat show were very much Addison's underlings. I knew the producers of *BGT*, who were also the producers of *The X Factor*, but they were obviously otherwise engaged. There was literally only one other TV producer I vaguely knew, called Dan Baldwin. Dan is married to daytime TV sweetheart Holly Willoughby and is often referred to as 'TV producer husband' in countless fascinating *Daily Mail* articles about Holly walking to the shops or getting out of a taxi. I interviewed Holly on my (ill-fated, much-maligned) chat show and she told the story of how they met when she was hosting, and he was producing, *Ministry of Mayhem*. The Saturday morning show was live with producer Dan communicating with Holly through her earpiece. She said she fell in love with him when he was guiding her through items such as Stephen Mulhern throwing custard pies in her face. Producing live TV and seducing Holly Willloughby all at the same time struck me as impressive.

What also struck me as impressive was that he had recently started his own production company, backed by Peter Jones from the TV show *Dragon's Den*, where multimillionaires invest in new businesses. Peter Jones had always been the hardest Dragon to impress and obviously had an excellent eye for a good business. Only Peter saw the potential in Levi Roots's recipe for Reggae Reggae Sauce. If Peter thought Dan had the recipe for TV success, maybe I should be 'in' too. Dan also had experience of making successful shows with comedians, having produced the BAFTA-winning *Celebrity Juice* with Leigh Francis since it began. What also appealed about Dan was that I knew he was a fan of mine. Holly had told me during an ad break on *This Morning* that her husband had pre-ordered my DVD (I do love a pre-orderer), and I ran into him at a party once and he drunkenly told me he listens to my *Desert Island Discs* episode over and over again in his car.

Other than those few occasions I didn't know Dan Baldwin, although he had recently texted me for the first time and asked me if it was true I had a Ferrari. I replied that I did, to which he replied, 'Excellent behaviour.' I found that expression funny, and I found it funny he had texted me for the first time ever, just to ask if I had a Ferrari. I don't even know how he got my number. So I found that old text and phoned him.

'Hi, is that Dan Baldwin?'

'Yes,' replied Dan.

'It's Michael McIntyre from the *Desert Island Discs* you listen to in the car.'

'Ah, Michael. Yes. I remember you. You have a Ferrari. What can I do for you?'

'Make me a Saturday night TV show on BBC1 from a West End theatre, please,' I explained.

'Anything else?' Dan asked.

'A BAFTA and beating Simon Cowell in the ratings would be nice,' I said.

'I'd love that,' said Dan. 'I'd love to make a TV show with you. I've got lots going on but I'd drop everything for you. Seriously. Let's meet up as soon as you can.'

'Excellent behaviour,' I replied.

20

'Komedikonge Michael McIntyre is coming' read the headline on the front page of a Norwegian daily newspaper with a picture of my smiling face. Typing komedikonge into Google Translate, I was thrilled to learn it meant 'comedy king'. Now, I've often said in this book that the levels of success I experienced were beyond my wildest dreams, but if I ate a cheese platter before bed and had a high fever, I'm not sure I would ever have dreamt of becoming Norway's komedikonge.

The internet can be a scary place for people in the public eye, but YouTube and Facebook meant that my comedy routines could be shared around the world, and the result was that Joe kept getting calls from abroad for me to perform. These weren't just shows for a few hundred expats mixed in with some curious locals, they were arena events for tens of thousands. Nothing has ever surprised and thrilled me more than visiting countries for the very first time and finding I had such a big following. My first trips were to Norway, South Africa, Australia and New Zealand. There is some logic to going to South Africa, Australia and New Zealand, they are all major English-speaking countries. But for some reason I was a big hit in Norway. It's something I often bring up around the house. 'Hey, you can't talk to the komedikonge like that.' 'The komedikonge will exit the bathroom when he is good and ready.' 'Budge up, the komedikonge is here.'

Joe booked all of my live shows at home and abroad and often came to see the show, but his uniquely unassuming nature meant he never told me he'd be there. When Addison came to shows he would be announcing it for weeks in advance: 'Don't forget, Michael, I'm coming down to that one, I might bring Scott with me and the dogs, let's book a nice restaurant for afterwards.' Joe would just duck into my dressing room after a show and apologize repeatedly for his being there. 'Don't mind me, Michael, I know you're busy,' Joe would say, umbrella and *Guardian* in hand, humbly bowing between every word. 'Great show tonight. I won't keep you.' Once he opened a self-closing fire door to my dressing room, said he loved the show and then backed out of the door apologizing as it self-closed in front of him. Many times I didn't even know he was in my dressing room, as he didn't say a word and just stood in the corner while I would be talking to far less important people. I once lifted my spare suit and shirts off a free-standing clothes rail in my dressing room to find Joe behind them. 'Don't mind me, Michael. I'll be out of your way.' When Joe told me he was coming to all my gigs abroad I thought it would be lovely to finally spend some time with him, especially on the sixteen-hour flight to Australia. Along with Joe, I headed to Australia with my wingman Paul Tonkinson (rare to have a wingman on the plane with you), who was supporting me both emotionally and professionally as he was performing twenty minutes' warm-up before I went onstage. Paul and I took our seats on the plane but there was no sign of Joe. The plane was moments from take-off. He's cutting it a bit fine, isn't he? So I phoned him.

'Sorry, Michael,' he said, apologizing for picking up the phone.

'Joe, where are you? The plane's about to take off,' I said.

'Don't mind me, Michael. I didn't want to get in your way. I'll make my own way there. I won't keep you.'

I really didn't know what that meant. How can you make your own way to Australia? And how can Joe think he'll get in my way on an Airbus A380, the biggest passenger airliner in the world?

My success abroad did mean that I eventually spent more and more time with Joe, especially after shows when Paul, Joe and I would share a bottle of red wine in the hotel bar, Paul and Joe talking politics and me talking about myself. It was Danny and Joe who brought me to Off The Kerb before Addison swooped in and did what Addison does. Now Danny and Joe were running the business and bringing through fantastically funny new comics like Rob Beckett, Romesh Ranganathan and Josh Widdicombe. I've never known anyone to dominate a room more than Addison and although I would forever miss his presence, I was so lucky to have Danny, the kindest, hardest-working and most positive man I've ever known, and (when he finally emerged from behind the clothes rail) Joe, or Josephine as I started to call him for no apparent reason.

Like with the *Comedy Roadshow* my trips abroad were filled with Paul and me prowling for potential jokes. Even before we arrived in Australia, while filling out the landing card, Paul had started.

'It says here, "Do you have any criminal convictions?" Is that still a prerequisite of going to Australia? If I tick "No" will they not let me in?' Paul said, followed by, 'Is that usable? Maybe a bit offensive? Funny though. Write it down.'

In the queue to hand in our landing cards at the airport in Perth the immigration officer was making sure nobody was importing any food that might contain diseases. He was asking everyone as they passed through, 'Do you have any fruit, vegetables or meat products?' in his dry Australian drawl. Following a chorus of nos from those in front of us, it was the turn of Paul and me. 'You're so hungry, aren't you? I wish I had something to give you. You poor thing,' I said, and then Paul shouted down the line, 'Has anybody got any fruit, vegetables or meat products for this man? He's starving. Here, mate, have a chewing gum, it's all I've got.'

Is that funny? Can I use that? Write it down.

Very soon it became apparent that every Australian we encountered asked, 'How you going?' instead of 'How are you?'

When we asked the cab driver to take us to our hotel he said, 'No worries. How you going?'

'How are we going?' I said from the back seat. 'In this car I hope.'

All these little jokes and ideas were compiled and endlessly discussed between Paul and me, and then shared with thousands of Aussies who were so unbelievably welcoming. It's a long way to go but more than worth it. I've spent so many gigs trying to be funny enough so that audiences would return, but I got the feeling in Australia that they wanted to show me so much love that I too would return. It was the same in every country I went. I never thought I would be there and they never thought I would come, and it made for some wonderful nights. I say nights, but due to the time difference for me it was the morning, which meant that I was finally able to fulfil my dream of being 'morning guy' onstage. Anyone who has travelled to Australasia will know about the extreme jet lag. I struggle very badly with jet lag. Even when the clocks change for British Summer Time it takes me a while to adjust. I watch ITV +1 a few days before to try and prepare myself. On those long-distance trips I never adjusted to the local time as I was so full of adrenaline after the show I had no chance of getting to sleep. So I was up all night and asleep all day.

When I went to perform in Hong Kong we arrived at the luxurious Intercontinental Hotel at about midnight local time, which was the middle of the day for me. I spent the whole night wide awake in my room. Now, it's no secret I have an unexplained Asian appearance. I do look like a Chinese person. Nobody else in my family resembles Chinese people. Lucas once mistook me, his own father, for a Chinese gentleman. I was cycling behind him in the park and I took a secret little detour; the plan was to pedal hard and emerge in front of him to make him jump. I did indeed give him a fright, although such a fright he burst into tears.

'What's wrong? What's wrong? It's me,' I said, trying to calm him.

'I thought a Chinese man was attacking me,' he said, through his tears.

I too mistook myself for an Asian man in that Hong Kong hotel room after a sleepless night. Behind the bed in my Intercontinental suite was the bathroom. Despite trying for a few minutes, I couldn't find the switch that turned off the lights. I needed the light off as it was spilling into the bedroom that I wanted to be pitch black to give me the best chance of convincing my fully conscious daytime brain that it was the middle of the night. Unable to switch the light off I decided to close the mirrored sliding door to the bathroom instead. I stripped to my pants and began several hours of restlessness in bed. At about 6 a.m., having not slept a wink, I gave up, turned on my bedside light, got out of bed and headed to the bathroom, forgetting that I had closed the mirrored door. I smashed my face against the mirror, but just before I did there was a split second when I saw my reflection and thought a partially naked overweight Asian man was running at me head first, like at the start of a sumo wrestling fight.

Although it was 6 a.m. Hong Kong time, for me it was 10 p.m. I knew I would soon be getting tired but was starving hungry as I had missed dinner. With the mini-bar Pringles and Toblerone long since consumed (I'm ashamed to say, I even poured the hot chocolate powder down my throat for a sweet snack), I decided to go down to breakfast. I lazily threw on the same suit I had been wearing the day before with a fresh white shirt.

'I'm sorry, sir, but breakfast isn't open for another ten minutes, but you are welcome to take a seat here and wait,' the hotel receptionist informed me.

So I took a seat on a large leather sofa in the lobby just outside the restaurant. I could see the restaurant staff through the door busily preparing. I was all alone until a Chinese businessman exited the lift, walked to the reception, had a conversation in Chinese and then walked over to me and bowed. I felt I should respond so I bowed back from my seat on the sofa. He then sat on a chair next to me. No sooner had he sat down when the lift doors opened once more and another Chinese businessman walked out of the lift and straight over to us, said something in Chinese and bowed to the chap on the chair, bowed to me, I bowed back, and he then sat next to me on the sofa. This pattern continued until I was surrounded by Chinese businessmen, all of whom I had bowed to and all of whom were wearing dark suits and white shirts just like me. It soon dawned on me that I had been mistaken for a Chinese businessman and was now in the midst of a breakfast meeting. All the other men were nattering in Chinese around me as I sat in the middle of the full sofa. The maître d' from the restaurant then announced in Chinese that breakfast was open and ushered us all in. Trying to get away from the businessmen I quickly moved to the front so that I would be first in and could break free, but that backfired when they all followed me and all sat around me. I ended up having a meeting with at least ten Chinese businessmen, my contribution limited to profuse nodding and cackling when anyone else laughed.

Luckily Paul, who was also jet lagged and hadn't slept all night, then showed up for breakfast but although I was frantically waving at him he didn't recognize me as I blended in so well with my mistaken colleagues. Why is that Chinese man waving at me, is what he later told me he was thinking. I eventually extricated myself from the meeting and joined Paul, where things went from weird to worse. As I was hungry for dinner and not breakfast I ordered something called a seafood laksa. Now, it's best not to go into too many details here other than to say I feel the dish should be renamed a seafood arse re-laksa. The impact of the laksa wasn't immediate. I had booked myself in for a massage in the spa later that day and midway through I realized something was terribly wrong in my bowel area. My stomach was making stranger and louder sounds than the whale music being pumped into the massage room. The situation was worsened by the tiny female masseuse of Herculean strength vigorously pummelling me. In a part of the world famed for 'happy endings' this was nearly the unhappiest of them all.

I can't say I wasn't a bit nervous about going to South Africa. I was due to perform in Cape Town and Johannesburg. Whenever I told anyone I was going they always replied that Cape Town was beautiful and that I would love it there, but when I asked them about Johannesburg they tended to go a bit quiet. Cursory internet research revealed Johannesburg to be the murder capital of the world and that more people are shot there than anywhere else. I went on Google Maps to have a look at the venue I would be playing. If you've been on Google Maps you will know there is a little yellow man who you pick up with your cursor and drop onto any road in the world and then an image of that road is revealed as if you are there. So I picked up the little yellow man and dropped him onto the road in Johannesburg outside the venue, and he got shot. No he didn't. That's a joke. He was fine and so was I. The shows in South Africa were incredible. I played the Coca-Cola Dome in Johannesburg for over 10,000 people, which I was told was the biggest comedy show ever held in South Africa. In Cape Town there had been a drought that had lasted months and was making headlines all over the world. In our five-star hotel we were limited to one-minute showers and the plugs in all the baths had been removed so you couldn't use them. It was a very serious situation but Paul and I couldn't stop laughing as Joe still insisted on bringing his umbrella wherever we went.

When I played Dubai, Joe forwarded me a list of things I

wasn't allowed to say onstage. This wasn't just advice, it was a list of subjects that had come from the government of Dubai as being illegal to talk about. I was categorically not allowed to use any foul language, talk about sex or drugs, or be critical of the Dubai government. The consequences of breaking these rules didn't bear thinking about. I asked the promoter how serious the rules were and he told me he had been arrested and spent a night in jail when he foolishly brought Snoop Dogg to Dubai a few years prior. Within seconds of Snoop's performance it became apparent he probably hadn't read the government guidelines.

'Whassup, motherfuckers,' opened Snoop, prompting the authorities to head backstage brandishing handcuffs.

Paul and I went through our sets making sure there was nothing that could get us into trouble. Paul was a bit worried about a routine depicting his wife getting drunk on a night out with the girls and then coming home horny, waking him up when he was fast asleep and not in the mood for her drunken advances. He did a hilarious impression of her turning the bedroom door handle and falling into the room, and her waking him up with make-up running down her face from her sweaty night out. 'It was like getting a lap dance from a sad clown.'

Everyone, including the ex-con promoter, said the routine was fine and harmless but Paul was worried. As soon as he went onstage I said to Joe and the promoter that I wanted to play a joke on him. We gathered the backstage security guards and briefed them about my plan while he was onstage for the 5,000 strong audience at the World Trade Centre in Dubai. He performed the joke about his wife at the end of his set to huge laughs, thanked the audience and told them I would be on after the interval, and left the stage to thunderous applause. But as soon as he reappeared backstage a congregation of security staff and the promoters were awaiting him.

'Everything all right?' Paul asked.

'I'm so sorry, Mr Tonkinson,' the promoter said, 'but the Ruler of Dubai just had a children's party and his son hated the clowns, so clowns have been added to the list only this morning. I had no idea.'

Another one of the promoters then chipped in, 'The idea of a clown lap dancing has caused great offence.'

'Disgusting,' said one of the security guards.

'An abomination,' said another.

At this point I approached, like Jeremy Beadle.

'What's going on?' I asked.

'I'm being arrested mate,' Paul said, red faced with panic. 'It was the clown joke. Clowns have been added to the list mate.' He then turned to the 'fake' authorities and said, 'Mike had nothing to do with this. Please leave Mike out of this. Take me. He's innocent.'

If I didn't know already, that was proof that Paul is truly the sweetest of men and such a good friend to me. Facing jail time in the Middle East, his immediate concern was that I would not be implicated. He would take the rap. I could bear it no longer and told him it was a prank as we all laughed hysterically. Paul congratulated us all on our acting skills and called me a fucking arsehole, which then nearly got him arrested for real.

'Paul, please be careful,' said the promoter, 'swearing in a public place is number fourteen on the list.'

Globetrotting with Paul was always a laugh and invaluable for working on material together, normally over breakfast in various hotels. Everywhere we went was so different, and stimulating in different ways. When I, the komedikonge, finally made it to Norway we were well into the groove of picking up material to immediately share with the crowd. Although English was their second language they were as good as any audience in the world. It was my first time in Scandinavia and everything I knew about it came from watching box sets of Scandi crime dramas, which meant that every person I saw in Norway looked to me like a suspect in a gruesome murder. Also, the language is so peculiar I questioned whether Norwegian is a real language and not just the result of the freezing weather. 'It sounds like you're trying to speak English with frozen faces,' I told them.

Paul and I played arenas in Oslo, Stavanger and Trondheim. We also went to Bergen to play a few nights at a smaller theatre. I googled Bergen and found out it was one of the rainiest cities in the world. Joe was giddy with excitement at the prospect of finally opening up his brolly. But when we arrived, although cloudy, it was dry. In the taxi from the airport the driver had his windscreen wipers on and they were making that terrible screeching sound on the bone-dry windscreen.

'Why are your windscreen wipers on? It's not raining,' I asked the driver.

'It will,' came his reply.

Having a following abroad was such an amazing bonus. Comedy really is universal. Parents all over the world are struggling to leave the house when they have kids, husbands are annoying their wives globally by putting their dirty plates next to the dishwasher and not in it, women throughout the earth look silly putting their tights on. The internet had literally opened up the world to me. But in America I still remained unknown. Whenever I had a great gig abroad the subject of going to America would dominate our post-show hotel bar boozing. America is the home of stand-up. All the stand-up I watched and loved as a kid was from American comics like Richard Pryor, Jerry Seinfeld, Eddie Murphy, Jackie Mason. But unlike other countries around the world, Americans don't look to the small island of the UK for their entertainment. If I wanted to make it there, I would have to go there and build myself up. I had mentioned it to Addison during the conversation we had that resulted in my chat show, but he dismissed it. I think because it was out of his jurisdiction and comfort zone and, like me, he was a nobody there. But it was a growing dream of mine to see if I could make Americans laugh.

For my first two arena tours I didn't have a support act; Paul was someone I would chat to constantly on the phone and meet up with between shows. But I'd loved having him with me abroad, so asked if he wanted to carry on and be the warm-up for my *Happy & Glorious* arena tour in 2015. It was so much better having him with me on what was another mammoth tour of the UK with the same daily pattern continuing: wake up and have breakfast in the hotel with Paul to go through notes from the night before and any new thoughts for jokes, wander around the city we were in looking for more gags, sleep in the afternoon, do the show, have a drink back at the hotel and talk about breaking America.

'They're laughing all over the world mate,' Paul would say. 'Australia, New Zealand, South Africa, Dubai, Norway.'

'I know. I'm the komedikonge,' I replied, not for the first time.

'You're the fucking komedikonge,' Paul would repeat. 'America is waiting for you, mate. They're gonna love you. You're made for America.'

Breaking America has long been considered the pinnacle for entertainers. I worried about failing like so many before. Addison worried about failing. But you only live once. I had to go for it.

But before that, I had unfinished business on TV. Like Lennox Lewis, I had to avenge the defeat my chat show represented.

My new TV show had to work and be a success, although I did now have a back-up plan.

Moving to Norway!

21

I didn't want to take too many risks with the format of the TV
show I was developing with Dan Baldwin for the BBC. I knew I
wanted to make the show at a West End theatre, I knew I was
going to be opening the show with stand-up, and I knew I would
be introducing a variety of acts onstage. But I wanted to inte-
grate other ideas within the fabric of a traditional variety show.
The one success from my chat show was undoubtedly the Send
to All game that culminated in the final show with my guest
James Corden and I swapping our own phones and sending a
message to all of each other's contacts, inviting everyone we
knew to a lap-dancing club. Send to All had been fun playing
with the audience, but playing with a celebrity and having
famous people reply as well as more obscure acquaintances
made it all the more hilarious. Harry Styles, Jeremy Clarkson,
Alan Carr and David Walliams were all up for a night of lap
dancing, only the then England football manager Roy Hodgson

wasn't, although he seemed to misinterpret the text as he replied, 'My dancing days are long gone.' I don't think either James or I fancied a lap dance from Roy himself. My mother-in-law replied, 'Are you sure this was for me? If so, we need to talk.' My kitchen designer asked when we could put a date in and said, 'I'm liking where your head's at.' I had literally only met him once, for less than half an hour, and talked solely about my new kitchen.

Although the memory of the chat show made me shudder and I didn't want any reminders, it was clear that Send to All worked as a game and had the perfect narrative for a TV format, sending out the text early in the show and then coming back to it later to reveal the replies. Any idea that gives viewers a reason to stay watching until the end is a good one. So Dan and I discussed playing Send to All with an audience member. It was Kitty however who suggested we played it with a celebrity. It was a brilliant idea and supersized Send to All, taking it from the Monday night graveyard to Saturday night glamour.

The other idea for the show was more high-concept and, unlike Send to All, hadn't been trialled before. I thought of it at one of the corporate events that Big Fee Fay had been steadily booking since my debut at the Kitchen and Bathroom Awards. After a rocky start I did mostly enjoy them. I also started performing at a lot more private parties for wealthy people. I performed at countless birthdays, anniversaries, weddings, bar mitzvahs, even a christening. I have to say they were almost all great fun as, unlike business events, the people who booked me were obviously big fans and in a great mood. Also, more often than not I was a surprise, so the gig always began with a wave of goodwill for me to ride for the duration of my act. I was also doubly determined not to spoil someone's special day. It did feel strange being a 'comedian for hire', when I was selling out arenas all over the world. But everybody has their price. The first time I got offered a bar mitzvah Big Fee Fay called me to ask if I was interested.

'Absolutely not,' I said. 'I'm not a children's entertainer. It'll be a disaster.'

'But you haven't heard the offer yet,' Fay said.

'That's irrelevant. I have to draw the line at birthdays for thirteen-year-olds,' I reiterated.

I was steadfast. There was no amount of money that would get me to do it so I said no. They offered more money. I said no. They offered even more money. I said no. This story predictably ends with me wearing a kippah on my head and dancing in a circle with several Jewish men singing 'Hava Nagila' and, honestly, having the time of my life. By the end of the night I felt like one of the family. I was sitting and chatting with an eighty-nine-year-old lady who had flown over from Florida for the occasion when I was interrupted by a hilariously cocky twelve-year-old boy.

'I'm considering hiring you for my bar mitzvah. Good job tonight . . . on the whole,' he said in his unbroken voice.

He then held out a business card, which I took. He was a twelve-year-old with a business card. It reminded me of that bit in *Pretty Woman* when Julia Roberts is having a lovely day at the polo until Richard Gere's lawyer reminds her she's a hooker. The card just had his name and mobile phone number on it.

'Thank you, Daniel. I hope to see you on your big day too,' I said.

'Maybe,' he said, walking away. 'There are a few others in the mix.'

I'm not sure what the purpose of giving me his card was. Surely he needed my card, not that I had one. Was I supposed to keep phoning him and enquiring whether he had made a decision about wanting me for his bar mitzvah?

Sometimes I was hired to entertain people who weren't celebrating a special occasion. They were just so rich they couldn't be bothered to go to the O2 Arena so they paid for me to come to them. I was once flown onto a yacht in the French Riviera to entertain a family of twelve, including a little three-year-old girl who sat at the front with big headphones on, watching an iPad in her pyjamas. Just before I got to my first punchline she lifted up one headphone and shouted, 'Is it finished yet, Mummy?'

The smallest event I have done was for eight friends at a private residence in Mayfair. I stood at the end of their dining room table and basically took the piss out of them for being absurdly rich. One of the guests was notorious for driving around London with a motorcade, an actual motorcade like the President of the United States. He himself drove a Lamborghini with two black Range Rovers in front and another two black Range Rovers behind, filled with security. All five cars had similar personalized licence plates. This level of vanity and eccentricity can only be applauded, although I'm not sure Greta Thunberg would applaud his carbon footprint. I mercilessly mocked him and he fortunately found it hilarious, otherwise I probably wouldn't be here today to tell the tale. I did impressions of him looking for a place to park five cars in a row and trying to pay for them all at the pay and display, and imagined him calling his wife on the way home from work: 'The bad news is that I'm stuck in terrible traffic, the good news is they're all my own cars.'

At another private gig at another billionaire's residence I experienced something for the first time since I swept hair in a hairdresser's salon as a weekend job when I was seventeen. I got tipped. I may have been a TV star and arena-selling comedian, but to them I was just another staff member. I was standing at the doorway saying goodbye to the hosts following my after-dinner performance for them and their friends, when one of the friends approached me.

'Good show, buddy,' he said as he stuffed something in my suit pocket.

I had no idea what it was so I reached in and lifted out wads of fifty-pound notes. There were so many and I was so shocked, half of them fluttered to the floor, resulting in me literally falling to my hands and knees in their hallway and crawling around picking up fifties and stuffing them back in my pockets. I remember the hosts turning away in embarrassment. I suppose if there was ever a scene to define corporate entertainment, that was it. I gave half to my driver who drove me home and the rest as tips of my own in restaurants for the forthcoming weeks. Although I enjoyed being so generous and behaving like a billionaire it meant that we could never revisit those restaurants, as the waiters would now be expecting fifty-quid tips every time I went.

In among these private shows I hosted the Domino's Pizza Awards at the NEC in Birmingham. I know, who knew there was such a thing? This was a glittering night for over a thousand shop managers and staff as well as a table in the front for the CEO and other Domino's top brass. I remember there was even an award for the delivery driver who had averaged the fastest delivery times over the past year. While onstage I had the idea of ordering a pizza from the local Domino's on my mobile phone. I put my phone close to the microphone so the whole audience could hear and placed an order for me and all the Domino's executives, adding extra toppings of comedy throughout the call. When later in the show the helmeted Domino's delivery driver arrived at the NEC, he was sent straight onto the stage with over a thousand of his Domino's Pizza colleagues and senior management all on their feet going wild and loving the surprise. It was a wonderful and impromptu moment.

After the show my driver held the back door open for me, and held open his free hand, hoping for another massive post-corporate tip. Sorry, not this time. For the whole journey back to London I kept thinking, was there a way of recreating the surprise I just gave the Domino's delivery man for my TV show? And before I arrived home I had the whole idea, fully formed. I could dupe people into coming to the theatre where we were to record the TV show under false pretences, as part of their work.

I had the idea of a locksmith who had to unlock a locked door. He would be led through the back of the theatre, maybe not even knowing he was at a theatre, and have to open a locked door. On the other side of the door would be the huge, hushed theatre audience. As soon as the locksmith opened the door the audience would be revealed and erupt. What a surprise! But why surprise them? What if they had a talent? What if they were singers and then performed on the stage at the end of the show? They would have to be secretly nominated. It wasn't going to be easy finding the right people and setting everything up, but if it worked it would surely be amazing.

I called Dan first thing in the morning and told him about what happened at the Domino's Pizza Awards and how it had given me an idea for a segment of the show I wanted to call the 'Unexpected Star of the Show'. Dan loved it. Kitty loved it. The BBC loved it. I ordered Domino's pizza to celebrate, and asked the delivery driver if he could sing.

The format for my new TV show was complete: it would be a variety show with these two big ideas, Celebrity Send to All and the Unexpected Star of the Show. We booked the Theatre Royal, Drury Lane, where I only had good memories from the *Christmas Comedy Roadshow* I made, with Addison hopping on and off his taxi bike. Lucas and Ossie were going through a phase (that thankfully passed) of loving WWE wrestling and always shouting 'Big Show' during their play fights with toy figures or each other. Apparently Big Show was the name of one of the wrestlers and I liked the sound of it for my TV show. Simple and self-explanatory and a subtle nod to my kids. So I went for it. *Michael McIntyre's Big Show*.

Working with Dan Baldwin was obviously a gamble. We didn't know each other, let alone have experience of working together. But it soon became clear that, although he was chosen from a pool of one, I was incredibly fortunate to have found him. I think we surprised each other by how well suited we were. Dan is super ambitious, creative and industrious but most of all he's really fun. Every phone call and every meeting we had we were laughing away as we strived to make the best show we could. Dan was very proud of his team. 'I only hire the best people,' he kept saying, whenever I complimented someone to him. Everyone working on the show, the producers, the bookers, the casting department, the runners, all of them were smart, talented, hardworking and pulling together for the common goal of making an excellent TV show. Everyone was so invested from day one, and that all trickled down from Dan, his drive, his energy and his enthusiasm. Peter Jones was right. If I was a Dragon I would definitely invest in Dan Baldwin.

The only part of the format that concerned me was the Unexpected Star of the Show. This was the one brand-new idea and, as it was to be the finale, a lot depended on it working. This is why Dan and his team are so good. I had a crazy idea in my mind and they were actually able to make it happen. For the first show, the casting team found a young Welsh hairdresser called Natasha whose dream was to be a singer. Natasha thought she was coming to the backstage of the theatre to style hair for a convention. The props department built an actual room on the stage that resembled a hair salon and a fake corridor that led to it, so Natasha would have no idea she was actually walking to the stage. I sat inside on a hairdresser's chair wearing a big blond wig and cloak, facing the mirror supposedly waiting for a trim. But behind the mirror was the entire audience in hushed silence, and on the edge of their seats. Natasha entered the fake room and no sooner had she plonked down her hairdressing bag, the wall of the room collapsed and the mirror Natasha and I were facing was replaced by 2,000 people on their feet cheering. The thud the wall made when it landed on the stage was almost as shocking as the view. I had set the whole thing up telling the audience Natasha would get the surprise of her life and that's exactly what happened. It had worked. I don't think I've ever been more relieved. Natasha was so sweet and adorable and beside herself. I introduced Michael Ball and told her they would be duetting at the end of the show.

Natasha was transformed from hairdresser to superstar as she brought the house down singing 'The Prayer'. I implore you to watch it on YouTube right now. She was sensational. Goosebump avalanche. I stood backstage watching her on the monitor with genuine emotion. It had worked. This girl's dream had come true; beautifully and totally unexpectedly we had given her this extraordinary experience. It was magical. Dan and I picked over every shot in the edit to best capture Natasha's performance, watching it over and over again, welling up every time. We couldn't wait for the show to be broadcast. Thank you, Domino's Pizza.

Dan and his family came to stay with us at Breach House to watch the first show go out on BBC1. While Dan and I were making final edits to the show in London, Jason from Pest Control spent the week fumigating the bedrooms in preparation for our visitors. I was so excited and confident about the show I even bought a brand-new 78-inch TV to watch it on. Dan and I wanted to create a programme for the whole family to enjoy. That's what Saturday night TV is all about. I was reminded, however, as we all settled down in front of my new TV – Dan, Holly, his three kids, Kitty and my two boys – that families don't sit and watch TV together like Mark Kermode watches a new arthouse release. They are not forensically focused on every frame, like Dan and I had been in the edit. It's pandemonium. The kids are shuffling around, checking their phones, fighting over crisps, needing the loo, bickering over nothing. Nobody was concentrating on the show at all. 'I was sitting there.' 'I'm hungry.' 'Put your phone down.' 'I'm just checking the football score.' 'Why are there no adverts?' Even Kitty was idly chatting to Holly: 'I love the colour of your nail varnish.' Meanwhile Dan and I were in panic free fall, stressing over every decision that we'd made. 'Is the pace right?' 'Does it look too bright to you?' 'Is it just me or is the sound a bit tinny?'

The show ended and all the confidence I had before evaporated; I was left with raw fear that the show was a disaster and I should strap myself in for another media mauling. Kitty reassured me all night that the show was great and I did receive several positive texts. But the sleepless countdown was now on for 9.36 a.m. the following morning when the all-important ratings would be in.

'What do you think the ratings will be?' I asked Dan at breakfast as the clock ticked into the final hour before we'd have our result.

'I'd be happy with anything over 4 million,' Dan said.

He was being conservative. He wanted more. I wanted more. I wanted the rating to be over 5 million. The sky is the limit for ratings on a Saturday night show. In general terms, over 4 million is strong, over 5 million is a proper hit, and beyond that is the dreamland where shows like *Strictly Come Dancing*, *The X Factor* and *Britain's Got Talent* can average around 10 million. *Britain's Got Talent* was in fact on ITV the same night but thankfully not at the same time as the *Big Show*. If I didn't know already that *Britain's Got Talent* was on, I was soon reminded as everyone wanted to watch it afterwards. 'Weren't you a judge on this once?' Dan asked. Having forgotten like everyone else.

Our hearts were racing as Dan and I kept refreshing our inboxes at 9.36 a.m. 'Nothing.' 'Where are they?'

'I've got them,' Dan said.

'What are they?' I asked, about to pass out.

'4.9,' Dan said.

'That's OK. That's good,' I replied.

Neither of us quite knew whether to get excited or not. It felt like par. I had to be happy with par but I'd dreamt we'd get more.

But it was a good start. Solid. I wished it was 5 million, though. Close.

'What did *Britain's Got Talent* get?' I asked, although I knew I shouldn't.

'10 million,' Dan said.

The BBC were thrilled. Most Saturday night shows had been getting far less, especially when they launched. This was a good result but most satisfyingly the reviews were almost universally positive. Certain journalists who had been so scathing about the chat show that I got quotes to make voodoo dolls of them, were now so full of praise I wanted to make them into cuddly toys. They were just doing their job and giving their opinion, and now their opinion was in my favour it felt like a big win. It's hilarious how when the press are critical I argue they are clueless. Charlatans. Losers. But when their reviews are glowing then suddenly they really know exactly what they're talking about. Excellent journalism. Spot on.

The ratings remained consistent until the sixth and final show where they fell off a cliff. I was actually mountain walking in Austria at a weight-loss clinic when I heard the ratings and nearly fell off an actual cliff for real. Kitty had decided I needed to improve my health and sent me to the famous Mayr Clinic, where you pay a fortune to lose weight very quickly. I spent thousands and thousands of pounds to basically be trapped in a place with no food so I couldn't eat. This is no genius new breakthrough method of weight loss, it's commonly known as starving yourself. In addition to the starving I was given something called Epsom Salts to drink every morning. Epsom Salts basically prompt you to flush out your entire system on the loo. For far less money I could have stayed at home and asked the Intercontinental Hotel, Hong Kong, for their seafood laksa recipe. I couldn't face spending a week on my own at the clinic so I asked Paul if he would accompany me. 'It would be my treat,' I said, in one of the most misleading sentences of my life. The Mayr Clinic was no treat. Paul said he'd heard of the Mayr Clinic and the health benefits of an intensive detox. The elephant in the room however was that there was only one elephant in the room, me. I was fat and Paul, an exceedingly fit marathon runner, is a very slim man.

Poor Paul, whose metabolism is lightning fast, ended up losing more weight than me and told me on day four of our trip that he felt like he might actually die. Also, there was a moment on our trip we haven't been able to speak of since.

'Those Epsom Salts aren't working on me at all mate,' Paul said as we walked through the Austrian woodland.

'Are you kidding?' I said. 'I'm having quite an intense reaction just a few minutes after drinking mine. How odd.'

Later in our walk I turned to see no trace of Paul whatsoever. Where had he gone? He was right next to me just moments ago.

'Paul! Paul!' I cried out. 'Where are you?'

Scanning the woods I saw a figure crouched behind a tree and heard some terrible sounds that made birds and wildlife scatter like there had been a series of gunshots.

'Paul? Is that you?' I called out.

'Stand back! Stand back! Don't look! Turn away! Turn

away!' Paul yelled as his now impossibly slender frame cleared itself of what little remained.

I realized we had to cut short our trip. I had lost a good amount of weight and Paul was reduced to a skeleton shitting in the woods. I phoned my travel agent and begged him to get us out of there. When he called back and said he could get us on a Ryanair flight home in just a few hours we were both so overcome with joy we simultaneously burst into tears and shat our pants.

The final episode of my *Big Show* was aired during that horrific Austrian week. I had very low expectations for that final rating as there appeared to be a perfect storm of negatively influencing factors. First it was a Bank Holiday, meaning people would be away and not watching telly, secondly it was a heatwave, meaning people would be outside having fun not inside watching the telly, and thirdly we had been scheduled directly opposite not just *Britain's Got Talent* but the *Britain's Got Talent* final, meaning whoever was still watching telly would be watching that. I had actually convinced myself the rating might be in single figures.

The show got 2.6 million. Horribly low. If that was the rating for the first show it would have been a flop. But thankfully the *Big Show* was already deemed a success and a second series was being discussed with the BBC to go straight into production for that autumn.

'Why the autumn?' I said to Dan on the phone, now slim and

back in London. 'It's a bit crowded on Saturday nights in the autumn, isn't it?' I continued.

'We'd go after *Strictly Come Dancing*. A pretty plum slot,' Dan said.

'Yes, but what would be on the other side?' I asked.

'That's the downside. We'd have to go up against Simon Cowell and *The X Factor*.'

'Let's do it,' I said, with fire in my belly, if little else.

22

So much was learnt from the first series of the *Big Show*. Now we had more confidence, a solid foundation to take the show on to the next level. Our first unexpected star of the new series recordings was a firefighter called Andy Quinn. His profession was totally at odds with his extraordinary show-stopping singing voice. When I was shown some amateur footage of him singing I was blown away. Andy's wife told us that although it was his dream to perform on a West End stage he was naturally shy, he didn't have confidence in himself as a singer and would never put himself forward for anything like this. He was perfect. Everyone in the office was so excited about Andy. But we had to make it work. The ruse was that Andy, who was based in Nottingham, was coming to London to host a fire safety course in an office that, unbeknowst to him, was directly behind the Theatre Royal.

Everything was going to plan. Andy gave his fire safety talk to a group of people he had no idea were actors. Communicating with them through hidden earpieces, I got them to ask him silly questions for laughs. Then his boss told him he needed a hand fetching some fire extinguishers from a store cupboard. Andy was led out of the shop and down the alley that runs alongside it and to the back of the theatre. Once inside, he then entered our fake corridor that led to the fake storeroom we had built in the middle of the stage. The plan was for Andy to enter the store-room, cueing a fire alarm to sound, sprinklers to go off and douse him in water and the wall to collapse, leaving him where he's always dreamt of being, on a West End stage with the audience going wild.

Unfortunately nobody realized that it was vital Andy got all the way into the storeroom before the wall collapsed. So Andy opened the door, grabbed the fire extinguisher and when the fire alarm went off, walked straight out. The alarm was bellowing, the lights were flashing, the sprinklers shooting water everywhere and the wall collapsed, but Andy had gone. The 2,000-strong audience were on their feet cheering an empty storeroom. Eventually Andy, encouraged by a producer now at the other end of the corridor, reopened the door and saw the audience and I grabbed him. But the moment of true surprise and shock was missed. Damn. Andy was shy when I spoke to him onstage and seemed almost annoyed at his wife for nominating and duping him. You never know how people are going to react. Andy is a tough firefighter. He was in shock. He's a naturally reserved person. Our dream unexpected star hadn't quite played out how we hoped. Dan and I had long since earmarked Andy as the strongest unexpected star we had found. He would be the one to have in our all-important first broadcast show of the series. We were annoyed in the interval that we made a mistake and didn't put the fire extinguishers on the other side of the storeroom and that we didn't actually shut Andy into the storeroom before the wall collapsed. We would make the best of it in the edit, but the feeling was we'd missed our chance for Andy to be in the first show.

'This can't be show one now,' I said to Dan in my dressing room.

'No way,' Dan replied.

But all that changed when he sang. I know I asked you to stop and watch Natasha on YouTube, but I have to insist you now watch Andy too.

He was magnificent. He thought he was in London to give a fire safety talk and now look at him, breathtakingly blowing the roof off the Theatre Royal, singing 'Bring Him Home' from *Les Misérables*, and singing it as well as anyone ever has. Andy was fulfilling his dream. We weren't making a talent show, we were giving people a moment they never thought they would have, and in Andy's case a moment he never had the self-belief to go for. It was magical. For every big note Andy hit, the crew were backstage high-fiving. We were all gathered around a tiny monitor behind the stage watching note-perfect Andy and shots of his wife and father crying their eyes out with pride, when Dan tapped me on the shoulder.

'Show one?' he said.

'Oh yes,' I replied.

The whole team were buzzing after the show. I drank way too much celebratory wine and went home to be met by a beeping sound in my hallway. I had no idea what it was as I staggered around intoxicated and talking to myself. 'Hello? What's that noise?'

It was the smoke alarm. The batteries needed changing. Owing to the high levels of alcohol in my system I forgot the alarm needed to be disabled with the monitoring station before being tampered with in any way. So as soon as I unscrewed it, the alarm went off, the deafening noise waking up my whole family.

'It's a sign. It's a sign,' I kept drunkenly repeating as Kitty staggered down the stairs in her nightie, confused, not being able to hear me over the racket as she put our code into the alarm control panel to stop the noise.

The phone rang. It was the monitoring station asking if I needed them to send the fire brigade.

'Can any of them sing?' I slurred down the phone, sounding like Dudley Moore at the beginning of the film *Arthur*. 'Do you know Andy Quinn? He's a firefighter based in Nottingham. Incredible voice. Do you watch *The X Factor*? Don't! Watch my show instead,' I rambled whilst opening another bottle of wine from the fridge.

Kitty snatched the phone from me as I began another chorus of 'It's a sign!'

'Hello? Sorry. We don't need the fire service, it was an accident with the smoke alarm,' she explained.

'But is your husband OK?' came the reply. 'Maybe you need an ambulance instead?'

For my own health I made it a point to stay off social media whenever I was on TV. But I couldn't resist after the first show of the series aired with Andy the firefighter. Everyone loved Andy. His story and his voice had touched their hearts. I scrolled through what seemed like endless glowing comments, a unique experience indeed. People were loving Send to All and loving the Unexpected Star. At the top of the show I said there would be big stars, big laughs and big surprises, and that's what we delivered. Lucas and Ossie seemed to enjoy the show too but as soon as it ended they immediately watched *The X Factor* on catch-up. They loved *The X Factor*. I loved *The X Factor*. The previous year the boys had actually gone to watch one of the live shows at Fountain Studios in Wembley. But *The X Factor* wasn't the big hitter it once was. The ratings had declined gradually but the show still commanded an audience of over 6 million, much more than the peak of our first series, 4.9 million, and over three times the rating of our last show when the *Big Show* lost viewers faster than I was losing weight in Austria.

Dan and I had the usual pre-ratings chat before the Sunday morning 9.36 a.m. reveal. We just wanted to get close to *The X Factor*, to have them in our sights, not be embarrassed. My phone rang at 9.37 a.m. It was Dan. Here we go.

'Have you seen them?' Dan asked.

'No. I haven't. Have you got them? I haven't got them. Is it bad?' I asked, my pulse racing, prepared for the worst.

'It's good. It's really good,' Dan said.

'What did we get?'

'6.18 million!' Dan announced.

'Fuck. That's amazing!' I said, cueing disappointing groans in the background from my kids because of my bad language. 'Daaaad.'

'6.18,' I said, 'that's very specific.'

'I know,' said Dan, 'because *The X Factor* got 6.13 million. We beat them.'

'We didn't just beat them, we thrashed them,' I joked.

'A win is a win, and we won,' said Dan.

The main thing was that the show was a smash hit on a Saturday night. So many shiny-floor entertainment shows had tried and failed to make that slot their own. This was a big achievement for Dan and everyone who worked on the show. My resurrection from the chat show was complete. I was so happy. Beating *The X Factor* was an added and satisfying bonus. Addison was all about setting big goals and achieving them. There's no doubt his relentless drive had rubbed off on me. He was such a force of nature that I could still hear him in my head, like a slightly cockney Obi-Wan Kenobi. I missed him. I missed sharing big wins with him. The rest of the series continued to be a success and the ratings grew to a high of over 7 million. The *Big Show* beat *The X Factor*, including the *X Factor* final, every single week with an ever-increasing margin.

Whereas the *Big Show* went from strength to strength, I didn't, as I continued to suffer with some kind of ache or pain.

This doesn't improve with age. For the first few years of my relationship with Kitty, I would wake up in the morning and when she asked how I'd slept I would simply say, 'Fine,' and we would start our day. As the years ticked on our morning conversation became more like a medical consultation. 'How did you sleep?' was replaced by, 'How's the back?' 'How's the eye?' 'Your throat?' 'Your ankle?' A lot of my pain was inadvertently self-inflicted. The pain in my calf muscles was caused by my inability to walk heel to toe like a normal person. I walk, and run, toe to toe. After years of discomfort I was given corrective shoes that miraculously introduced my heel to the concept of walking and the pain disappeared. But the damage was done; my years of toe-to-toe walking had resulted in my having gigantic calf muscles, bigger than my thighs. As I recounted on my *Happy & Glorious* tour, a child once saw me by the swimming pool on holiday and said to her mother, 'Mummy, why are that man's legs on upside down?'

My latest injury was in my shoulder. This again was a self-inflicted injury, although I had no control over its self-infliction. When I sleep I manage to get myself in the most insane positions, as if I'm dreaming I'm playing Twister every night. Many breakfasts have been spent with Kitty laughing as she shows me photos she's taken of me asleep. I am convinced, although my doctor isn't totally, that my shoulder problems stem from my sleeping every night with my arm wedged awkwardly behind my head. The second series of the *Big Show* had ended at Christmas 2016 and another series was commissioned for the following autumn, again running through to Christmas. It was on our now annual Easter holiday to Disney World that my shoulder pain became agony. Sleeping in positions that resembled someone who had fallen onto the pavement from a high-rise building, in conjunction with the constant high-fiving of Disney characters, made the pain unbearable. I also seemed to be experiencing more and more limited movement of my arm, which would on occasion become completely stuck in one position.

I phoned my doctor from Orlando, who tentatively diagnosed me with a frozen shoulder. The worst-case scenario was that it would take eighteen months to unfreeze. Defrost? Thaw? I don't know the correct terminology. There was an injection I could have but obviously had to wait until I was back in London. I was advised to take painkillers and to ice it regularly. I strapped ice onto my shoulder and typically made things worse. I had no idea that if you leave ice on your shoulder for too long, it burns. Burns? Only I could burn myself with ice. It's called an ice burn. Who knew? Barmen warn you to be careful when they pass you a flaming Sambuca, but never issue the same warning when serving a drink on the rocks. Now my arm was covered in burn blisters and I was in even more pain, spending all day riding rollercoasters, holding on with one arm and screaming far louder than everyone else.

Due to the time difference in Orlando I always made sure my phone was on silent overnight, otherwise I'd be receiving calls and texts in the early hours from the UK. It was actually quite fun to wake up to nearly an entire day's worth of messages. One morning, mid-holiday, I reached for my phone on the bedside table in my Disney hotel (with my right arm, not my blistered frozen left one) and was met with a sea of texts, mostly starting with the word 'Congratulations'. It was the day of the BAFTA nominations. I had no idea. The *Big Show* had been nominated for Best Entertainment Programme and I had been nominated for Best Entertainment Performance.

Eight years after my disasterclass in how to present a BAFTA, I was nominated for two.

I fist pumped the air with my good arm and replied to everyone that I was over the moon just to be nominated.

That was, of course, a lie.

I wanted to win.

Badly.

23

'Will it hurt?' I asked Professor Emery as his syringe full of steroid approached my frozen shoulder. As the former president of the British Elbow and Shoulder Society (before they gave him the elbow) he was universally recommended to be the best.

'Little prick,' the professor replied in a vaccination moment that never fails to amuse.

'Your arm will feel quite heavy for the next few days, and tender, but the pain should greatly subside as long as it isn't touched or prodded and you don't lift anything heavy,' the professor informed me.

'Well, I am nominated for a BAFTA tomorrow night, they're quite heavy,' I said, failing to resist showing off.

'Just use your right arm and you'll be fine. Very best of luck for tomorrow,' said the professor.

Kitty again bought a new dress for the occasion and I cheekily rang the jewellery shop Boodles asking if they would lend me something unaffordable for her to wear for fun. They agreed to let Kitty borrow a necklace for the night that cost, wait for it, a quarter of a million pounds. Addison had bought me a Rolex for my birthday a few years ago. It was a vintage Rolex from 1976, the year of my birth, and he engraved it 'From the Captain' on the back. He also bought me a pair of gold cufflinks to replace my grandfather's, which I had been forced to sell. Righting a wrong that had so upset him. He, of course, told me how much he paid for both for 'insurance purposes'. I strapped the watch on the wrist of my frozen left arm and, with Kitty's assistance, put on the cufflinks too. For luck. Kitty looked insanely beautiful in her designer dress and diamond necklace.

I was a nervous wreck. For the Best Entertainment Programme we were up against *Ant and Dec's Saturday Night Takeaway*, *Strictly Come Dancing* and *Britain's Got Talent* and for the Entertainment Performance I was up against, among others, Graham Norton. I feared the night would go like this: I would lose to *Britain's Got Talent* and lose to Graham Norton, who would then remind the audience of my career-threateningly bad sitcom joke, and then Kitty would lose her borrowed diamond necklace. In the car en route to the ceremony I found myself holding the back of Kitty's necklace like it was a dog collar. The BAFTA invitation said that invitees must bring their passport to prove their identity. Dan said I didn't need my passport as this didn't apply to me as I was famous and nominated. But after my Sheffield Arena experience I wasn't going to take any chances. Kitty and I pulled up at the red carpet and I grabbed both of our passports but couldn't put them in any pockets of my suit as they were all sewn up. So I walked down the red carpet holding our passports. I had to hold them in my left hand, belonging to my sore arm, as my right hand was clamped behind Kitty's neck, tightly holding onto her diamond necklace in case it fell off. It must have looked like I was escorting a glamorous prisoner through an airport.

The event was held at the Royal Festival Hall, the same venue where I had been ignored by the entire audience when I enquired whether any of them needed a pee eight years earlier. When we sat down in the auditorium Kitty kept asking me if I myself needed a pee and I couldn't work out why. Then I remembered the aspiring actors who work as seat-fillers when anyone leaves their seat.

'Is this because you want some handsome man to come and sit next to you while I'm gone?' I asked.

'Don't be silly, you're being paranoid,' she said. 'But why don't you go anyway, just to see if that does happen.'

Dan and Holly sat directly behind us, along with the other producers of the *Big Show*. My mind was spinning with apprehension as I looked for the only clues available as to whether I had won, namely the seating plan. I had been up for awards before and realized I hadn't won as soon as I discovered my seat was closer to the exit than the stage. Once I was seated not just near the back, but in the middle of a row. I knew immediately I hadn't won. Have you ever seen anyone at the Oscars win in the middle of a row? And then have to force the whole row to stand as they shuffle along, 'Excuse me, thank you, excuse me, thank you.' So I was feeling positive as I was sitting at the end of the third row. Easy access to the stage. I've won. Hurray. Then I realized all the other nominees were in the first two rows, and Graham Norton was already on the stage. I've lost. Shall we just go home?

When you're nominated for an award the rest of the ceremony is an anxious blur of nervous laughter and applauding things you're not really listening to. I was nervously laughing at everything. It made me realize just how bad my sitcom joke was, given that I couldn't even get a few nervous laughs from that night's nominees. Nobody knows the order the categories are going to be announced, which leads to even more tension.

The whole ceremony seems so slow but when it's your category everything moves at lightning pace.

Suddenly it was happening.

'To present the award for Best Entertainment Programme please welcome Joan Collins . . .'

This is it. I braced myself for glory or despair. Kitty and I grew up watching Joan Collins play Alexis in *Dynasty*. Kitty was obsessed with Cristal Carrington; Alexis was Cristal's nemesis. It's a bad sign. It doesn't look good.

'The nominations are *Strictly Come Dancing* . . .' Joan Collins said.

Clips from all the nominated shows came up on the big screen. My heart pounded.

'And the winner is . . .'

This was the moment. I clenched my fist, forgetting I was

still holding Kitty's necklace. She choked out the words, 'You're strangling me.' I loosened my grip. Time stood still. Come on.

'*Ant and Dec's Saturday Night Takeaway*.'

Of course Ant and Dec won. They always win. They deserve to always win. They're the best. I turned to see them shaking hands with their production team and others as they made their way to the stage. When Dec saw me he very kindly squeezed my shoulder as if to say, bad luck, mate. It was a sweet gesture totally in keeping with his extremely generous personality. Unfortunately, and he wasn't to know this, my shoulder was frozen and his squeezing caused a stabbing pain.

'Owwwwww!!' I screeched.

He did a quick double take on his way past, presumably thinking the loss of the BAFTA for Best Entertainment Programme had caused me so much stress I was in physical pain. I turned to Dan behind me and we acknowledged each other's glances of disappointment.

I had one more chance not to go home empty handed. Well, my left hand was medically advised to go home empty handed, but for my right hand, it was all to play for.

'He's very handsome,' Kitty said, pointing to Ant's seat-filler. 'The other one not so much,' she said, referring to Dec's.

The real Ant and Dec were backstage with their BAFTA trophy, being interviewed by the press and basking in their latest success. The ceremony doesn't half drag on. I don't know if you've seen the BAFTA trophy, it's a face with one eye closed. Even he's falling asleep.

'To present the award for Best Entertainment Performance please welcome Kim Cattrall.'

Here we go. It's happening. Last chance.

It's Samantha from *Sex and the City*, another one of Kitty's favourite shows. Alexis Colby had cruelly overlooked me, would Samantha do the same?

'The nominations for Best Entertainment Performance are, Claudia Winkleman for *Strictly Come Dancing . . .*' said Kim Cattrall.

I held Kitty's hand, tighter and tighter as the nominations were read out and clips shown of each on the big screen. Lucas and Ossie were at home in our bed with Lorraine looking after them. Lucas, who was twelve now, had filmed the Best Entertainment Programme category on his phone but then deleted it when I didn't win. You see fathers do the same thing when they film their kids taking a penalty in a football match. If their child misses they turn away, immediately deleting the footage. Lucas pressed record again on his phone and held it up to the screen, panning to Ossie and Lorraine and to himself. 'Come on, Dad,' he said.

'And the winner is . . .' Kim Cattrall said as she opened the envelope.

When she put her lips together I knew I'd won. That's what I was waiting for. To say the names of the other nominees Adam Hills, Claudia Winkleman and Graham Norton, you don't put your lips together. Unless Kim Cattrall is also a ventriloquist, I've won this.

Michael McIntyre

'Michael McIntyre,' she said.

BAFTA rewards the best TV and films every year, but for me the best film of any year was the footage on Lucas's phone of me winning. Lucas and Ossie and Lorraine jumping on the bed with joy and in the background seeing the look on Kitty's face on the big TV in our bedroom as my name was announced. She was so happy, so full of pride. Everyone has their own story going on and this felt like a defining moment in ours. A real triumph. What a journey we had been on together, from having less than nothing to having more than we would ever need. But with success came a fear. Fear that I would contrive to lose it all. Fear that the doubters, the critics, the trolls were right and I would soon disappear. Losing Addison magnified that fear. I missed him. I missed him every day. But in that moment I knew for sure that I could stand on my own two feet and not just survive but thrive without him, and because of him.

I was handed the BAFTA and of course forgot all about my shoulder and held it in the wrong hand, but Dr Showbiz made sure I didn't feel a thing.

'Does anyone need to pee?' I said.

No, I didn't.

I thanked Dan and the team, but mostly my wonderful wife Kitty. Eight years before I had searched for her on that very stage while I was dying on my arse with jokes she told me not to do. Now it was easy to spot her with a quarter of a million pounds' worth of diamonds around her neck, and I was relieved that she was now sitting next to Dec's seat-filler and not Ant's. We met twenty years before when we were both twenty years old. Half our lives had been spent together. What a journey. What an adventure. What fun. For years we struggled to keep our heads above water and then, in the most extraordinary and unexpected way, our fortunes turned. It took a while to make sense of it all and to keep the fear of losing it all at bay. But what I've learnt is that there is no losing. Losing is just a detour on the road to winning.

I ended my speech by saying to my boys, who I knew were watching at home, 'Daddy won.'

If this was a film, a biopic, it would end there with a freeze frame of me triumphantly holding my trophy aloft. Well, my shoulder was already frozen, but the rest of me would need to be frozen too.

Then onscreen writing would update you on what happened next in the life of the main character. I love this bit but always have to pause it, as you know what a slow reader I am. I did a similar thing at the end of my first book, *Life & Laughing*.

So here goes . . . Imagine me paused, standing at the podium in my suit and bow tie, beaming a big smile as I clutch my trophy, lapping up the applause of the audience.

Michael embarked on a big world tour, creatively named: Michael McIntyre's Big World Tour. *Selling over 800,000 tickets in 20 countries.*

He finally made it to America, selling out the legendary Radio City Music Hall in New York, but nearly didn't make it, following a misunderstanding when the immigration officer at JFK Airport mistook his reason for travelling 'to break America' as a terrorist threat.

Michael became the biggest-selling artist in the history of the O2 Arena, selling out 28 shows in total. He was awarded the keys to the O2, along with Prince, Take That and One Direction. An incredible achievement but a bit annoying when the alarm goes off in the night and he has to drive to Greenwich to make sure everything's OK and reset it.

He continues to live a funny life in the same house in Hampstead with Kitty, Lucas and Ossie and their new dog Mr Mcfluffintyre.

Then the image of me smiling and holding my BAFTA would fade to black and these words would appear.

In Loving Memory of Addison Cresswell.

I do love the memories of Addison. My story would be so different without him. He changed my life before he sadly lost his.

His gravestone is inscribed 'Champion of Comedy' and below it in quote marks, 'I'll end on this . . .'

And I will too.

Picture Acknowledgements

A Funny Life

Page 7 top © Michael McIntyre, middle © Scott Welch, bottom courtesy of Ellis O'Brien and Open Mike Productions © Open Mike Productions Ltd

Page 8 top © Anthony Caveney, bottom © Michael McIntyre

Page 9 top courtesy of Ellis O'Brien and Open Mike Productions © Open Mike Productions Ltd, bottom © Shutterstock

Page 10 top courtesy of Ellis O'Brien and Open Mike Productions © Open Mike Productions Ltd, bottom © Hungry McBear

Page 11 © Hungry McBear

Page 12 top left © Dan Baldwin, top right © The O2 Press team, bottom © Neil Macdonald

Page 13 © Andy Hollingworth

Page 14 top © Danny Julian, bottom © Kitty McIntyre

Page 15 © Michael McIntyre

Page 16 © James Gourley/Shutterstock